ROMANCE
LINGUISTICS

ROMANCE LINGUISTICS

The Portuguese Context

**Edited by Dale A. Koike and
Donaldo P. Macedo**

Bergin & Garvey
Westport, Connecticut • London

Copyright Acknowledgments

The author and publisher are grateful for permission to reprint the following material:

"Interpretação de dezembro" by Carlos Drummond de Andrade from the original book *A Tosa do Provo*. Copyright © 1992 by Heirs of Carlos Drummond de Andrade.

Roy C. Major, "Stress and Rhythm in Brazilian Portuguese," *Language* 61, 2 (1985): 259-82.

Library of Congress Cataloging-in-Publication Data

Romance linguistics : the Portuguese context / edited by Dale A. Koike
  and Donaldo P. Macedo.
      p.   cm.
  Includes bibliographical references and index.
  ISBN 0-89789-297-6
    1. Portuguese language—20th century—Grammar.   I. Koike, Dale April.
  II. Macedo, Donaldo P. (Donaldo Pereira).
  III. Title: Portuguese context.
  PC5064.R66   1992
  869.5—dc20   92-19868

British Library Cataloguing in Publication Data is available.

Library of Congress Catalog Card Number: 92-19868
ISBN: 0-89789-297-6

First published in 1992

Bergin & Garvey, 88 Post Road West, Westport, CT 06881
An imprint of Greenwood Publishing Group, Inc.

Printed in the United States of America

The paper used in this book complies with the
Permanent Paper Standard issued by the National
Information Standards Organization (Z39.48-1984).

10 9 8 7 6 5 4 3 2 1

In memory

of

Dana Wheeler

Contents

SECTION IV   PRAGMATICS

SECTION V   TEXT AND DISCOURSE ANALYSIS

Introduction

As we began to write this introduction, we were confronted with a bit of a quandary. On the one hand, we were tempted to follow the traditional course and write an introduction highlighting the major issues raised in the articles, discussing the relation of these issues to current theories in linguistics. On the other hand, we were intrigued by the underdevelopment of Portuguese linguistics and language studies in the United States. In the end we chose not to pursue the former, more traditional route, but rather to consider the latter in more depth. We want to investigate why Portuguese has been granted little more than a footnote in the annals of linguistics. In so doing, we hope to explain why the study of Portuguese has little importance in the curriculum of American colleges and universities (Nitti, 1972, p. vi).

Although over one hundred million people on various continents use Portuguese as their major language, the academic community in the United States has almost totally neglected the study of Portuguese linguistics. Hardly any texts on this subject have appeared in the U.S. despite the presence of a large Portuguese-speaking population in the United States. Sizable Portuguese populations can be found in Massachusetts, Rhode Island, Connecticut, California, New Jersey, New York, and smaller numbers of Portuguese people reside in Florida (see Figure 1). The influx of Portuguese speakers has been especially marked over the last quarter-century, since Congress enacted changes in immigration quotas in 1965.

The largest groups of limited English speakers have arrived from Portugal, the Azores and the Cape Verde Islands. The 1975 Annual report of the Immigration and Naturalization Service, Department of

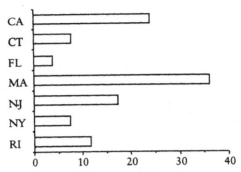

Figure 1. Portuguese Population Distribution
1980 Census Report

Justice, dramatically documents the tremendous influx of arrivals whose country of allegiance has been Portugal. Between 1820 and 1975 a total of 411,136 immigrants arrived in the United States from Portugal or territories controlled by Portugal. Of this total, 113,773 or 28 percent arrived in the ten-year period of 1951-60; the number of immigrants from Portugal placed it 15th out of thirty-two countries considered Europe by the Immigration and Naturalization Service. During the period 1961-65 it ranked 10th. Between 1966 and 1973, it ranked 4th each year as the country of allegiance. In 1974 it had moved to 2nd place and in 1975, immigrants from Portugal exceeded those from all other countries considered Europe. (The Need to Develop a System for the Assessment/Testing of Portuguese-speaking Students, 1977)

We will argue that the weakness of Portuguese language and linguistics studies in the United States comes mainly from two sources: first, the tradition of viewing Portuguese language study as only a vehicle by which to appreciate the literature of the Portuguese world; and second, the xenophobic climate in this country toward foreign languages in general and Portuguese in particular.

Traditionally, colleges and universities have seen the study of foreign languages only as a doorway to literature, and not as an avenue to communicative competence in the language under study. In fact, some institutions have advised students that if they want to gain fluency in a foreign language they should enroll in commercial language schools such as Berlitz. As John Rassias notes:

> Language training was not conceived primarily as an instrument to teach conversation or communication in any mundane sense; it concentrated largely on reading skills so vital to the appreciation of literature in the original language.... [It was thought that] language learning, a more mechanical process, ought not therefore to be taken seriously by a responsible institution. (1970, p. 4)

As Rassias points out, it is not at all uncommon to find literature professors who view language teaching "of such unsophisticated intellectual stature as to preclude it from ever being taken seriously, and a language teacher cannot consider distinguished instruction in this area a reason for promotion." Language teaching texts, for example are seldom considered as scholarly works. Rassias maintains that "This form of reasoning is still widespread in our universities and some language departments treat books by grammarians as inferior pedagogical garbage; further, they assign the most inexperienced staff members to the instruction of language" (1970, p. 4).

Against the landscape of negative attitudes toward foreign language teaching, it is hardly surprising that an alarmingly high number of foreign language students cannot communicate in the language—even after years of formal study. Karl Diller speaks to this issue:

> The history of foreign language teaching often appears to have been a history of failure. In fact, very few language majors in American colleges get even halfway to the level of "minimum professional proficiency." In 1965, 90 percent of the graduating French majors failed to reach the level of minimum professional proficiency in speaking, and only half of them reached that level in reading. (1978, p. 1)

Diller attributes this failure to methodological factors. An over-reliance on the Audiolingual and Grammar-Translation Methodologies, for example, prevents students from practicing real communication in the classroom. But we suggest that methodology is not the only issue. We think great emphasis should be given to the inhibitory influence of negative attitudes towards language study in general, and the study of Portuguese, in particular.

The failure to address socialized reality points the study of Portuguese toward a head-on collision with failure. There is a large body of research showing the vital relationship between language learning and general societal attitudes toward the particular language that is being learned. Yet, more often than not, Portuguese language programs do not concern themselves with the societal context of the Portuguese language in the United States—in particular, the overt and covert discrimination practice against speakers of Portuguese. In some instances, Portuguese language programs may even perpetuate linguistic discrimination in the community at large, simply by being blind to the ways language discrimination manifests itself in social interactions. Since language is the vehicle by which people best express their cultural characteristics, it follows that, by downgrading language, one is simultaneously depreciating culture. As a result, a people's cultural values come to be associated with an inferior social status bringing about a very low self image. An illustration of this process emerging in reality reveals itself in the following anecdote: In a meeting with Portuguese bilingual teachers in Massachusetts, an Azorean teacher pointed out that "The Azorean parents don't come to the Parent Advisory Council meetings because they are ashamed of the Portuguese they speak."

Therefore, we believe that it is of paramount importance not only to gain a thorough understanding of the nature of language and language acquisition processes as this understanding impacts on choice of methodology, but also to understand the dialectical relationship between language and society. The latter may have as great an impact on language learning as the former.

In order to better understand the status of Portuguese studies in the United States, we sent a questionnaire to over 50 Portuguese programs around the country, with a 95 percent return rate. The hypothesis with which we started was one that at first glance might seem to make little sense—that enrollment in these programs would be lower in areas with a sizable Portuguese-speaking minority in the nearby population. The reason, we hypothesized, was that in these areas, higher concentrations of Portuguese-speaking people would proportionately invite discriminatory attitudes toward the Portuguese community. In these situations, we predicted that non-Portuguese speakers would be less disposed to undertake the study of a language, culture, and literature that was associated with a group perceived to be inferior and non-prestigious. In fact, our data showed that Portuguese programs tend to develop better in areas with little or no concentration of Portuguese immigrants (see Figures 2 through 4).

As shown in Figures 5 and 6, students of Portuguese and Brazilian ethnic backgrounds enroll in Portuguese literature programs more than their American counterparts in areas of high concentrations of Portuguese-speaking communities. On the other hand, the reverse is true: American students outnumber their Portuguese and Brazilian counterparts in areas of a low concentration of Portuguese-speaking communities.

We conclude that the statistical data gained from the questionnaire support our general assumption that discriminatory attitudes hurt the development of Portuguese language and culture studies in areas which contain high concentrations of Portuguese-speaking populations in this country. Clearly, American students are disinclined to take Portuguese language and linguistics courses when these courses are offered in institutions located in areas in which high concentrations of Portuguese-speaking immigrants live. American students are far more inclined to take courses in Portuguese language and linguistics in areas in which there are low concentrations of Portuguese-speaking immigrants.

Despite the general context of indifference towards Portuguese language studies, there have, nevertheless, been some significant developments within the field of Portuguese linguistics in the United States. The present text represents a collection of papers which discuss not only the formal aspects of the Portuguese language, but also those aspects dealing with the social reality

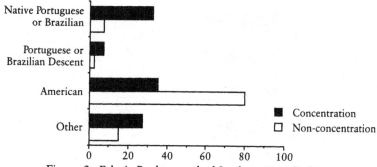

Figure 2. Ethnic Background of Students Enrolled in
Portuguese/Brazilian Literature Programs
Concentration vs. Non-concentration of
Portuguese Immigrants

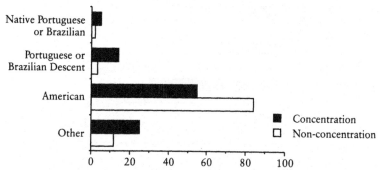

Figure 3. Ethnic Background of Students Enrolled in
Portuguese Language Programs
Concentration vs. Non-concentration of
Portuguese Immigrants

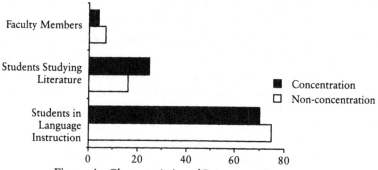

Figure 4. Characteristics of Portuguese Programs
Concentration vs. Non-concentration of
Portuguese Immigrants

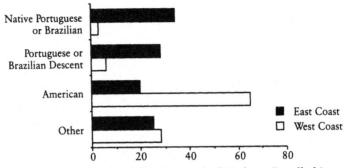

Figure 5. Ethnic Background of Students Enrolled in
Portuguese/Brazilian Literature Programs
East Coast vs. West Coast

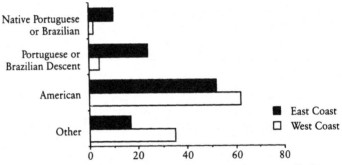

Figure 6. Ethnic Background of Students Enrolled in
Portuguese Language Programs
East Coast vs. West Coast

of the Portuguese language in context. In other words, this text seeks to link
the formal linguistic study of Portuguese with the social context in which
Portuguese is used and studied. We believe that this text will not only address
the paucity of research in the area of Portuguese language and linguistics, but
will provide also a better understanding of a language which has been
unjustifiably neglected by the academic community in the United States. We
hope that our humble contribution will stimulate future research which will
shed more light on the myriad issues raised by the contributors of this text.

Dale A. Koike
University of Texas at Austin

Donaldo P. Macedo
University of Massachusetts at Boston

REFERENCES

Diller, K. 1978. The Language Teaching Controversy, Rowley, MA: Newbury House Publishers.

The Need to Develop a System for the Assessment/Testing of Portuguese-speaking Students. 1977. Providence, RI: Curriculum Research and Development Center, The University of Rhode Island.

Nitti, John J. 1972. 201 Portuguese Verbs. New York: Barron's Educational Series.

Rassias, John A. 1970. New Dimensions in Language Training: The Dartmouth College Experiment. Washington, DC: Peace Corps Faculty Paper No. 6.

Section I–Phonology

1

Stress and Rhythm in Brazilian Portuguese

Roy C. Major
Washington State University

1. Introduction[1]

1.1. STRESS AND RHYTHM have long been recognized as important factors in phonology. Syllable-timed languages—such as Spanish—generally do not undergo as many reductive processes as stress-timed languages such as English, in which these reductive processes aid isochrony by reducing the durations of unstressed syllables occurring between major stresses. Furthermore, DEGREES of stress govern English reductive processes; e.g., the first syllable of *tomato* is much more reduced than the first syllable of *Pandora*, because of differences in stress.

Metrical theory has attempted to formalize these rhythmic hierarchies that exist in natural languages (Liberman 1975; Liberman and Prince 1977;

Selkirk 1980; Hayes 1981, 1984; Halle and Vergnaud 1980, 1984; Prince 1983). As originally proposed by Liberman and Prince, the theory uses two basic concepts in prosodic representation: relative prominence, represented on s[trong]/w[eak] trees, and linguistic rhythm, which results from alignment of tree relations to the metrical grid. This alignment to the grid is essentially a 'formalization of the concept of stress-timing.

Prince notes that, as theory has progressed, the metrical grid has almost disappeared; and if it exists, it seems to be outside linguistic theory. He argues against this trend by proposing that surface structure is directly related to the grid, without a level where s/w calculations occur on trees. Although considerable differences have been expressed by theorists regarding these formal rhythmic hierarchical relationships, the result of this line of research has been to provide a better theoretical base for otherwise arbitrary characterizations of stress patterns and linguistic rhythm.

1.2. BRAZILIAN PORTUGUESE STRESS There has been little work on the organization of the BP stress system. Câmara (1969, 1972a,b) uses impressionistic data of perceived prominence to propose three degrees of stress. In the structuralist tradition, he cites minimal pairs such as the following:

(1) /sélèbrìdàdì/   *celebridade*   'celebrity'
    /sélèbrìdàdì/   *célebre idade*   'renowned age'

Although his examples illustrate stress intuitively, he goes no further to give evidence for degrees of stress.

Maia (1981) uses metrical theory to characterize BP stress by constructing trees to fit the perceived relative prominence of syllables, as shown in Figures 1–3. Maia does not suggest how many degrees of stress exist nor does she attempt to justify these structures, some of which are questionable—e.g., in *carcará*, stressed *rá* is assigned w on her tree; and in *máquina*, stressed *má* is also w. Alternative structures for these syllable types are discussed in §4.1, below.

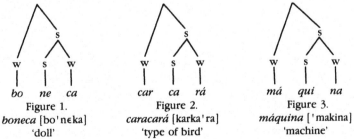

Figure 1.
boneca [bo'nɛka]
'doll'

Figure 2.
caracará [karka'ra]
'type of bird'

Figure 3.
máquina ['makina]
'machine'

Major (1981) and Cintra (1982) present evidence that BP is stress-timed; but they do not discuss degrees of stress, or how the syllables would be mapped onto a metrical grid.

The present paper will argue that BP prosody is organized in a rhythmic hierarchy which profoundly affects the phonology of the language. Instrumental and phonological evidence will demonstrate that this rhythmic patterning is present both synchronically and diachronically, and that it operates as style changes from formal to casual. Because there is little previous research to draw upon, the data here will mainly be limited to the word level. It is hoped that, in the future, this line of inquiry will be expanded to include larger utterances.

2. Instrumental Evidence

2.1. THE ACOUSTIC CORRELATES OF STRESS in natural languages are one or more of the following: pitch, intensity, and duration. English stress or linguistic accent includes all three factors: a stressed syllable is higher pitched, more intense, and longer (Lehiste 1970). In BP, the data given below show the same three correlates of stress, although duration is the most consistent.

2.2. DURATIONS OF TRISYLLABIC PAROXYTONES To control for intrinsic segmental differences in pitch, intensity, and duration, I have used a method of mimicry similar to that of Liberman and Streeter (1978), who employed a nonsense syllable /ma/. However, the use of /ma/ would not be satisfactory in BP, since stressed /a/ is raised before a nasal to become [ɐ] or [ɐ̃], but in unstressed position before a nasal the pronunciation alternates between [ɐ], [ɐ̃], and [a]. After experimenting with various syllables, I finally decided upon /la/, which speakers found easy to imitate.

Native speakers were asked to utter the sentence *Repita a palavra BA-TATA de novo* 'Repeat the word POTATO again.' Immediately after each utterance, the speakers repeated this frame sentence, but imitated the key word *batata* [ba'tata] using /la/ syllables; i.e., first *Repita a palavra BA-TATA de novo,* and then *Repita a palavra LALALA de novo.* Measurements were taken from a Mingograph 42B of the speakers' productions of the syllables in la'lala [la'lala]. The results are shown in Table 1.

Table 1

	Average Durations (msec)			Durational Ratios			Standard Deviations (msec)			
	S_1	S_2	S_3	S_2/S_1	S_2/S_3	S_1/S_3	S_1	S_2	S_3	
Speaker 1 (Bahia)	148	240	99	1.62	2.42	1.50	17	25	18	(N = 30)
Speaker 2 (Minas Gerais)	168	235	125	1.40	1.88	1.34	22	30	19	(N = 17)
Speaker 3 (Paraná)	164	255	111	1.55	2.30	1.48	20	26	17	(N = 38)

Levels of significance: mean durations between all syllables (for each speaker) are significant to > 0.01.

Table 1 clearly demonstrates that the tonic syllable is the longest, the posttonic the shortest, and the pretonic intermediate. In round figures, the durational ratios of the syllables for the paroxytone *lalala* are 3:4:2 or 3:5:2. If these figures roughly represent the ideal or preferred durations of paroxytones, this suggests that two degrees of stress exist, i.e., làlálå. In addition, native speakers often intuit these two degrees (cf. §4.1, below). If these durational differences reflect two degrees of stress, additional evidence should be present in the phonology (this is discussed in §3).

In the productions of the nonsense word *lalala*, the primary-stressed syllable typically showed a higher pitch, intensity, and length than either of the unstressed syllables. However, pitch and intensity were not always reliable correlates of stress. In some utterances, mingograms revealed that the intensity of the pretonic was approximately equal to that of the posttonic, though the posttonic was shorter; or that the intensity and pitch of the pretonic were approximately equal to that of the tonic, though the pretonic was shorter; or that the intensity and pitch of the posttonic were approximately equal to that of the tonic, though the posttonic was shorter. Thus the relative pitch and intensity of the syllables may vary considerably, while the durational ratios remain fairly constant. This indicates that the primary correlate of stress in BP is length.

3. Phonological Evidence

3.1. PHONOTACTICS In many languages, lack of stress is associated with the simplification of syllable structures—e.g., a decrease in the number of possible segments, consonant cluster simplification, or change from heavy to light syllables. BP shows large differences in phonotactic pattern among pretonic, posttonic, and tonic syllables: the largest number of combinations occurs tonically, a smaller number pretonically, and the smallest number posttonically. These differences support the acoustic data (§2.2) which suggest two degrees of stress in trisyllabic paroxytones—i.e., primary stress on the tonic syllable, secondary stress on the pretonic, and no stress on the posttonic (in what follows, G = glide, L = liquid, O = obstruent).

3.1.1. SYLLABLE STRUCTURE Harris (1983) presents evidence that the two immediate constituents of a syllable are the ONSET and the RHYME (which unites the nucleus and coda into a single superordinate constituent).[2] In this framework, BP syllable structure can be described as follows: the pretonic and tonic syllables have a maximum of five segments, and posttonic syllables a maximum of four. Onsets for all positions contain 0–2 elements; rhymes contain 1–4 segments in pretonic and tonic syllables,[3] and 1–3 segments in posttonic syllables. There are further stipulations when non-syllabic sonorants are involved: GVG is possible in pretonic and tonic position, but not posttonically. When the rhyme ends with /r/, GV*r* is permitted pretonically and tonically, but not posttonically:

(2) [kwaw'kɛr]   *qualquer*   'any'
     ['kways]   *quais*   'which'
     [kways'kɛr]   *quaisquer*   'whichever'
     ['agwas]   *águas*   'waters'
     but *['agway]
     [des'trɔys]   *destróis*   'destroy'
     [ẽ'kõtrẽw̃]   *encontram*   'they meet'
     [či'atrus]   *teatros*   'theaters'
     [perspek'čiva]   *perspectiva*   'perspective'
     [kwar'tɛw]   *quartel*   'headquarters'
     ['kwartu]   *quarto*   'room'
     but *['tukwar]

These examples raise the interesting question of whether prevocalic liquids (in initial OL clusters) belong to the onset or the rhyme. For Harris they are part of the onset (as in earlier traditional approaches), while glides in the same environment (OG) are part of the rhyme. However, if we consider the liquids as part of the rhyme instead of the onset, we can generalize that all sonorants (prevocalic and postvocalic) are in the rhyme; i.e., pretonic rhymes are all ([+son]) V ([+son]) ([+strid]), while posttonic are ([+son]) V ([+son]) or ([+son]) V ([+strid]). Furthermore, the claim that pretonic and tonic rhymes have 1–4 segments, while posttonic have 1–3, still holds. In addition, we correctly predict that /OLVVVs/ will be pronounced as disyllabic [OLV $VGs] (e.g., *cruéis* [cru'ɛys]) rather than monosyllabic *[OLGVGs], which would violate the four-segment maximum in rhymes. (If the liquid were part of the onset, such a monosyllable would be expected, since the rhyme would have only four segments.) Thus, because the behavior of the liquids and glides is similar, both might be considered part of the rhyme.[4]

3.1.2. ORAL VOWELS The distribution shown in Table 2 results from a tensing process which causes /ɛ ɔ/ to become [e o] when they lack primary stress, and from a raising process by which posttonic /e o/→ [i u] (see §3.23, below).

Table 2

PRETONIC	TONIC	POSTTONIC
i	i	i
e	e	
	ɛ	
a	a	a
	ɔ	
o	o	
u	u	u
['pɛ]	*pé*	'foot'
['mači]	*mate*	'type of tea'
[me'ninu]	*menino*	'boy'

3.1.3. NASAL VOWELS Five nasal vowels occur in tonic and pretonic positions; posttonically, only two occur, as shown in Table 3.

Table 3

PRETONIC	TONIC	POSTTONIC
ĩ	ĩ	
ẽ	ẽ (OR [ẽỹ])	ẽ (OR [ẽỹ])
ệ	ệ	
õ	õ (OR [õw̃])	õ (OR [õw̃])
ũ	ũ	
[sẽ'tar]	sentar	'to sit'
['sệ]	sã	'saint'
['nɛwsõ]	Nelson	'Nelson'

3.1.4. ORAL DIPHTHONGS[5] Twelve diphthongs occur tonically, eight pretonically, and three posttonically; see Table 4.

3.1.5. NASAL DIPHTHONGS Three nasal diphthongs occur in tonic and pretonic positions, and one in posttonic position; see Table 5. In many instances, the diphthongs result historically from deletion of intervocalic *n*, e.g., *panes* > *pães* 'breads'.

3.1.6. SUMMARY There is a noticeable simplicity in possible posttonic structures as compared with pretonic and tonic positions. These phonotactic patterns, in addition to the durational differences discussed in §2.2, further suggest two degrees of stress.

Table 4

PRETONIC	TONIC	POSTTONIC
uy	uy	
iw	iw	iw (from /il/)
ey	ey	ey (only in [eys])
ew	ew	ew (from /el/)
	ɛy	
	ɛw	
ay	ay	
aw	aw	
	ɔy	
	ɔw	
oy	oy	
ow	ow	
[dey'tẹmus]	deitamos	'we lie down'
['doys]	dois	'two'
['dɔys]	dóis	'hurt'
[ǰi'fisyu]	difícil	'difficult'
(→[ǰifisiw])		

Table 5

PRETONIC	TONIC	POSTTONIC	
ẽỹ	ẽỹ		
ẽw̃	ẽw̃	ẽw̃	
õỹ	õỹ		
[pẽỹ'zĩɲus]	pãezinhos	'rolls'	
['pẽw̃]	pão	'bread'	
['põỹ]	põe	'puts'	
['falẽw̃]	falam	'they speak'	

3.2. PHONOLOGICAL PROCESSES In many languages, presence of stress is associated with lengthening and strengthening processes, while lack of stress is associated with shortening and weakening. In American English these tendencies are apparent in the form of vowel reduction and deletion of unstressed syllables, but lengthening and diphthongization of stressed syllables. Thus, in many American dialects, /e o/ are diphthongized to [ey ow] (or [ɛ yʌw]) with primary stress, e.g., ['dey] *day* and ['now] *no*, but are monophthongized or reduced in the absence of primary stress, e.g., [ve'keyšən]~[və'keyšən] *vacation*, [no'teyšən] *notation*.

In addition, duration can affect the phonology independently of stress. For example, in many American dialects shortening of the stressed syllable in disyllabic words can prevent diphthongization, as in [dæɾi] *Daddy* beside [dæɡd] Dad, Southern [dæyd], Northern urban [deɡd]. Similarly, in Frisian (Cohen et al. 1961:118-21), a falling diphthong VG in a monosyllabic word undergoes a shift in syllabicity when it occurs in a disyllabic word—e.g., ['doɡs], ['dwaskɡ] *doas, doaske* 'box, little box'.

3.2.1. STYLES USED IN THIS STUDY In addition to stress and rhythm, the phonology of a language is affected by STYLE. For the purposes of this analysis, it is divided into three categories: CIT[ATION], NOR[MAL], and CAS[UAL]. I shall define these operationally in the following manner: CIT is the careful style of speech typical of reading a list of words or sentences in a slow, deliberate manner. NOR is the natural speech used in settings which vary from slightly informal to formal—such as a lecture, a newscast, or consultation with one's colleagues; it is the style which the layman considers good or correct pronunciation. CAS is used in very informal, casual, or intimate settings, e.g., conversation between good friends and lovers. The layman often considers this style to be incorrect or sloppy.

3.2.2. DIPHTHONGIZATION OF STRESSED SYLLABLES Both synchronically and diachronically stressed syllables in BP show a tendency to diphthongize. In Rio de Janeiro (the Carioca dialect), syllables with primary stress typically lengthen and develop a [y] or [ɡ] glide, depending on the environment.

In this dialect, syllable-final /s/ is [š], and word-final /Vs/ with primary stress is pronounced ['Vyš]:

(3) $[\theta] \rightarrow \begin{bmatrix} -syl \\ +hi \\ -bk \end{bmatrix}$ / $\begin{matrix} V \\ [+1\ stress] \end{matrix}$ __ [+strid] #

(/'Vs/#→['Vys])

e.g., ['payš]   paz   'peace'
      ['nɔyš]   nós   'us'
      but ['bašta] basta 'enough'

For many American English speakers, a similar process occurs; but it is usually limited to the vowels /æ/ and /ɛ/ with primary stress, e.g., ['mæyš] *mash*, ['preyšɹ̥] *pressure*. However, in Rio de Janeiro the glide [y] develops regardless of the vowel.

Again in the Rio dialect, especially in younger speakers, a shwa offglide [ə] occurs after a vowel with primary stress (except when it is followed by /s/, as above):[6]

(4) $[\theta] \rightarrow \begin{bmatrix} -syl \\ -bk \\ -hi \\ -lab \end{bmatrix}$ / $\begin{matrix} V \\ +1\ stress \\ -lo \end{matrix}$ __ [-strid]

(['V]→['Və])

e.g., [a'loə]   alô   'hello'
      ['friəta]   frita   'fries'
      but [fri'tar] fritar 'to fry'

In most dialects, the nasal vowels /ẽ õ/ are diphthongized when they have primary stress and are word-final: [bõw̃] *bom* 'good', [a'lẽỹ] *alem* 'besides', but [bõ'daʃi] *bondade* 'goodness', [sẽ'tar] *sentar* 'to sit'. Historically, diphthongization also occurred when /an/ changed to what is presently /ẽũ̃/, e.g., *pan* > *pão* [pẽw̃] 'bread'.

3.2.3. UNSTRESSED RAISING A number of reductive and shortening processes occur in syllables lacking primary stress. Just as pretonic and posttonic differences in phonotactics reflect stress differences, so differences in reductive processes provide further evidence for two degrees of stress. The conditions of Rule 5 are given in Table 6a, with examples in Table 6b.

(5) $\begin{bmatrix} V \\ -lo \\ -nas \end{bmatrix} \rightarrow [+hi]$

(/e o/ → [i u])

Table 6a

	CIT	NOR	CAS
Pretonic	–	–	±
Posttonic	±	+	+

Table 6b

CIT	NOR	CAS		
['fɛsta]	['fɛsta]	['fɛsta]	*festa*	'party'
[fes'čivo] [fes'čivu]	[fes'čivu]	[fis'čivu]	*festivo*	'festive'
[po'lido] [po'lidu]	[po'lidu]	[pu'lidu] *[pu'lido]	*polido*	'polite'
[me'nino] [me'ninu]	[me'ninu]	[mi'ninu] *[mi'nino]	*menino*	'boy'
[pe'dɛstre] [pe'dɛstre]	[pe'dɛstri]	[pi'dɛstri]	*pedestre*	'pedestrian'

Raising is obligatory posttonically in NOR, but pretonically it occurs only in CAS. For many speakers, non-raised [e o] occur posttonically in CIT. The difference in the operation of this raising process is undoubtedly influenced by stress differences realized by differences in durations of the pretonic and posttonic syllables. Since [i u] are intrinsically shorter than [e o] (Lehiste 1970), the raising process in the posttonic syllable reduces the length of the syllable where a short duration is required. In the pretonic position, which has a longer duration, the raising process occurs only in CAS. Since the tempo of CAS is generally faster than NOR, the operation of this process pretonically also has the effect of shortening.

In CIT, some speakers produce non-raised posttonic [e o], while others show [i u]. For the speakers who produce [i u], one might consider that the raising process is now a lexical constraint as the result of an historical process, the motivation of which seems to be shortening. In contrast, the other speakers produce [e~i] and [o~u] alterations. But since the posttonic is shorter than the pretonic, why would [e o] occur in CIT, if shortening is the motivation for raising? The explanation lies in the difference between CIT and NOR. My data on syllable durations were based on NOR, where *lalala* occurred in the middle of a sentence. Since many languages show prepausal lengthening (e.g., English; cf. Klatt 1975), this possibility must be considered for the CIT utterances, where each word is produced in isolation and is followed by a pause. To test this, I asked Speaker 3 (Paraná) to produce *batata* 'potato' in isolation with *lalala* imitations. Table 7 shows the results, and compares CIT (isolated productions) with NOR (uttered in a sentence).

Table 7

	Average Durations (msec)			Durational Ratios			Standard Deviations (msec)			
	S_1	S_2	S_3	S_2/S_3	S_2/S_3	S_1/S_3	S_1	S_2	S_3	
Citation	168	276	169	1.64	1.63	0.99	14	20	19	(N = 30)
Normal	164	255	111	1.55	2.30	1.48	20	26	17	(N = 38)

Levels of significance: for CIT, mean durations between S_1 and S_2, and between S_3 and S_2, are significant to > 0.01; durations between S_1 and S_3 not significant. For NOR, mean durations between all syllables are significant to > 0.01.

Table 7 demonstrates that BP has prepausal lengthening; in fact, the differences in duration between pretonic and posttonic syllables are not significant. This suggests that non-raised [e o] are permitted posttonically in CIT precisely because, in that style, the posttonic syllable is much longer than in NOR.

Clearly, speakers who show posttonic [e~o o~u] alternations (in CIT and NOR) have underlying /e o/; [i u] can be derived by Rule 5. In contrast, some speakers produce only [i u] in CIT, which might lead one to conclude that these speakers have underlying /i u/. Even if this were true, the phonetic motivation of the historical change would be shortening, since [i u] are shorter than [e o]. Raising, then, would be a lexical constraint rather than a process which produces surface alternations. However, even for this group of speakers, evidence exists that raising is a productive synchronic process, when one considers verb forms and compounding (cf. Redenbarger 1976, Major 1979):

(6)	/kom + e/	['kɔmi]	*come*	'eats'
	/kom + e + mos/	[ko'memus]	*comemos*	'we eat'
	/sono/	['sonu]	*sono*	'sleep'
	/sonoterapia/	[sonotera'pia]	*sonoterapia*	'sleep therapy'

Raising also occurs for the nasal vowels, but only in very casual speech. The conditions of Rule 7 are given in Table 8a, with examples in Table 8b.

$$(7) \quad \begin{bmatrix} V \\ -lo \\ +nas \end{bmatrix} \rightarrow [+ hi]$$

$(/\tilde{e}\ \tilde{o}/ \rightarrow [\tilde{i}\ \tilde{u}])$

Table 8a

	CIT	NOR	CAS
Pretonic	−	−	±
Posttonic	−	−	±

Condition: The process will operate in pretonic CAS if and only if [õ] is not derived from /ɐu/ (see Rule 12, below).

Table 8b

CIT	NOR	CAS		
['õtẽỹ]	['õtẽ]	['õtẽ] ['õčĩ]	*ontem*	'yesterday'
[sẽ'tar]	[sẽ'tar]	[sẽ'tar] [sĩ'tar]	*sentar*	'to sit'
['nɛwsõw̃]	['nɛwsõ]	['nɛwsõ] ['nɛwsũ]	*Nelson*	'Nelson'
[kõ'tar]	[kõ'tar]	[kõ'tar] [kũ'tar]	*contar*	'to tell'

Clearly, nasality is an inhibiting factor in the raising process. In addition, BP has a diphthongization process which changes word-final /ẽ õ/ to [ẽỹ õw̃] (both tonically and posttonically for some speakers). This diphthongization process may further inhibit the operation of raising for the nasal vowels. A possible explanation for the limited raising of the nasal vowels is in terms of their phonemic status. An old controversy among scholars of BP is whether the nasal vowels are underlyingly nasal /Ṽ/, or vowel plus nasal consonant /VN/. Heavy syllables generally undergo reduction less readily than light syllables, which tend to be shorter in duration. Maia has presented instrumental evidence that BP nasal vowels are longer than the oral counterparts—which, taken in conjunction with the fact that the nasal vowels undergo raising much less readily than the oral vowels, suggests that the former are phonemically heavy syllables, and should be represented as /VN/.

Raising may also occur when /e o/ are followed by a tautosyllabic glide, but only posttonically in CAS. The conditions of Rule 8 are given in Table 9a, with examples in Table 9b.

$$(8) \quad \begin{matrix} V \\ [-\text{lo}] \end{matrix} \rightarrow [+\text{hi}]/\underline{\quad} G$$

([ey ew oy ow ẽỹ õw̃] → [i iw uy u ĩ ũ])

Table 9a

	CIT	NOR	CAS
Pretonic	–	–	–
Posttonic	–	–	+

Table 9b

CIT	NOR	CAS		
[ǰi'fiseys]	[ǰi'fises]	[ǰi'fisis]	*difíceis*	'difficult' (pl.)
[dey'tḛmos]	[de'tḛmus]	[de'tḛmus] *[ǰi'tḛmus]	*deitamos*	'we lie down'
[vow'tḛmos]	[vo'tḛmus]	[vo'tḛmus] *[vu'tḛmus]	*voltamos*	'we return'
[fa'larẽỹ]	[fa'larẽ]	[fa'larĩ]	*falarem*	'will speak' (subj.)

3.2.4. MONOPHTHONGIZATION Unstressed diphthongs may be shortened to monophthongs. The conditions of Rule 9 are given in Table 10 (see examples in Table 9b, below).

$$(9)\quad \begin{bmatrix} V \\ -hi \\ \alpha bk \end{bmatrix} \begin{bmatrix} V \\ +hi \\ \alpha bk \end{bmatrix} \rightarrow \begin{matrix} V \\ \\ \end{matrix}$$

$$\quad\quad\quad 1 \quad\quad\ 2 \quad\quad\quad 1$$

(/ei ou ai/ → [e o a]; [ẽỹ õw̃] → [ẽ,õ])

Rule 9 feeds the raising Rule 5; but raising of /ei ou/ is limited to posttonic CAS, as stated above. It is possible to eliminate Rule 8 if pretonic raising is ordered before monophthongization; this would account for the non-occurrence of *[ji'tẽmus] and *[vu'tẽmus] in CAS:

Table 10

	CIT	NOR	CAS
Pretonic	−	±	+
Posttonic	−	+	+

(10)	/dei'tamos/	/vou'tamos/
Raising	[dey'tẽmus]	[vow'tẽmus]
Monophthongization	[de'tẽmus]	[vo'tẽmus]

Posttonically, the correct output would result if both processes applied simultaneously and iteratively (or by ordering monophthongization before raising). However, a counterfeeding order can be interpreted as a restriction on iteration, rather than ordering (Donegan and Stampe 1979). In that case, if raising and monophthongization are operable at the same time, only monophthongization can apply, since raising does not occur before a tautosyllabic vowel. If raising can apply only once, the result will be non-raised [e o]:[7]

(11)		/dei'tamos/	/vou'tamos/
	Raising and monophthongization	[de'tẽmus]	[vo'tẽmus]

Rule 9 deletes a glide after a syllable nucleus. Monophthongization also occurs with /au ẽũ/, but the resultant monophthongs are intermediate between the initial and final segments, i.e., [o õ]. The conditions of Rule 12 are given in Table 11a, with examples in Table 11b.

$$(12)\quad [+lo] \begin{bmatrix} V \\ +hi \\ +bk \end{bmatrix} \rightarrow \begin{bmatrix} V \\ -hi \\ -lo \\ +bk \end{bmatrix}$$

$$\quad\quad\ 1 \quad\quad 2 \quad\quad\quad\ 1$$

(/au ẽũ/ → [o õ])

Table 11a

	CIT	NOR	CAS
Pretonic	–	–	+
Posttonic	–	+	+

Table 11b

CIT	NOR	CAS		
[fa'larẽw̃]	[fa'larõ]	[fa'larũ]	*falaram*	'they spoke'
[pẽw̃'ziɲu]	pẽw̃'ziɲu]	[põ'ziɲu] *[pũ'ziɲu]	*pãozinho*	'roll'
[maw'risyo]	[maw'risyu]	[mo'risyu] *[mu'risyu]	*Maurício*	'Maurice'

Since there is a lexical constraint against posttonic /ai au/, their monophthongization is not observable synchronically. However, all loanwords with posttonic diphthongs are restressed so that stress falls on the diphthongs, e.g., *playgróund, handóut, playbóy*. These examples show that, rather than generating an unpronounceable representation in prosodic processing (i.e., stress assignment) and then repairing it by segmental processing via monophthongization, BP assigns stress according to the normal rule which stresses final diphthongs. Thus posttonic monophthongization of /ai au/ may be considered obligatory.

3.2.5. SYLLABICITY SHIFTS Underlying unstressed /VV/ sequences are potentially either disyllabic or monosyllabic on the surface; and some sequences which are disyllabic in one style may become monosyllabic in another, because of glide formation, e.g., [pie'daʝi] (NOR) → [pye'daʝ] (CAS) *piedade* 'pity'. This type of shift or desyllabification, which involves vowels of different heights, can be considered a shortening process, since it reduces the number of syllables from two to one.[8] The higher vowel becomes the glide; this follows from a universal sonority hierarchy which predicts that the less sonorous element will become non-syllabic. The rule for desyllabification is as follows; conditions are given in Table 12a, and examples in Table 12b.

(13) V_1V_2
     ↓
     G
   Condition: height $V_2 > V_1$

Table 12a

	CIT	NOR	CAS
Pretonic	+	+	+
Posttonic	+	+	+

Table 12b

CIT	NOR	CAS		
[koy'tado]	[koy'tadu]	[koy'tadu]	*coitado*	'poor guy'
[dow'rado]	[do'radu]	[do'radu]	*dourado*	'golden'
[ji'fiseys]	[ji'fises]	[ji'fisis]	*difíceis*	'difficult' (pl.)

Note that in some of the examples above, monophthongization and raising apply after glide formation (Rules 9 and 5). The conditions of Rule 14 are given in Table 13a, with examples in Table 13b.

(14) V_1V_2
    $\downarrow$
    G
    Condition: height V1 > V2

Table 13a

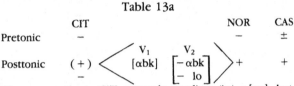

	CIT			NOR	CAS
Pretonic	−			−	±
Posttonic	(+) / −			+	+

The condition on posttonic CIT correctly predicts /io/ → [yo], but otherwise /VV/ → [V$V].

Table 13b

CIT	NOR	CAS		
['labyo]	['labyu]	['labyu]	*lábio*	'lip'
['sabia]	['sabya]	['sabya]	*sábia*	'wise' (fem.)
[pie'dade]	[pie'daji]	[pye'daj]	*piedade*	'pity'
[sua'jiɲa]	[sua'jiɲa]	[swa'jiɲa]	*suadinha*	'sweaty'

For those speakers who in CIT raise final unstressed vowels, /io/→[yu] (in accordance with Rules 15–16, below).

A sequence of stressed vowel plus high vowel is monosyllabic on the surface in all styles; it is pronounced [VG], not *[GV]. If the syllable becomes destressed and both vowels are high, the syllabicity can shift from [VG] to [GV]. Such syllabicity shifts have been associated with shortening resulting from lack of stress (see §3.2); such a shift never occurs in BP on a tonic syllable. However, because of sentence-level stress, a whole word may become destressed, which results in a syllabicity shift for the normally tonic syllable, e.g., ['čia'marsia] → [čya'marsya] *tia Márcia* 'Aunt Marcia'. Either the first or second vowel yields the glide, depending on whether raising applies in CIT for a given speaker. In the first case, Rule 15 applies, with style conditions as in Table 14.

(15) V_1V_2
      $\downarrow$
      G
Condition: height $V_1 = V_2$

Table 14

	CIT	NOR	CAS
Pretonic	–	–	±
Posttonic	$(+)\langle V\# \rightarrow [-hi]$ in CIT $\rangle$ –	+	+

In the second case, Rule 16 applies, with style conditions as in Table 15.

(16) V_1V_2
      $\downarrow$
      G
Condition: height $V_1 = V_2$.

Table 15

	CIT	NOR	CAS
Pretonic	–	–	±
Posttonic	$(+)<V\# \rightarrow [+hi]$ in CIT$>$ –	–	–

The style conditions on 15–16 state that either may apply, but not both. Examples are given in Table 16.

Table 16

CIT	NOR	CAS		
['žemyo] ['žemyu]	['žemyu]	[žemyu]	*gêmeo*	'twin'
[siu'mẽto]	[siu'mẽtu]	[syu'mẽtu] [siw'mẽtu]	*ciumento*	'jealousy'

These glide formations, involving underlying vowels of equal height, indicate that the posttonic has a decided preference for GV. Posttonically, VG occurs only in CIT, and only for those speakers who obligatorily raise final V; otherwise GV occurs. By contrast, pretonic position shows GV only in CAS, where it also alternates with VG; either vowel may raise and subsequently form a glide. However, this prevents the other vowel from raising (as in the other two glide-formation processes discussed above). Since experimental data on syllable durations show that the posttonic syllable is considerably shorter than the pretonic, the shorter duration may be a causal factor in the operation of these shortening processes.

The durational measurements, however, were for trisyllabic paroxytones (SŚS), but not words with two pretonic and/or two posttonic syllables (SSŚSS), which Rules 15–16 include. My implicit argument is that if, in $S_1S_2S_3$, we find $S_1 > S_3$, then in $S_1S_2\acute{S}_3S_4S_5$ (or $S_1S_2\acute{S}_3$, $\acute{S}_1S_2S_3$, etc.), we should find $S_1S_2 > S_4S_5$. However, no experimental evidence exists to support this. Therefore, I made a very limited study of words of the type SSŚ and ŚSS, to look for differences between durations of pretonic and posttonic disyllabic sequences, using the method of nonsense-syllable mimicry. In the frame *Repita a palavra lalalá/lálala de novo,* Speaker 2 pronounced [lala'la] and ['lalala] with the following durations (in microseconds):

(17) $S_1S_2\acute{S}_3$: 210, 175, 262
     $\acute{S}_1S_2S_3$: 238, 135, 148
                   Pretonic: $S_1 + S_2 = 385$ msec ($N = 4$)
                   Posttonic: $S_2 + S_3 = 283$ msec ($N = 6$)

Since the sample size was extremely small, these results should be taken only as tentative or suggestive. They do, however, support the hypothesis that pretonic and posttonic differences are factors governing VV shortening processes, since #SS sequences are longer than SS# sequences.

Other shifts in syllabicity involve syllable-final /l/, which phonetically is realized as [w]; e.g., *mal* 'badly' and *mau* 'bad' are both pronounced [maw]. In /il/ sequences, the syllabicity can shift from [iw] to [yu]. The conditions of Rule 18 are given in Table 17a, with examples in Table 17b.

$$(18)\quad \begin{bmatrix} +\text{syl} \\ -\text{cns} \\ +\text{hi} \\ -\text{bk} \end{bmatrix} \begin{bmatrix} -\text{syl} \\ -\text{cns} \\ +\text{hi} \\ +\text{bk} \end{bmatrix} \rightarrow [-\text{syl}]\,[+\text{syl}]$$
$$\qquad\qquad 1 \qquad\quad 2 \qquad\quad 1 \qquad 2$$
$$(/il/ \rightarrow [iw] \rightarrow [yu]$$

Table 17a

	CIT	NOR	CAS
Pretonic	−	−	±
Posttonic	−	+	+

Table 17b

CIT	NOR	CAS		
[fiw'mẽmos]	[fiw'mẽmus]	[fiw'mẽmus] [fyu'mẽmus]	*filmamos*	'we film'
['abiw]	['abyu]	['abyu]	*hábil*	'skillful'

Unstressed /el/ also can undergo a syllabicity shift, but only posttonically. The conditions of Rule 19 are given in Table 18a, and examples in Table 18b.

(19) $\begin{bmatrix} +syl \\ -cns \\ -hi \\ -lo \\ -bk \end{bmatrix} \begin{bmatrix} -syl \\ -cns \\ +hi \\ +bk \\ 2 \end{bmatrix} \rightarrow [+hi] \rightarrow [-syl] \ [+syl]$

          1   1 2   1   2

(/el/ → [ew] → [iw] → [yu])

Table 18a

	CIT	NOR	CAS
Pretonic	−	−	−
Posttonic	−	−	+

Table 18b

CIT	NOR	CAS		
[a'mavew]	[a'mavew]	[a'maviw] [a'mavyu]	*amável*	'loveable'
[dew'gado]	[dew'gadu]	[dew'gadu] *[jiw'gadu] *[jyu'gadu]	*delgado*	'slim'

Since syllabicity shifts involving /il el/ are favored posttonically, it appears that the lack of phonological stress (phonetically realized as a short posttonic syllable) is a factor which influences the operation of these shortening processes.

Figures 4–7 demonstrate syllabicity shifts. In general, these spectrograms show that the most prominent part of the diphthong or syllabic portion has a longer steady state and shorter transition than the non-syllabic (glide) portion—which has a shorter steady state or none at all, and a relatively longer transition.

3.2.6. SUMMARY The shortening processes of raising, monophthongization, and syllabicity shift are clearly favored in posttonic position: the conditions for the processes may be summarized quite simply as pretonic ⊃ posttonic. In other words, if one of these processes applies pretonically (in a given style), then one of them necessarily applies posttonically as well, but not vice versa. Thus a process that applies posttonically in NOR may apply pretonically only in CAS, or not at all, e.g., in Rule 15 above: /VV/ → [GV], ['labyu] (NOR) *lábio* 'lip', but [pyo'neru] (CAS only) *pioneiro* 'pioneer'. However, the converse does not hold true: it is never the case that pretonic shortening processes occur posttonically in CAS, but not in NOR or CIT.

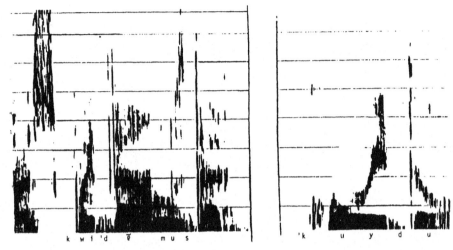

cuidamos 'we take care of' (NOR) *cuido* 'I take care of' (CIT)

k w í 'd ẽ m u s   'k u y d u

Figure 4. Speaker 4 (Matto Grosso).

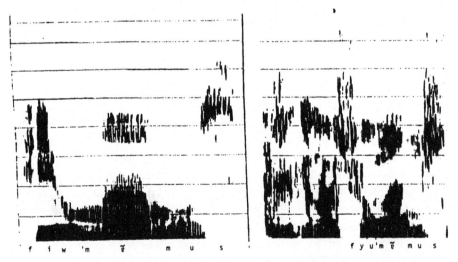

filmamos 'we film' (CIT) *filmamos* 'we film' (CAS)

f í w 'm ẽ m u s   f y u 'm ẽ m u s

Figure 5. Speaker 4 (Matto Grosso).

20

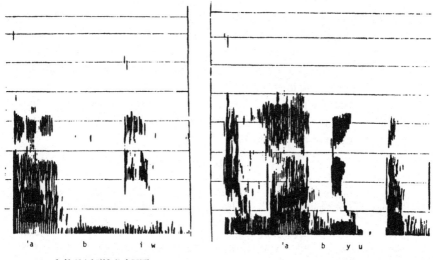

hábil 'skillful' (CIT)   *hábil* 'skillful' (NOR)

Figure 6. Speaker 1 (Bahia).

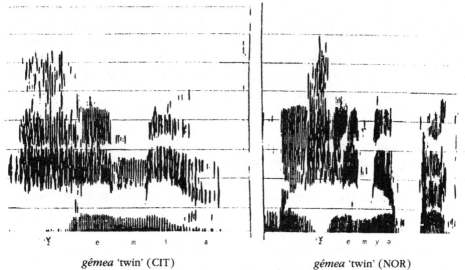

gêmea 'twin' (CIT)   *gêmea* 'twin' (NOR)

Figure 7. Speaker 1 (Bahia).

Rules 15–16 deserve comment. Rule 16 is optional pretonic in CAS, but does not occur in posttonic CAS. Because it is a shortening process (desyllabification), this appears to be a counter-example to the claim that pretonic⊃ posttonic. However, Rule 15 applies posttonically in CAS and NOR, but pretonically only in CAS. Rule 16 produces [VG], while Rule 15 produces [GV]; and although both are shortening processes, 15 produces a shorter (open) syllable than 16 (which produces a closed syllable). Therefore, the preference for 15 over 16 posttonically demonstrates the susceptibility to shortening in this position.

The implication pretonic⊃ posttonic is illustrated in Table 19, where more than one process can apply to a given word. The numbers in parentheses refer to the rules in §§3.23-3.25.

Table 19

CIT	NOR	CAS			
[pay'zežēȳ]	[pay'zažē] (7, 9)	[pa'zaži]	*paisagem*	'scenery'	*[pa'zažēȳ]
[fiw'miɲo]	[fiw'miɲu] (5, 18)	[fyu'miɲo]	*filminho*	'little film'	*[fyu'miɲo]
[se'naryo]	[se'naryu] (5, 14, 18)	[si'naryu]	*cenário*	'scene'	*[si'naryo]
[maw'risyo]	[maw'risyu] (5, 9, 14, 16)	[mo'risyu]	*Maurício*	'Maurice'	*[mo'risyo]
[saw'davew]	[saw'davew] (8, 9, 19)	[so'davyu]	*saudável*	'healthy'	*[so'davew]
[leo'pardo]	[leo'pardu] (5, 15, 16)	[lew'pardu] [ʎo'pardu]	*leopardo*	'leopard'	*[lew'pardo] *[ʎo'pardo]
[kõ'tarẽw̃]	[kõ'tarõ] (7, 12)	[kũ'tarũ]	*contaram*	'they told'	*[kũ'tarẽw̃]
[pẹ̃w̃'ziɲo]	[pẹ̃w̃'ziɲu] (5, 12)	[põ'ziɲu]	*pãozinho*	'roll'	*[pūziɲu]

The starred forms in Table 19 emphasize the pretonic⊃ posttonic relationship. These forms are tantamount to mixing styles, e.g., *[mi'nino] would be equivalent to pretonic CAS + posttonic CIT, a phenomenon nonexistent in natural speech. The examples demonstrate that the shortening processes are favored as one goes from CIT to NOR to CAS, and that they are favored in posttonic over pretonic position.

The data in this section demonstrate how rhythmic structure at the word level governs the phonology of a language. Since a shortening process necessarily operates posttonically before it operates pretonically, and since the posttonic syllable is considerably shorter than the pretonic, I conclude that phonological stress is a causal factor for these phenomena. This, in addition to the instrumental and phonotactic evidence discussed above, provides strong evidence that two degrees of stress are present in trisyllabic paroxytones; primary stress on the tonic syllable, secondary stress on the pretonic, and no stress on the posttonic. This hierarchical relationship is represented in a metrical tree structure shown in Figure 8.

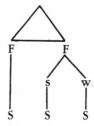

Figure 8. F = foot, S = syllable; s = strong, w = weak.

4. Other Stress Patterns and Longer Utterances

4.1. PROPAROXYTONES AND OXYTONES The data from trisyllabic paroxytones in §§2–3 above provide phonological and instrumental evidence that BP has two degrees of stress. Further evidence emerges when one considers other stress patterns.

The behavior of the penultimate and ultimate syllables in proparoxytones indicates that they contain no stress. In these positions, only a single segment is permitted in the rhyme (except for /Vs/#), e.g., nonsense *pábanta, *pábasta, *pábarta, *pábatar, *pábatan, *páboita, but pábatas (cf. Maia). In addition, words of this type almost always show penultimate /e o/ reduced to [i u] in NOR and CAS, e.g., [ʝi'alugu] diálogo 'dialog', ['trafigu] tráfego 'traffic'; in trisyllabic paroxytones, the pretonic syllable is reduced only in CAS (§3.23). In addition, the penultimate syllable has a tendency to be deleted in CAS, e.g., [a'bɔbora] → [a'bɔbra] abóbora 'pumpkin', ['arvor-i] → ['arvri] árvore 'tree', ['asidu] → ['asdu] ácido 'acid'. These data strongly suggest that the penultimate and ultimate syllables in proparoxytones have no stress; this is represented in Figure 9.[9]

Figure 9.

In oxytones, the pretonic syllables may contain two segments in the rhyme, e.g., importar 'to import'. These syllables do not undergo reduction as readily as posttonic syllables; thus the raising of pretonic /e/ to [i] in [sili'sẽw] seleção 'selection' would occur only in extremely casual speech, if at all. In contrast, ['trafigu] tráfego 'traffic' occurs in NOR. Furthermore, the vowel in the pretonic syllables of trisyllabic oxytones is deleted only in extremely casual speech, e.g., [mere'ser] → [mer'ser] *merecer* 'to deserve'. This suggests that both pretonic syllables carry secondary stress—in contrast to the posttonic syllables, which carry no stress.

In English, vowel quality and syllable weight are important factors bearing on surface stress assignment; e.g., the first syllables of *dynamic* and *canteen* carry more stress than those of *fanatic* and *container.* In BP, however, the evidence up to this point suggests that there are predetermined rhythmic types; and both vowel quality and syllable weight result from stress, rather than vice versa. The data on oxytones, paroxytones, and proparoxytones demonstrate that posttonic syllables (as compared to pretonic ones) readily undergo vowel reduction, and have limitations regarding syllable weight. This strongly suggests that pretonic syllables carry greater stress.

This conclusion is further supported by native speakers' intuitions. When I asked several consultants to distinguish relative degrees of stress, their responses were quite uniform. In paroxytones, e.g., [ba'tata] *batata* 'potato', they felt that the pretonic was stronger than the posttonic. In proparoxytones, e.g., [ʝi'alugu] *diálogo* 'dialog', they were unable to decide which of the posttonic syllables was weaker, but they felt that both were weaker than the pretonic syllable(s). In trisyllabic oxytones, speakers felt that both pretonic syllables were of equal strength, and that this did not depend on syllable weight; the pretonic syllables were perceived to be of equal strength in *emprestar* 'to loan', *vatapá* 'type of food dish', *seleção* 'selection', and *importar* 'to import'.

My conclusion, based on instrumental and phonological data as well as intuitions of native speakers, is that BP has two degrees of stress. After primary stress is assigned (which is variable), the remaining syllables receive secondary stress or no stress in a predictable manner. Examples of the various word types are shown in Figures 10–12.[10]

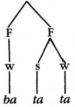

Figure 10. S'SS: *bătătă* 'potato'

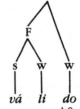

Figure 11. 'SSS: *vălidŏ* 'valid'

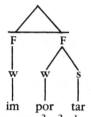

Figure 12. SS'S: ímportar 'import'

When one considers that relative stress changes when words are combined in a sentence, it is possible to distinguish three degrees of stress.[11] Thus in *Comprei quinze batatas* 'I bought fifteen potatoes', the stressed medial *ta* in *batata* is somewhat stronger than the stressed syllable *quin* in *quinze*. Using numerical notations, this difference could be represented as *quinze batatas*. Word compounds can also create a third degree of stress, e.g., *beija-flor* 'hummingbird' vs. *beija Márcia* 'kiss Marcia'. However, this third degree emerges only in utterances of two or more words; there is no evidence for three degrees on the single-word level, as in Eng. *intelligentsia* and *ambassadorial*.

4.2. ALTERNATING STRESS PATTERNS In many languages, such as English, stress tends to be repeated at regular intervals. Maia has noted this tendency in BP for relatively long words, as in Figure 13.

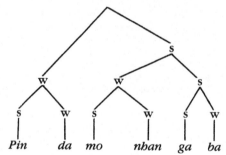

Figure 13. Pindamonhangaba (name of a city).

Other data reveal a similar tendency. Thus the pretonic *cul* in *faculdade* 'college' tends to be much more reduced than when it occurs in *culpado* 'guilty'—suggesting that, in the former case, *cul* is actually posttonic in a preceding foot. Similarly, the pretonic *pa* in *Ipanema* (a placename) is often reduced to [pə]; but in *palito* 'toothpick' it is never reduced to *[pə'litu]*.

To test this further, I asked native speakers to pronounce several nonsense words with penultimate stress and unstressed /e/ in pretonic positions, e.g., *pinelico, penilico, panelaco,* and *penalaco.* They showed a greater tendency to reduce /e/ to [i] when it immediately preceded the primary-stressed syllable than when it was two syllables before; e.g., *pane-laco* → [pani'laku], but *penalaco* → [pena'laku]. However, sometimes speakers did not reduce /e/ at all in either pretonic position, as shown in Figure 14.

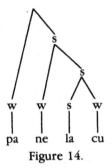

Figure 14.

These observations suggest a tendency for an alternating s/w pattern; but it is not so overwhelming as to cause a necessary disruption in the stress patterns of Figures 10–12, which assign secondary stress to all pretonic syllables.

There is also a slight tendency for stress to shift to alternating patterns in a sentence. Thus, although *você* 'you' is normally pronounced [vo'se], the stress may shift to ['vose] to accommodate an alternating s/w pattern:

(20) *Ténho certéza que vo'cê falóu.*
      'I'm certain that you spoke.'
(21) *Ténho certéza que 'você fói p'ra cása.*
      'I'm certain that you went home.'

However this is only a tendency; *você* in 21 can also be pronounced [vo'se].

4.3. Stress-Timing Considerable work on English has dealt with stress alignment to a metrical grid at the sentence level, in order to accommodate stress-timing (Liberman and Prince 1977; Prince 1983). Investigations of this type have not yet been undertaken in BP; however, I can offer some preliminary observations.

Major (1981) presents instrumental, phonological, and perceptual evidence that BP has a tendency toward stress-timing. The data also reveal a greater tendency for intervals to be isochronous if they differ in the number of posttonic, rather than pretonic, syllables. This follows logically from the preference for posttonic over pretonic shortening. However, because these pretonic and posttonic differences are lessened as style changes from CIT to NOR to CAS (allowing pretonic syllables to be reduced, and perhaps with a concomitant decrease in stress), the language becomes increasingly stress-timed as style becomes more casual. These observations suggest that sentence-level rhythmic tendencies (i.e., stress-timing) can disrupt or alter word-level rhythmic patterns. The formalization and other specifics of this await further work.

4.4. SUMMARY Data on different word types, showing that posttonic syllables are weaker than pretonic ones, suggest two degrees of stress; data on longer utterances suggest three degrees. Word-level stress can be disrupted to accommodate a tendency toward stress-timing and an alternating s/w pattern.[12]

5. Conclusion

This paper has argued that Brazilian Portuguese prosody is organized in a rhythmic hierarchy which governs the phonology of the language synchronically and diachronically, and which follows style changes from formal to normal to casual. At the word level, two degrees of phonological stress are proposed: the tonic syllable carries primary stress, pretonic syllables carry secondary stress, and posttonic syllables carry no stress. This conclusion is supported by instrumental data on durations, which show that tonic syllables are longest, posttonic are shortest, and pretonic are intermediate. Phonotactic data lend further support. Posttonically, the allowable structures are fewer and simpler than in other positions; e.g., there are 15 tonic dipthongs, of which 11 occur pretonically, but only 4 posttonically.

The strongest evidence for two degrees of stress comes from data on phonological processes. The operation of the reductive or shortening processes of raising, monophthongization, and syllabicity shifts is inversely proportional to the proposed degrees of stress. This hierarchical relationship can be expressed as pretonic ⊃ posttonic; i.e., in a given style, any process which occurs pretonically will necessarily occur posttonically, but not vice versa. This implicational hierarchy strongly suggests that pretonic syllables carry more stress than posttonic ones.

The data on phonotactics and phonological processes indicate that words are organized in certain rhythmic types which govern vowel quality and rhyme structure. In longer utterances, the rhythmic patterning of single words can be disrupted, because of tendencies toward an alternating s/w pattern and stress-timing. Since the tendency toward stress-timing increases as style becomes more casual, word-level patterns can become increasingly disrupted. Other hierarchical principles which may be involved, and the specifics of mapping these relationships onto a metrical grid, have not yet been worked out. However, the data on longer utterances suggest that this is a promising area for further research.

NOTES

[1] I wish to thank Mary Clayton, Lynn Gordon, and Ellen Kaisse for their useful suggestions and comments. Reprint from LANGUAGE, Volume 61, Number 2 (1985).

[2] Although the term 'coda' may be used for convenience in this system, Harris argues that it is not theoretically significant.

[3] This contrasts with possible rhymes in Spanish, which contain a maximum of three segments (cf. Harris). Thus GVGs occurs in Portuguese, but not Spanish, rhymes.

[4] This proposal would require further conditions, by which a single prevocalic sonorant consonant would be in the onset rather than in the rhyme. One possibility might be that empty onset positions are preferentially filled by non-syllabics before any prevocalic filling of the rhyme.

[5] These phonetic [VG] sequences are derived from /VV/, discussed in §3.2.5.

[6] The process also will not operate when the primary-stressed vowel is followed by another vowel. This is because a glide develops which precludes [ə] insertion, since syllable structure will not permit two postvocalic glides in a rhyme.

[7] Another solution would appear possible if the raising process were stated differently. Although the processes above indicate that monophthongization is an intermediate stage to raising, i.e., [ey] → [e] → [i] and [ow] → [o] → [u], it is conceivable that [ey ow] could go directly to [i u] (thus being assimilated to the following glide). In that case, the raising process would be:

$$
\begin{matrix} \text{V} \\ \begin{bmatrix} -\text{lo} \\ \alpha\text{bk} \end{bmatrix} \end{matrix} \rightarrow [+\text{hi}]/\underline{\quad} \begin{matrix} \text{G} \\ [\alpha\text{bk}] \end{matrix}
$$

Stated thus, the process would be restricted to posttonic position. However, this solution would not prevent pretonic [e o] (from monophthongization of /ei ou/) from being raised to non-occurring *[i u]. Thus the only reasonable course is to order raising before monophthongization, or to restrict the iteration of the two processes.

[8] Although this is a shortening process, one might suspect that the real motivation is to remove the hiatus between vowels, in which case shorten-

ing would merely be accidental. However, the fact that glide insertion is not used to break hiatus, i.e., *[piye'daji] *piedade* 'pity', suggests that the motivation for the desyllabification is shortening.

[9] The instrumental results also support this to some extent; but since the sample size is extremely small, the data are merely suggestive.

[10] No other stress patterns are possible; i.e., stress must fall on one of the last three syllables of a word.

[11] See the works of Câmara, discussed in §1.2.

[12] There seems to no obvious reason why shortening processes are favored in posttonic position over pretonic position. This pattern in BP is the mirror image of English—where, in trisyllabic paroxytones, the pretonic syllable is reduced before the posttonic, e.g., *potato* [po'teto], [pə'teɾo], [pə'teə], *[po'teɾə].

REFERENCES

Câmara, Joaquim Mattoso, Jr. 1969. Problemas de lingüística descritiva. Petrópolis: Vozes.

———. 1972a. Estrutura da língua portuguesa. Petrópolis: Vozes.

———. 1972b. The Portuguese language. Translated by Anthony J. Naro. Chicago: University of Chicago Press.

Cintra, Geraldo, 1982. Duração de segmentos fônicos em português. Paper presented at the VII Encontro Nacional de Lingüística. Rio de Janeiro: Pontifícia Universidade Católica.

Cohen, A., et al. 1961. Fonologie van het Nederlands en het Fries. 2nd ed. The Hague: Nijhoff.

Donegan, Patricia J., and David Stampe. 1979. The study of natural phonology. In Daniel A. Dinnsen (ed.), Current approaches to phonological theory, pp. 126–73. Bloomington: Indiana University Press.

Halle, Morris, and Jean-Roger Vergnaud. 1980. Three-dimensional phonology. Journal of Linguistic Research 1.83-105.

———. 1984. Three-dimensional phonology. Ms.

Harris, James W. 1983. Syllable structure and stress in Spanish: A non-linear analysis. Cambridge, MA: MIT Press.

Hayes, Bruce. 1981. A metrical theory of stress rules. Bloomington: Indiana University Linguistics Club.

———. 1984. The phonology of rhythm in English. Linguistic Inquiry 15.33-74.

Klatt, Dennis H. 1975. Vowel lengthening is syntactically determined in a connected discourse. Journal of Phonetics 3.129-40.

Lehiste, Ilse. 1970. Suprasegmentals. Cambridge, MA: MIT Press.

Liberman, Mark. 1975. The intonational system in English. Dissertation, MIT.

——, and Alan Prince. 1977. On stress and linguistic rhythm. Linguistic Inquiry 8.249-336.

——, and L.A. Streeter. 1978. Use of nonsense-syllable mimicry in the study of prosodic phenomena. JASA 63.231-3.

Maia, Eleonora Albano Da Motta. 1981. Hierarquias de constituentes em fonologia. Anais do V Encontro Nacional de Lingüística, 260-89. Rio de Janeiro: Pontifícia Universidade Católica.

Major, Roy C. 1979. Prosody in Brazilian Portuguese phonology. Dissertation, Ohio State University.

——. 1981. Stress-timing in Brazilian Portuguese. Journal of Phonetics 9.343-51.

——. 1982. Influências prosódicas na fonologia do português no Brasil. Paper presented at the VII Encontro Nacional de Lingüística. Rio de Janeiro: Pontifícia Universidade Católica.

Prince, Alan S. 1983. Relating to the grid. Linguistic Inquiry 14.19-100.

Redenbarger, Wayne J. 1976. Portuguese vowel height and phonological theory: A generative re-analysis based on tongue-root features. Dissertation, Harvard University.

Selkirk, Elisabeth O. 1980. The role of prosodic categories in English word stress. Linguistic Inquiry 11.563-605.

2

A Spectrographic Analysis of Portuguese Stressed and Unstressed Vowels

Willis C. Fails
J. Halvor Clegg
Brigham Young University

1. Studies done to date on Portuguese vowels have been useful but incomplete. The vast majority have been largely intuitive in nature and have basically followed the same timeworn patterns. The tremendously complex phonological system has been reduced to generalizations, which, though commendable in their effort and intent, do not present the reality of detail and thorough investigation that Portuguese merits. There remain many areas of Portuguese phonology that have not been researched. As Godínez (1981) states in his preliminary report, the need for further analysis is clear.

The few instrumental studies have focused on the stressed vowels. Neither the unstressed vowels nor the nasal vowels have been adequately researched to date. This paper will focus on the unstressed vowels in Brazilian Portuguese because of the importance of their unique evolution. It will present data available on tonic and nasal vowels for comparison as well as examine unstressed pretonic, posttonic, and final vowels in both open and closed syllables.

2. Tonic Vowels

Linguists familiar with Portuguese would generally agree that in tonic position the vowel system of Brazilian Portuguese is comprised of seven oral vowels. Pottier et al. (1973) and Azevedo Filho (1968, 1975) both present the same basic schema. In graphic form it appears this way:

Figure 1. The tonic vowels of Brazilian Portuguese.

These vowels were first studied acoustically by Lacerda and Canellada (1942) in a comparative work on Spanish and Portuguese vowels. They made recordings of their own voices and analyzed the acoustic signals using a chromograph, an early type of oscilloscope. They examined not only the tonic vowels, but the atonic vowels as well. However, no conclusions could have been drawn from their research because of the primitive nature of their equipment. Their findings were first published serially in the *Revista de Filología Española* beginning in 1942, and in book form in 1945. In 1950, Lacerda published a book analyzing the sounds of Portuguese utilizing the same research techniques.

During this period, great strides in the area of experimental phonetics were being made in the United States. In 1941, a spectrographic development project was begun by Bell Telephone Laboratories. By 1943, an experimental model had been completed and was being used to explore 'visual hearing' possibilities. The most significant feature, for our purposes, was its ability to separate the compound sound wave into its unique components, allowing phoneticians readily to distinguish vowel quality.

Only a few researchers have applied spectrographic techniques to the study of Portuguese vowels. Among the more significant studies dealing with tonic vowels are Head (1965), Martins (1964 and 1973), Fails (1977), Godínez (1981), and Clegg and Fails (1983). A review of most of these articles is found in Godínez (1981).

Head's research was phonemic in nature but based on acoustic results. He did a distinctive feature analysis of Carioca and Lisbon speech. Martins' study was a careful, controlled analysis of Peninsular tonic vowels. She chose eight university-educated males and had them repeat a sentence (*Digo a palavra X outra vez*), inserting 69 different test words to provide both syntactic and phonetic control. The pattern was varied in situations where the desired word was a verb. The results from Martins (1964 and 1973) appear in Table 1.

Table 1

Vowel	F1	F_2
i	294	2344
e	403	2084
ɛ	501	1893
ɐ	511	1602
a	626	1326
ɔ	531	994
o	426	864
u	315	678

The formant frequencies of Portuguese tonic oral vowels according to Martins (1964 and 1973).

Godínez patterned his investigation somewhat after that of Martins. He analyzed 9 male speakers from different regions of Brazil who repeated a set of 7 words (*se, sesta, sexta, sa, só, sou,* and *zuzu*) within Martins' model sentence. Then, as in Martins' study, the frequencies were averaged. Results were presented in the form of a graph.

In our previous research (Fails 1977; Clegg and Fails 1983), we obtained formant frequencies for the tonic oral vowels which compare favorably with the results of Martins and Godínez. The averaged results of Clegg and Fails (1983) are given in Table 2.

Table 2

Vowel	F_1	F_2
i	280	2187
e	402	1824
ɛ	522	1770
a	709	1342
ɔ	514	983
o	435	857
u	318	832

The formant frequencies of Portuguese tonic oral vowels according to Clegg and Fails (1983).

The results of these previous studies aid in understanding certain aspects of the tonic vowel system. This paper will explore vowel timbre in *atonic* position, since both Martins and Godínez, as well as most others, examined only tonic vowels. We will add spectrographic evidence to substantiate the existing data and to provide new information on atonic vowels.

Most traditional analyses suggest a set of five oral vowels in atonic non-final position, as in Câmara (1973). There is some controversy as to whether this is really a five-vowel set or if there are *seven* vowel phonemes as in tonic position. There is also some question as to the timbre of the phoneme /a/. A summary of this discussion is presented in Azevedo (1981). His own conclusion is that, in general, atonic vowels are reduced to a raised five-vowel system. A graphic representation of the five-vowel set looks like this:

Figure 2. A reduction of the atonic non-final vowel system (Azevedo 1981).

In final atonic position, consensus provides a set of three oral vowels as well. However, no acoustic data are available for these vowels either. A graphic representation looks like this (Câmara 1973:34):

$$i \qquad\qquad u$$
$$a$$

To obtain our data, we designed a wordlist including examples of each vowel in tonic, initial atonic, pretonic, posttonic, and final atonic positions. We also provided examples of each of these categories in both open and closed syllables. In order to test for open /e/ and /o/ in atonic position, the sentences *Um café pequeno é um cafezinho* and *Uma bola pequena é uma bolinha* were included. Finally, a series of words with consonant clusters was added that could trigger the *i intercalada*.

We followed general procedure in the selection of our informants to ensure their normal speech capability, and a uniform age, sex, and socio-economic background. Past research indicated, as might be expected, that there was a sharp difference between male and female speakers. We therefore chose 10 male informants who ranged in age from 20 to 29 and came from 5 different regions of Brazil (São Paulo, Rio de Janeiro, Brasília, Paraná, and Paraíba).

Recordings were made using the condenser microphone of a Sony 5600 cassette recorder. The cassettes were then played through a Harman/Kardon CD301 tape deck into a Digital Sona-Graph™ model 7800. We first made 3D Sonagrams displaying from 0 to 4000 Hz. through a 250 Hz. analysis filter. We also ran power spectra on one speaker to corroborate the 3D spectrograms and to provide additional information on the intensity. The nucleic vowel formants were measured with a calibrated hand ruler and were recorded. F_1 and F_2 were subsequently plotted on Koenig graph charts for visual facility.

3. Findings

3.1. TONIC The formant frequencies we obtained for the tonic oral vowels compared favorably with results of other scholars and with our own previous research. The only area of difference was in the second formant of phoneme /u/, for which results in this study indicated a higher second formant. No appreciable differences were found in formant frequencies between tonic vowels in open syllables and those in closed syllables. The averaged results are given in Table 3 and are graphed in Figure 3.

3.2. PRETONIC We found no appreciable differences between the formant frequencies of initial atonic versus pretonic vowels, nor between open and closed syllables for these two positions. Our results showed a five-vowel system. The averaged formant frequencies for pretonic vowels are given in Table 4 and graphed in Figure 4. The neutralization of the mid vowels does not take place midway between the tonic mid vowels. Instead, these vowels have the same degree of frontness as the tonic vowels but a middle degree of openness.

The test words (*opção, optar, repugnante,* and *advogado*) designed to elicit the *i intercalada* produced varying results. There were several instances where there were no *intercaladas*. Those cases where a high vowel was produced resulted in a first formant frequency of 315 and a second formant frequency of 2042, which compares to a tonic /i/.

We also included in our study the two sentences that examined the open /ɛ/, /ɔ/ in pretonic position. Azevedo (1981:12) notes that while the opposition between open and closed /e/, /o/ is systematically neutralized in atonic position, the open vowels may occur in pretonic position in mor-

Table 3

Vowel	F_1	F_2
i	293	2149
e	383	1936
ɛ	539	1659
a	713	1264
O	545	939
o	399	780
u	318	896

The formant frequencies of Portuguese tonic oral vowels.

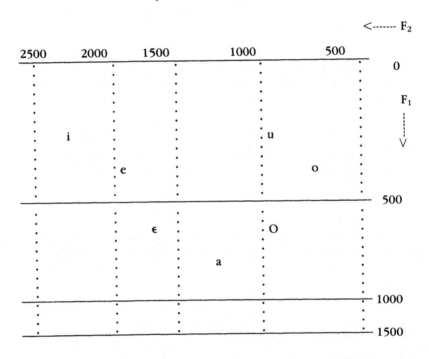

Figure 3. The tonic vowels of Portuguese.

phological derivations. In the pairs *café/cafezinho* and *bola/bolinha*, we found that the second formants of both vowels compare favorably with the second formants of their tonic counterparts. However, the first formants are situated midway between the first formants of the tonic open and closed phonemes /e/ and /o/. This produces mid vowels that have the same degree of fronting but with a neutral middle degree of opening, shown graphically in Figure 5.

Table 4

Vowel	F_1	F_2
i	286	2120
e	364	1940
a	635	1319
o	388	779
u	292	821

The formant frequencies of Portuguese pretonic oral vowels.

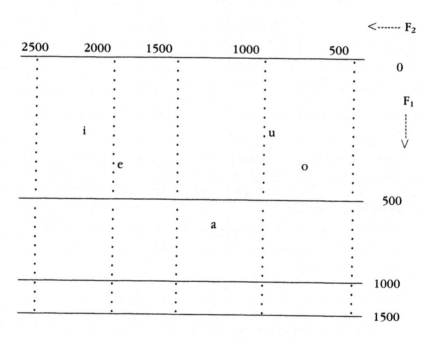

Figure 4. The pretonic vowels of Portuguese.

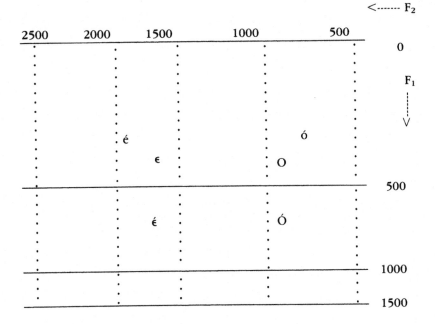

Figure 5. The pretonic vowels of *cafezinho* and *bolinha* compared with open and closed tonic /e/ and /o/.

3.3. POSTTONIC The formant frequencies of posttonic vowels are shown in Table 5 and graphed in Figure 6. The results indicate that the high and mid vowels seem to be moving toward neutralization. The low vowel is considerably raised.

Table 5

Vowel	F_1	F_2
i	303	1942
e	348	1900
a	408	1340
o	328	918
u	300	822

The formant frequencies of Portuguese posttonic oral vowels.

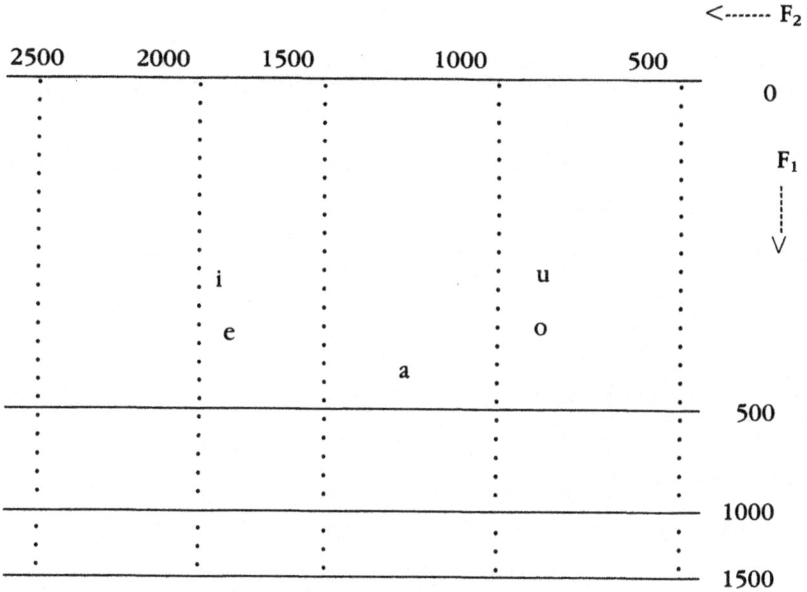

Figure 6. The posttonic vowels of Portuguese.

3.4. FINAL ATONIC We found no appreciable difference in vowel formant frequencies between open and closed syllables in final atonic position. The formant frequencies of final atonic vowels are shown in Table 6 and graphed in Figure 7.

Table 6

Vowel	F_1	F_2
i	290	2039
a	445	1416
u	329	809

The formant frequencies of Portuguese final atonic oral vowels.

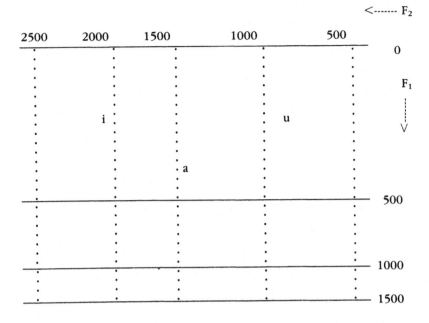

Figure 7. The final atonic vowels of Portuguese.

4. Conclusions

The results of our study are summarized below and placed on a graph (Figure 8) to provide a comparison.

(a) There is no appreciable difference in vowel formant frequencies between open and closed syllables in any position.

(b) There is no appreciable difference in vowel formant frequencies between initial atonic and pretonic vowels.

(c) There is a seven-vowel system in tonic position in Brazilian Portuguese, as shown by an acute accent mark [´] in Figure 8. The tonic vowels are included to provide a point of comparison for the atonic vowels.

(d) There is a five-vowel system in pretonic position shown by the symbol [°] in Figure 8. In this system, the high vowels /i/ and /u/ are comparable to their tonic counterparts. The mid vowels /e/ and /o/ are comparable to tonic closed /O/ and /ɛ/. They do not converge to a point midway between the open and closed mid vowels. The low vowel /a/ is slightly raised as compared with its tonic counterpart.

(e) The posttonic vowels are shown by the symbol [□] in Figure 8. There is a merging of the high and mid vowels in posttonic position. These vowels appear to be moving towards a neutralization. The low vowel /a/ is highly raised to a position above that of the final atonic /a/.

(f) There is a three-vowel system in final atonic position. The final vowels are shown by the symbol [+] in Figure 8.

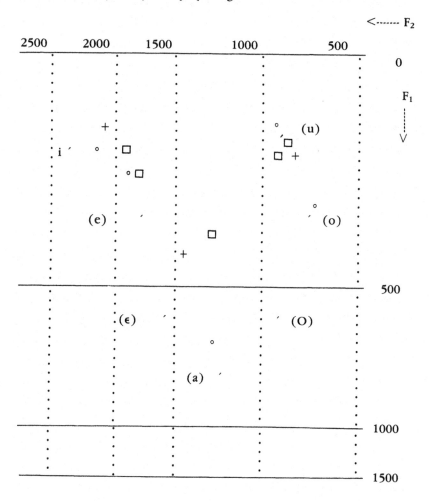

Figure 8. Summary of the vowels of Portuguese.

REFERENCES

Almeida, Antonio. 1971. Die portugiesischen Nasalvokale: Versuch einer phonetischphonologischen Untersuchung. Marburg: Philipps-Univ.

————. 1976. The Portuguese nasal vowels: Phonetics and phonemics. In Jürgen Schmidt-Radefeldt (ed.), Readings in Portuguese linguistics, pp. 349–96. Amsterdam: North-Holland Publishing.

Azevedo, Milton M. 1981. A contrastive phonology of Portuguese and English. Washington, D.C.: Georgetown University Press.

Azevedo Filho, Leodegário de. 1968. Estudo da gramática portuguesa: Fonologia. Revista de Portugal 33(267).318–43.

————. 1975. Para uma gramática estrutural da língua portuguesa. 2.ed. Rio de Janeiro: Gernasa.

Câmara, Joaquim Mattoso, Jr. 1973. Estrutura da língua portuguesa. Petrópolis: Vozes.

Clegg, J. Halvor, and Willis C. Fails. 1983. A spectrographic analysis of the vowels of Portuguese. Paper presented at AATSP Annual Convention, Boston, August 1983.

Fails, Willis C. 1977. An acoustic comparison of the vowels of Spanish and Portuguese. Master's thesis, Brigham Young University.

Godínez, Manuel, Jr. 1981. An acoustic study of Mexican and Brazilian Portuguese vowels. Hispania 64.594–600.

Head, Brian F. 1965. A comparison of the segmental phonology of Lisbon and Rio de Janeiro. Doctoral dissertation, University of Texas at Austin.

Lacerda, Armando de. 1950. Análise de expressões sonoras da compreensão. Coimbra: Universidade de Coimbra; Acta Universitatis Conimbrigensis.

————, and María Josefa Canellada. 1942. Comportamientos tonales vocálicos en español y portugués. Revista de Filología Española 26.171–220, 469–85; also (1943) 27.256–391; also (1944) 28.190–256.

————, and María Josefa Canellada. 1945. Comportamientos tonales vocálicos en español y portugués. Revista de Filología Española, Anejo 32.

————, and Brian F. Head. 1966. Análise de sons nasais e sons nasalizados do português. Revista do Laboratório de Fonética Experimental (Coimbra) 6.5–71.

Martins, Maria Raquel Delgado. 1964 and 1973. Análise acústica das vogais orais tónicas em português. Boletim de Filologia 22.303–14.

Pottier, Bernard, Albert Audubert, and Cidmar Teodoro Pais. 1973. Estruturas lingüísticas do português. São Paulo: Difusão Européia do Livro.

Section II–Morphology

3
Nomes Aumentativos Denominais em Português

Maria Carlota Amaral Paixão Rosa
Universidade Federal do Rio de Janeiro

1. Em português, a indicação de maior tamanho ou intensidade para os nomes—o chamado *grau aumentativo*—pode ser feita por dois modos: pela adjunção de um adjetivo indicador de tamanho ou intensidade maior do que um padrão de normalidade tomado como referente, mas não expresso lingüisticamente, ou pelo acréscimo de sufixos especiais a uma base nominal. Assim, um nome considerado de grau normal, como, e.g., *gato*, passaria ao grau aumentativo se a ele se juntasse um adjetivo como *grande* ou sinônimo (*gato*: *gato grande*), ou se recebesse um dos sufixos considerados aumentativos, como *-ão*, por exemplo (*gato: gatão*). Neste artigo, nosso interesse estará voltado para os aumentativos formados por derivação sufixal. Analisaremos, numa abordagem gerativa, a situação de produtividade de dez sufixos comumente listados como aumentativos, a saber, *-oila, -ola, -orro, -orra, -arrão, -eirão, -alhão, -az, -aço* e *-ão*.

2. Nas gramáticas tradicionais de língua portuguesa, o aumentativo é apresentado como um dos graus dos nomes. Indica 'um aumento do ser (i.e., do substantivo) relativamente a seu tamanho normal' (Lima 1965: 89). Seguem-se à definição uma lista de sufixos aumentativos e exemplos. Não há qualquer indicação acerca da produtividade de cada um dos elementos listados, mas apenas observações gerais sobre a pequena possibilidade de formação de aumentativos derivacionais.

Para analisar a produtividade dos sufixos acima citados, precisaremos dar conta de dois aspectos da competência de um falante nativo no tocante ao léxico: (a) esses sufixos são interpretados como aumentativos? e (b) no caso de a resposta à pergunta anterior ser *sim*, esses sufixos formam novas palavras?

As questões (a) e (b) serão formalizadas, respectivamente, por dois tipos de regras: *regras de análise estrutural* (doravante *RAE*s) e *regras de formação de palavras* (doravante *RFP*s). A distinção entre ambos os tipos foi proposta por Basílio (1980), com o intuito de evitar dois problemas de inadequação descritiva: (a) impedir a pressuposição de que apenas os processos produtivos de criação vocabular podem conter redundâncias identificáveis pelos falantes; e (b) afastar a possibilidade de considerar-se como obrigatoriamente produtiva qualquer redundância passível de identificação.

As RAEs representam a possibilidade de interpretação de itens morfológicamente complexos. As RFPs refletem a possibilidade de formação de novos itens lexicais.

Qualquer RFP tem como contraparte uma RAE, uma vez que, se os falantes podem criar novos itens com determinada estrutura, devem ser capazes de analisá-la. As RAEs, ao contrário, podem existir isoladamente na gramática, porque, embora indiquem que determinadas redundâncias são passíveis de reconhecimento, não implicam que tais estruturas são necessariamente produtivas.

A fim de neutralizar a influência de nossas características idioletais na análise, lançamos mão de uma testagem informal. Entrevistamos falantes nascidos no Rio de Janerio e os dividimos em dois grandes grupos: (a) adolescentes, de 13 e 14 anos, matriculados na sétima série do 1° Grau; e (b) adultos, de 20 a 62 anos, todos de nível universitário.

Os testes foram aplicados, na sua maioria, oralmente. Esta foi uma exigência que se impôs no decorrer do trabalho, uma vez que os falantes tendiam a negar a existência de formas usuais na fala coloquial carioca, tais como *homão*, *bifão*, sempre que estas lhes eram apresentadas por escrito. Os itens que compuseram os testes foram apresentados fora de contexto quando o objetivo era saber se os falantes os reconheciam como aumentativos. Quando a meta era a testagem da aceitabilidade ou a precisão de diferenças mais sutis de significado, os aumentativos foram colocados em frases.

Os testes de reconhecimento de redundâncias morfológicas consistiram na apresentação de aumentativos precedidos da pergunta 'O que você acha que essas palavras significam?' Para a análise dos resultados, subdividimos as respostas em quatro grupos: (a) *acerto*, quando base e sufixos eram reconhecidos; (b) *sufixo*, quando era percebido o significado 'aumentativo', embora não se percebesse a significação integral do item; (c) *base*, quando o informante conseguia isolar a base, mas não percebia o significado 'aumentativo'; (d) *erro*, quando o sufixo e a base não eram reconhecidos.

Para obtermos informações acerca da possibilidade de criação de novos aumentativos com determinados sufixos, criamos formas que foram colocadas em frases ao lado de outras já existentes. Precedemos as frases de um enunciado onde se pedia que fossem indicadas quaisquer palavras que parecessem estranhas.

Os questionários para precisarmos o significado dos itens formados a partir de uma mesma base tiveram sua apresentação por escrito, com opções em termos de múltipla escolha. Era deixada para o informante a possibilidade de apresentar resposta que divergisse das alternativas por nós apresentadas (Rosa 1982).

3. Dos sufixos apresentados no início deste trabalho, apenas seis são interpretados como aumentativos: *-arrão*, *-eirão*, *-alhão*, *-az*, *-aço*, e *-ão*.

3.1. Os sufixos *-oíla* e *-ola* aparecem em poucas e desusadas palavras. Encontramos apenas os seguintes exemplos:

(1) façoila 'face grande, larga'
(2) beiçola 'beiço grande'   dentola 'dente grande'
    festarola 'festa grande'   passarola 'pássaro grande'
    petarola 'grande peta, mentira'   sapatola 'sapato grande'

Além disso, tais sufixos apresentam identidade fonética com sufixos diminutivos. É com esse significado que *-oíla* aparece em *moçoíla* 'mocinha' e em *caçoíla* 'caço pequeno'. É como diminutivo que *-ola* aparece nos exemplos de (3):

(3) rapazola 'pequeno rapaz'   fazendola 'pequena fazenda'
    casinhola 'casinha pequena'   portinhola 'pequena porta'

Quando perguntados, os falantes diziam não ter idéia do que os aumentativos *X-ola* e *X-oila* (em que X representa a base) significavam, ou davam
respostas como as de (4) abaixo:

(4) *façoila*   'moça fascinante'
                   'moça muito fácil no dialeto de Portugal'
                   'diminutivo de fácil'
    passarola   'coletivo de pássaros'
                   'local com pássaros'
                   'feminino de pássaro'
                   'passagem pequena ou grande'

Não se pode, portanto, a rigor, falar em redundância com relação a esses
sufixos e, a partir daí, torna-se evidente que não faz sentido continuar a
considerá-los aumentativos. Conseqüentemente, *-oila* e *-ola* não reúnem
condições para serem produtivos, pois não se espera que novas palavras
sejam formadas com elementos não identificáveis.

3.2. Quanto aos itens *X-orro* e *X-orra*, também a eles os falantes não
conseguem atribuir o significado 'aumentativo', embora as gramáticas os
apresentem como 'aumentativos-pejorativos'. Nos testes foi alta a quanti-
dade de respostas em que se associavam tais terminações às palavras *cachorro, zorra* ou a outras com a seqüência /or/, como, e.g., *borrado*, como
se estes itens fossem o resultado de um tipo de formação vocabular encon-
trável na fala coloquial em que se juntam a seqüência fônica inicial de uma
palavra com a seqüência final de outra (e.g., *bótimo* 'bom com ótimo';
horrorível 'horroroso com horrível'), além de outros significados não aumentativos. Assim, *gatorro, beatorro* e *sapatorro*, respectivamente, *gato
grande, grande beato* e *sapato grande* tiveram como leituras:

(5) *gatorro*   'mistura de gato com cachorro'
                   'gato usando um gorro'
                   'gato'
    beatorro   'cachorro beato'
    sapatorro   'sapato para cachorro'
                   'sapato pequeno e velho'
                   'uma coleção de sapatos'
                   'homem muito grande'

Pelos exemplos, pode-se notar que *-orro* e *-orra* não estão sendo tratados
como sufixos aumentativos, mas como elementos do que se poderia considerar um tipo de composição. Desse modo, não se pode esperar que os
falantes os utilizem na formação de novos aumentativos.

3.3. Os vocábulos formados com *-arrão, -eirão, -alhão* e *-az* são reconhecidos como aumentativos, conquanto não sejam aceitas novas palavras formadas com eles. Desse modo, embora os falantes possam interpretar corretamente uma palavra criada por nós especialmente para a testagem, como é o caso de *sapatarrão* 'sapato grande', eles a rejeitam como estranha.

Há de se notar, porém, que há um pouco mais de dificuldades para identificar as bases das formações *X-eirão*, *X-alhão* e *X-az* do que para *X-arrão*, em especial no que diz respeito a falantes adolescentes:

(6)

Aumentativo	Significado	Respostas dos informantes
toleirão	'grande tolo'	'excessivamente tolerante'
		'grande tolerante'
parvoeirão	'grande parvo'	'grande pavor'
		'pavão grande'
facalhão	'faca grande'	'grande facada'
fradalhão	'frade grande'	'fraude grande'
		'fralda grande'
ladravaz	'grande ladrão'	'uma ladroagem enorme'
truanaz	'grande truão'	'uma TRU (Taxa Rodoviária Única) alta'

Este tipo de resultado pode dever-se a dois fatores. Em primeiro lugar, consideremos o fato de algumas bases, como *truão*, *vilão*, *rufião*, *parvo*, por exemplo, serem desconhecidas dos falantes, em especial, dos mais jovens. Em segundo lugar, a sílaba final de *-eirão* e *-alhão* poderia levar os falantes a classificar esses derivados como aumentativos, seguindo a regra mais produtiva; ao mesmo tempo, porém, a presença de uma seqüência fônica entre o radical e *-ão* dificultaria o reconhecimento da base. Com relação a *-az* pode-se observar que os exemplos fornecidos pelas gramáticas (e que se constituíram no corpus utilizado na testagem), ou apresentam uma seqüência fônica entre o radical e *-az* (e.g., ladr*av*az, fat*ac*az), ou mostram uma mudança fonética que consiste na transferência do travamento nasal posvocálico /N/ para a sílaba seguinte como consoante /n/, antes do acréscimo do sufixo (*vilão:vilanaz*, *rufião:rufianaz*). O único aumentativo em *-az* que não se enquadra nos casos acima, *lobaz*, não apresentou dificuldade de reconhecimento para os falantes adultos, embora não ocorresse o mesmo com adolescentes.

Constata-se, portanto, que existe probabilidade de análise correta para itens *X-alhão*, *X-eirão* e *X-az*, embora em declínio, como se depreende da comparação dos resultados de adultos e adolescentes.

3.4. Dentre os sufixos reconhecidos como aumentativos, apenas *-ão* e *-aço* emtram na formação de novas palavras. Quando formam derivados a partir de uma mesma base, não são exatamente sinônimos: *-aço* indica 'qualidade maior', ao passo que *-ão* indica 'dimensão maior'. Assim, um *apartamentaço* seria um 'apartamento bem decorado'; um *apartamentão*, um 'apartamento grande'. Do mesmo modo, um *mulherão* seria uma 'mulher fisicamente grande'; um *mulheraço*, uma 'mulher de corpo muito bonito'.

Essas respostas evidenciam que *-aço* está passando por um processo de mudança semântica. De um sufixo com significado pejorativo, passou ao valor oposto, i.e., a um indicador de qualidade em alto grau. Somente falantes na faixa dos sessenta anos de idade fizeram leituras como em (7) abaixo:

> (7) *mulheraço*   'mulher vagabunda'
>   'mulher vulgar'
>   *apartamentaço* 'apartamento mais ou menos'
>   *carraço*   'aumentativo de carro, mas bem pejorativo'

que coincidem com a descrição tradicional. O grau de produtividade de *-aço* também foi alterado: começa a aparecer com freqüência em discursos marcadamente informais, como, por exemplo, programas destinados ao público jovem na televisão e no rádio, onde se podem ouvir termos como *sonzaço, musicaço, rockaço, solzaço*.

No que diz respeito às formas *X-ão*, estas são aceitas e interpretadas sem problemas, sejam formas novas criadas para a testagem ou não. Para os adolescentes, *-ão* pode combinar-se com qualquer tipo de base. Para os adultos, não é produtivo com bases abstratas ou com noção coletiva:

> (8) *pessimismão
>   *cremosidadezona
>   *criadagenzona

O sufixo *-aço* combina-se apenas com bases primitivas concretas:

> (9) biquinaço
>   carraço
>   filmaço
>   golaço
>   jogaço

Formações *X-aço*, em que X é uma base abstrata ou concreta derivada são rejeitadas por unanimidade:

> (10) *nudezaço
>   *palidezaço
>   *ferimentaço

Há de se notar que a produtividade a que aqui nos referimos existe na fala coloquial. Os derivados aumentativos em -ão e em -aço são considerados gíria. Estariamos, assim, diante de um tipo diferente de gíria: a 'gíria morfológica'. Dizemos diferente porque o comum é o uso de determinadas palavras como gíria, ao lado de outras que não o são. Neste caso, porém, temos a formação de gírias através de regras do componente morfológico da gramática, não importando a que registro pertença a palavra base.

4. A análise dos dez sufixos em foco nos leva à proposição de algumas regras.

Se os falantes de português podem reconhecer a estrutura de itens X-arrão, X-eirão, X-alhão, X-az, X-aço e X-ão, incluiremos RAEs para eles:

(11)   *RAEs*

$$
\begin{array}{lll}
[X]_N & arrão &]N_{aumentativo} \\
[X]_N & eirão &]N_{aumentativo} \\
[X]_X & alhão &]N_{aumentativo} \\
[X]_N & az &]N_{aumentativo} \\
[X]_N & aço &]N_{aumentativo} \\
[X]_N & ão &]N_{aumentativo}
\end{array}
$$

As regras em (11) indicam que nomes aumentativos podem ser interpretados como formados a partir de bases nominais com cada um dos seis sufixos citados.

Como, porém, os falantes formam novos aumentativos apenas com -ão e -aço, teremos a inclusão de duas RFPs:

(12) $[X]_N \rightarrow [[X]_N$ ão $]N_{aumentativo}$
      $[X]_N \rightarrow [[X]_N$ ãço$]N_{aumentativo}$

As regras em (12) indicam que um nome existente pode servir de base a um nome aumentativo pela adjuncão de -ão ou de -aço.

Os grupos analisados nos levam à observação de que é necessário não identificar reconhecimento de redundâncias morfológicas com produtividade lexical. Formas derivadas com -arrão, -eirão, -alhão e -az, criadas para a testagem, foram rejeitadas, apesar de terem sido analisadas de modo correto. Isto indica que tais sufixos, em que pese a possibilidade de serem interpretados corretamente, não são utilizados pelos falantes na criação de novos vocábulos, o que nos leva à postulação de RAEs isoladas. Não vemos como dar conta da possibilidade de falantes analisarem estruturalmente itens formados com sufixos improdutivos sem este mecanismo ou qualquer outro que lhe seja equivalente.

REFERÊNCIAS

Aronoff, Mark. 1976. Word formation in generative grammar. Cambridge, MA: MIT Press.

Basílio, Margarida Maria de Paula. 1980. Estruturas lexicais do português: Uma abordagem gerativa. Petrópolis, Brazil: Vozes.

Jackendoff, Ray. 1975. Morphological and semantic regularities in the lexicon. Language 51(3).639-71.

Lima, Carlos Henrique da Rocha. 1965. Gramática normativa da língua portuguesa. Rio de Janeiro: F. Briguiet.

Rosa, Maria Carlota Amaral Paixão. 1982. Formação de nomes aumentativos: Um estudo da produtividade de alguns sufixos portugueses. Dissertação de Mestrado, Universidade Federal do Rio de Janeiro.

4

Capeverdean Diminutives

Donaldo P. Macedo
University of Massachusetts at Boston

1. The Capeverdean Diminutives

In this paper I analyze the Capeverdean diminutives which involve complex phonological operations such as vowel deletion, vowel shift, infixation of *inh* and *z*, and vowel harmony. My discussion of the diminutivization process in Capeverdean will draw from the work in Lexical Phonology as proposed by Kiparsky (1982), and Roca (1983). Because of the similarities between Portuguese and Capeverdean diminutives, I also found it necessary to address Maia's (1981) work on Portuguese diminutives.

The Capeverdean diminutives have been characterized by the attachment of suffixes *-inhu/a*, *-itu/a*, *-uchu/a* to nouns and adjectives. The *-inhu/a* suffixes are by far the most productive. Productivity is considered here to have the same theoretical status as in Aronoff (1983). The Capeverdean diminutive *-itu/a*, *-uchu/a* will not be discussed here. Masculine gender is represented by *u* in word final position; feminine gender by *a*.

The traditional analysis of Capeverdean offers a straightforward rule for the diminutive formation, as given in (1).

(1) Attach -*inhu* to masculine singular forms, and -*inha* to feminine singular forms.

Although this rule generates ungrammatical forms, for the purpose of my present discussion, I will assume that it will correctly generate the form in (2). Note that vowel harmony changes $o \rightarrow u$.

(2) *gordu*	*gurdinhu*	'little fat one'
pretu	*pritinhu*	'little black one'
capa	*capinha*	'little cover'

As can be seen in the data given in (2), the final vowel in *gordu, pretu, capa* was deleted before the application of rule (1). Thus, before rule (1) can apply, rule (3), which deletes the final vowel of the words, must apply first.

$$(3) \ V \rightarrow \theta \ / \text{—} \ \#$$

Rule (3) makes it possible for rule (1) to apply without generating ungrammatical forms such as **gorduinhu.*

I must note that rule (3) is not an independent rule and is intimately associated with rule (1). Otherwise, it will generate ungrammatical forms. Evidence from Spanish and Portuguese support this position. Roca (1983) concludes that the deletion rule (3) must be obligatorily followed by the diminutive formation rule as stated in (1), to avoid the erasure of final vowels which characterize all Spanish singulars.

A second proposal I could entertain is that the final vowel of the word is shifted to the rightmost position after the infixation of -*inh*. This is easily refuted since words that do not end in a vowel require that -*inh* take a final vowel -*u* or -*a*, as in (4):

(4) *mudger*	*mudgirinha*	little woman
dotor	*duturinhu*	'little doctor'

Further evidence that contradicts the above proposal is found in words ending in -*i* which require the affixation of the final vowels -*u* or -*a* to -*inh*:

(5) *penti*	*pintinhu*	'little comb'
boti	*butinhu*	'little boat'

Thus far, the diminutive formation has been described according to the following operations: (a) final vowel deletion from the stem; (b) -*inh* infixation; and (c) attachment of -*u* or -*a* to the right of -*inh* as given in (6).

(6) · word—altu
　　· vowel deletion—alt
　　-inh infixation—alt + inh
　　-u/-a insertion—alt + inh + u/a

The operations in (6) leave many unresolved problems, to which I will return later.

The proposal in (6) is embraced by Maia (1981) in her discussion of Portuguese diminutives. Maia's proposal treats *inho* (o = [u]) as a word and assumes that the initial Word Formation Rule (WFR) generates a compound formed with two types of words. One has the stress pattern and the morphological structure of a compound, while the other incorporates *inh* as an infix to the outermost stem. She argues that, in addition to bearing stress on both constituents, these words also resemble noun phrases in that they show internal agreement for gender and number. She gives the following examples:

(7)　　　　　　　　　　(a) *True compounds*
　　　Singular　　　　　　　Plural
　　obra-pr'ima　　　　*obras-pr'imas*　　　'masterpiece(s)'
　　amor-perf'eito　　　*amores-perf'eitos*　　'pansy(ies)'
　　terça-f'eira　　　　*terças-f'eiras*　　　'Tuesday(s)'

　　　　　　　　　　(b) *Diminutives*
　　　Singular　　　　　　　Plural
　　meninaz'inha　　　*meninaz'inhas*　　　'little girl(s)'
　　meninoz'inho　　　*meninoz'inhos*　　　'little boy(s)'
　　leaoz'inho　　　　*leoez'inhos*　　　'little lion(s)'
　　leoaz'inha　　　　*leoaz'inhas*　　　'little lioness(es)'

Number agreement is not relevant for our discussion, since Capeverdean pluralization does not require number agreement. Maia claims that in Portuguese diminutive number agreement is opaque because of the infixation of /z/ in the singular. The conditions which motivate /z/ insertion remain inexplicable. I will attempt to clarify this point as we proceed with our discussion. Another important point also unsatisfactorily explained by Maia (1981) concerns the words that end in final vowel /e/ and are unmarked for gender. I reproduce her examples in Portuguese, which show that only /o/ or /a/ can be affixed to *-inh*:

(8) *d'ente* (masc.) 'tooth'　　　*dentez'inho* 'little tooth'
　　p'onte (fem.) 'bridge'　　　*pontez'inha* 'little bridge'
　　d'oente (masc. fem.) 'patient'　*doentez'inho(a)* 'little patient'

The infixation of /z/ above is blocked in Capeverdean generating the forms *dintinhu, puntinhu,* and *duentinhu(a).* Maia accounts for the fact that /e/ does not attach to *inh* by proposing a vowel deletion rule to be applied in the diminutive formation process. However, she fails to differentiate between words ending in /e/ that maintain it in final position, such as *café* 'coffee'. I will later argue that the final vowel /e/'s in *café* -cafezinhu and *pente* -pintinhu 'comb' are different and trigger different rule application at different levels.

The approach for the Portuguese diminutivization discussed in Maia (1981) is plagued by a number of discrepancies, and she offers no solution for problems which hitherto were inexplicable. For example, there is no mechanism that guarantees gender agreements, particularly in cases such as *poema* 'poem' and *mapa* 'map' which keep the class marker vowels in the diminutives defying gender agreement. Portuguese gender agreement is generally determined by associating [o] with masculine forms and [a] with its feminine counterpart. The rules proposed by Maia are very uneconomical and involve the performance of two inverse operations, first erasing the final vowel in the base, and then making the same vowel surface through gender agreement (Roca 1983). The derivative sample shows that the class marker vowel /e/ is shifted to the right of *-inh* before it undergoes the vowel deletion rule, i.e., [[dent + inh + e] $_{NSt}$ z] $_N$. This operation is not possible since it fails to apply to base words which also end in /e/ such as *café* 'coffee' cafezinho and *pé* 'foot' pezinho. This word class requires obligatory /z/ infixation and never generates forms like *cafinhu.

The adjustment rule which inserts /z/ before the initial vowel of a stem with a left sister constituent ending in a vowel also fails to capture the generalization of the /z/ infixation rule. That is, it fails to account for words which trigger /z/ infixation but which do not end in a vowel. Words like *papel ~ papelzinhu* 'little paper' and *mar ~ marzinhu* 'little sea' also require obligatory /z/ infixation.

I have so far identified some obvious limitations to past analyses of diminutives in both Portuguese and Capeverdean. The discussion to ensue will draw from the proposals put forth by Roca (1983) in his analysis of Spanish diminutives.

Within Roca's proposals, I can now formulate a Capeverdean diminutive rule given below:

(9) Insert *-inh* in the environment ____] $_{stem}$

Rule (9) will correctly generate the following:

(10) [[car$_{\uparrow\uparrow}$] a]   [[sapat$_{\uparrow\uparrow}$] u]
      inh S   N   inh S   N

The examples given in (10) show the application of rule (9). This rule is further supported by the evidence given in (11), which partially solves the gender agreement problem:

(11)   (a) 'a poem'   (b) 'a map'
      un [[poem   ] a]   un [map   ] a]
            $\uparrow\uparrow$ S   N $\uparrow\uparrow$ S   N
            inh   inh

      un poeminha   *un mapinha*

Maia's rules would fail to predict the outcome in (11), since the gender agreement is solely determined by the class marker vowels /o/ or /a/. The Capeverdean examples given in (11) show that the diminutives in this language retain the class marker vowel of the base, in defiance of gender agreement.

Despite the economy and attractiveness of rule (9), it also fails to account for cases like *café, pé* since it generates the following ungrammatical forms:

(12) (a) [[cafe   ] θ]   (b) [[pe   ] θ]
            $\uparrow\uparrow$ S   N $\uparrow\uparrow$ S   N
            inh   inh

      cafeinh   *peinh*

In addition to the wrong predictions exemplified in (12a) and (12b), rule (9) also fails to trigger the obligatory /z/ infixation which is required by words such as *café, cal, pé*, etc. I will return to this question later.

To solve part of the problem presented by words that lack a class marker, Roca (1983) suggests the reformulation of 'the diminutive rule to take account of the principled separation between the CV-tier and the segmental tier.' Therefore, rule (9) should be rewritten as (13):

(13)   VC

      Insert $\bigvee$ in the stem, immediately to the right bracket

                μ

      [DIM]

Roca argues that since rule (13) requires that the diminutive rule apply to the stem domain, there will be no reference made to the class marker. Furthermore, it also predicts that the class marker of the base will be retained. In order to complete the derivation, Roca proposes a segmental rule of the type given in (14):

(14) In diminutives, associate -*inh* with VC.

Since the approaches so far discussed do not really account for words with no class markers, I will adopt a layered phonology model, usually referred to as 'Lexical Phonology', as described in Kiparsky (1982), in my analysis of words such as *café*, *capa*, and *poema* as seen in (15):

(15) (a) [uMASC]   (b) [uFEM]   (c) [mMASC]

μ   μ   μ
/|\   /|\   /|\
[[CVCV]]   [[CVC]V]   [[CVCV] V]
 | | | | | | | | | | |
c a f é   c a p   p o e m

Since (15a) does not have any slot for the class marker, deletion rule (3) does not apply, and *café* will surface without a class marker. In (15b) and (15c) the vowel insertion rule in (16) associates the unmarked vowel *a* with class marker V

(16) $O \rightarrow V / C \# \_ S$

in (15b), and the same vowel is also inserted in (15c), even though the base is marked for masculine. Roca (1983:78) contends that 'if the base form does not include a class marker, the diminutive invariably shows up with an unmarked vowel, i.e., with *o* if the base is masculine, and *a* if it is feminine ... It is reasonable to conclude that gender is an intrinsic property of all nominal lexical items, which must be diacritically specified, even though a limited number of semantic redundancies may exist.' This clearly points to the inadequacies of Maia's rules which fail to predict gender agreement correctly. The class marker V, as it has been amply demonstrated by Harris (1981), is not inherently marked for gender. It follows then that nouns are marked for gender in the lexicon. The linking of -*a* with the class marker V for feminine forms and -*o* for masculine forms is part of a redundancy rule. Thus, this redundancy rule juxtaposes the marked -*a* and -*o* with the class marker V. Then the diminutive derivation of *gordu* in (2) is given in (17):

(17)   [uMASC]

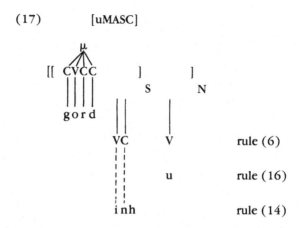

2. z Infixation

As observed in (12a) and (12b), rule (9) failed to generate the correct diminutive forms, which are as follows:

(18) cafe—cafi + z + inh + u   'little coffee'
        pe—pi + z + inh + u   'little foot'

The data given in (18) show the addition of a z segment between the stem and the infix *inh*. The forms in (19) cannot be predicted by any mechanism discussed thus far. Maia (1981) proposes that an optional z is part of the diminutive *inhu(a)* but she fails to specify clearly the environments which require the z infixation. In fact, since it is optional, it can apply in almost all environments, as shown in (19):

(19) (a) *dente—dentinho*   'little tooth'
        (b) *dente—dentezinho*   'little tooth'

In Capeverdean the z infixation in (19b) is blocked, since this addition takes place immediately after a root and not a class marker, as seen in (20):

(20) (a) dotor   duturzinhu   'male doctor'
        (b) dotora   duturinha   'female doctor'

Along the same lines as Maia, Jaeggli (1980) also treats $z = c$ in Spanish as an integral part of the diminutive *-inhu/a* (*-ito/a* in Spanish), which must be deleted in the appropriate environment. Roca (1983) argues that, if maximal simplicity is to be achieved, Jaeggli's proposal must be reinterpreted autosegmentally. He proposes the following rule:

(21) In diminutive, associate *-zinh* with VC.

Rule (21) accounts for the derivation in (22):

(22)   [uFEM]

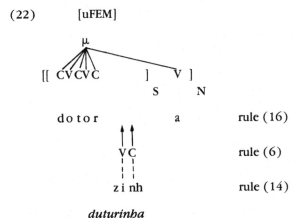

duturinha

In the derivation (22), the association between z and C is blocked, since C is already filled by r. Thus, rule (21) can only apply to (20a) and not to (20b). Roca (1983) solves the problem by reformulating rule (21) into rule (23):

(23)

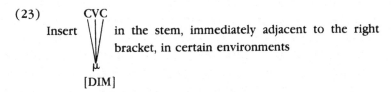

Rule (23) will enable the association of all elements in the segmental sequence *-zinh*, as seen in (24):

[uMASC]

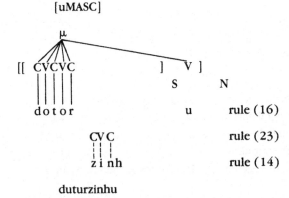

duturzinhu

I will now analyze the difference between (20a) and (20b) to determine

the environment which triggers *z* infixation. I can rule out the stem environment, since both *dotor* and *dotora* have the same stem. Then the only
observable difference is the class marker present in *dotora*. But since rule
(23) requires that the domain of its applicability be the stem, any reference
to the class marker as the appropriate environment for *z* infixation would
substantially alter rule (23). Any reference to class markers would also
raise serious problems if we were to adopt another model to analyze *z*
infixation.

The possible paradox inherent in the analysis of the *z* infixation remains
perplexing if I follow the Lexical Phonology model as proposed by Kiparsky (1982). In this approach we posit basic roots, and then posit two
layers of phonological rules. Phonological rules for each layer only apply in
'derived environments', that is, they are triggered only by segments found
either in a morpheme that has been affixed on that layer or otherwise
constitute segments that have just arisen as a result of some rule that
belongs to that layer.

The Lexical Phonology model refers to two layers 'derivational layer',
and the 'inflectional layer', though more for reasons of simplicity than for
any deep claim at this point concerning the nature of the affixes that
appear on each layer. The diminutive suffix is found in the derivational
layer, as in *gurdinhu*. An example of the inflectional layer suffix is the final
vowel class marker, such as *-u* or *-a* of *gordu* or *gorda*.

The Lexical Phonology framework, suggests the following rule:

(25) Insert a *z* after the radical when the radical will not take a
final vowel class marker or will take a null final vowel.

This generalization seems to be empirically correct, as illustrated in derivation (26). However, there is a discrepancy that needs to be worked out
for the affixation process to be theoretically acceptable. That is, if I am
correct in assuming that the diminutivization process takes place in the
Derivational Level, the *z* infixation which is part of this process does not
have any available information to trigger its realization, since the class
marker affixation takes place only in the Inflectional Level. This apparent
paradox raises serious problems for the Lexical Phonology model to the
extent that the level analysis fails to resolve the *z* infixation problem.

In order to account for all the processes involved in the *z* infixation rule,
it must be reinterpreted autosegmentally as proposed by Roca (1983)
where he suggested two different syllable structures:

(26)

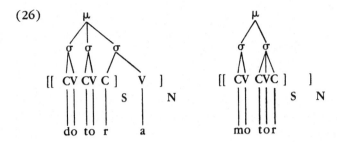

His analysis follows Clements and Keyser's (1981) propsal 'that all representations include a CV-tier and a syllable tier between the morphemic tier and the segmental tier of more traditional anlyses' (Roca 1983:85). From this proposal it follows that the information in (26) is easily accessible to Roca's diminutive prosodic template rule in (27):

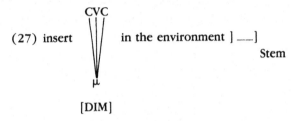

(27) insert [CVC] in the environment]___]
                                              Stem

[DIM]

From rule (27) we can easily derive *duturzinhu* since it inserts 'the specified material at CV-tier in cases where no extrasyllabic material intervenes between the stem-closing bracket and the preceding syllable—closing bracket' (Roca, 1983:85). The derivation of *duturzinhu* is given below:

(28)   [uMASC]

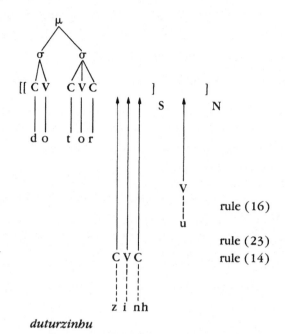

duturzinhu

Rule (27) accounts, in a straightforward way, for all cases of Capeverdean words with no final vowel class marker. In cases like *Djuninhu* and *Djunzinhu* 'little John', where two diminutives are possible, rule (27) applies correctly even though on the surface they appear to be structurally ambiguous. If I analyze *Djuninhu* as derived from *Djon*, I must analyze *Djunzinhu* as derived from something else. In fact, these two forms represent foreign borrowings which have been reanalyzed into the Capeverdean phonological system. *Djon* comes from John while *Djunzinhu* must be derived from *Djoni* (Johnny). Given American English influence on the dialect of Brava, particularly in reference to popular names, this assumption can easily be verified. *Maria* represents another case where two diminutives are possible. If *a* is analyzed as a final vowel class marker, the diminutive is *Mariinha*; if *Maria* is unanalyzed (i.e., just a stem), then the diminutive is *Mariazinha.*

Rule (27) also accounts for monosyllables in (29a) and for words which take a final vowel that is not a class marker, as shown in (29b):

(29) (a) *cruz—cruzinha*   'little cross'
         sol—sulzinhu   'little sun'
         pon—punzinhu   'little bread'

(b) *café—cafizinbu*   'little coffee'
    pé—pizinbu   'little foot'
    fé—fizinbu   'little faith'

REFERENCES

Arnoff, Mark. 1981. Word formulation in generative grammar. Cambridge, MA: MIT Press.

Harris, James. 1969. Spanish phonology. Cambridge, MA: MIT Press.

Jaeggli, Osvaldo. 1980. Spanish diminutives. In Frank H. Nuessel (ed.), Contemporary studies in Romance languages. Bloomington: Indiana University Linguistics Club.

Maia, Eleonora Albano da Motta. 1981. Phonological and lexical processes in a generative grammar of Portuguese. Doctoral dissertation, Brown University.

Roca, Ignacio. 1983. The category 'stem' and concatentative morphology. Unpublished manuscript, MIT.

Section III–Syntax

5

Tense and Binding
Theory in Portuguese

José A. Meireles
Faculdade de Letras
Universidade de Lisboa

Eduardo Raposo
University of California
Santa Barbara

1. Introduction and Theoretical Background[1]

Following a suggestion of George and Kornfilt (1981) for Turkish and Rouveret (1980) for Portuguese, Chomsky (1981:210) (*Lectures on Government and Binding*—henceforth *LGB*) proposes that the element AGReement in INFLection,[2] and not tense, is the relevant inducer of Opacity for the subject position of a clause, as far as the Binding Theory is concerned.

The key notion to this new approach to the Binding Theory is the notion of SUBJECT, extensionally defined as follows: the lexical subject of an infinitive clause, of an NP, and of a small clause is a SUBJECT; and the AGR element of a finite clause is a SUBJECT, but not the lexical NP subject of such a clause. The basic idea is that the SUBJECT is "the 'most prominent nominal element' in some sense, taking INFL to be the head of S" (*LGB*:209).

The concept of *governing category* (henceforth GC) is now built upon the notion SUBJECT:

(1) *B* is a governing category for *a* if and only if *B* is the minimal category containing *a*, a governor of *a*, and a SUBJECT accessible to *a*.

Finally, the Binding Theory makes a crucial use of the notion 'governing category':

(2) *Binding Theory*
Principle A: an anaphor is bound in its governing category.
Principle B: a pronoun is free in its governing category.
Principle C: an R-expression is free.

The Binding Theory (2)—via Principle B—accounts for the fact that in the European Portuguese (henceforth EP) sentence (3), the embedded pronominal subject *eles* 'they' may be coreferent with the matrix subject *os meninos* 'the children':[3]

(3) *Os meninos disseram* [@ *não terem eles partido o vidro*].
'The children said [not to have-AGR (they) broken the glass].'

@ in (3) is an inflected infinitival complement, whose INFL node dominates AGR but not [+ tense].[4] If tense were the relevant inducer of Opacity (as in the Tensed-S Condition of Chomsky [1973]), then we would expect obligatory disjoint reference between *os meninos* and *eles*. But since such is not the case, AGR must be taken as the relevant inducer of Opacity for the subject position. Under Principle B of (2) (itself based on definition [1]), @ is then the GC of *eles*, since it contains the governor of *eles*, which is the INFL node, and a SUBJECT accessible to *eles*, which is the personal infinitive AGR in INFL. *Eles* is free in this domain, and therefore may corefer with the matrix subject *os meninos*.

This paper will analyze the behavior of pronominal elements in the subject position of complement clauses and argue that in this case AGR is not the relevant inducer of Opacity, contrary to the position taken in *LGB*. Rather, an operator-like TENSE element is. This TENSE is not to be confused with tense in INFL.[5] TENSE is a semantic, operator-like linguistic element which is selected by matrix predicates. Thus, epistemic predicates like *acreditar* 'to believe'[6] and verbs of saying like *dizer* 'to tell'[7] (also known as declarative predicates) select for the TENSE operator ([+ TENSE]). Volitional predicates like *desejar* 'to wish',[8] on the other hand, do not (their complements are specified for [− TENSE]). Tense in INFL is always the reflex of a [+ TENSE] operator, but not necessarily one in the same simplex clause, as is the case with volitional predicates (see §4.1. below). Tense in INFL is responsible for whether a clause is finite or not (in the standard sense of 'finite clause'). Thus, if an INFL dominates tense, its clause is morphologically finite. If an INFL has no tense, then the clause is an infinitival (and, in Portuguese, possibly an inflected infinitival, depending on the further rewriting of INFL as AGR).

As a starting point, we assume the following rules for the expansion of S̄ and S, respectively:

$$(4) \quad (a) \quad \bar{S} \rightarrow COMP\ S$$
$$(b) \quad S \rightarrow NP\ INFL\ VP$$

Assuming that the selection relations between a matrix verb and a complement clause are mediated through the COMP node, we introduce the TENSE operator by the base rules in the COMP position. Therefore, one of the possible expansions for COMP will be as in (5):[9]

$$(5)\ COMP \rightarrow [\pm\ TENSE]$$

This paper is organized as follows. In the following section we will present the data under study, and show how they are problematic for the Binding Theory. In section 3, we will show that an account in terms of mood (indicative vs. subjunctive) is not sufficient to guarantee the correct results. In section 4, we will motivate the postulation of a selected [± TENSE] feature in the COMP position of the complement clauses of epistemic/declarative predicates vs. volitional predicates. We will correlate the [± TENSE] feature with the Opacity effects for pronominals in the subject position of a complement clause. In sections 5 and 6, we will provide further evidence that TENSE and not AGR or tense/mood is crucial in defining the domain of Opacity for pronominals in subject position. Inflected infinitival complements in EP will be analyzed in section 5, and factive predicates in section 6. In section 7, we will summarize our results.

2. Obligatory Disjoint Reference with Volitional Predicates

The phenomena under study concern the referential properties of pronominal elements in the subject position of a subordinate clause.[10]

Consider the following sentences:

(6) *O Manel pensa que ele ganha a corrida.*
'M thinks that he wins-Ind. the race.'

(7) *O Manel deseja que ele ganhe a corrida.*
'M wishes that he win-Subj. the race.'

In (6) the matrix verb *pensar* 'to think' is an epistemic predicate. Epistemic predicates, as well as declarative predicates, select for a complement clause whose verb is in the indicative mood. In (7) the matrix verb *desejar* 'to wish' is a volitional predicate. Volitional predicates select for complement clauses whose verb is in the subjunctive mood.

According to *LGB*, the GC for the pronominal subject in (6) and (7) is the embedded clause, since it is presumably governed and assigned case by the AGR element in the subordinate INFL mode, which is also its accessible SUBJECT. The pronominal is thus free in its GC, as required by Principle B of the Binding Theory, and should freely corefer outside of this domain. A possible coreferential reading with the main subject is therefore predicted in both cases.

However, the prediction is only borne out for (6). In (7), there is only one possible reading, in which the main subject and the pronominal in the embedded subject position must obligatorily be disjoint in reference. The *LGB* formulation of the Binding Theory does not predict this asymmetry, since in both cases it takes the complement S as the GC for the embedded subject. Crucially, in both cases, there is an embedded AGR element which may, in principle, be taken as an accessible SUBJECT.

There is a suggestion in *LGB* (p. 142) that the ungrammaticality of (7) under the coreferential reading should follow from the Avoid Pronoun Principle.[11] Thus, the impossibility of (7) (under the intended reading) would be due to the availability of a PRO option as complement subject in the case of a verb like *desejar*:

(8) *O Manel deseja* [PRO *ganhar a corrida*].
'M wishes to win the race.'

There are, however, several arguments against such an approach to this problem.

In the first place, the Avoid Pronoun Principle is intended to differentiate between preferred vs. non-preferred readings. For example, in *LGB* this principle is used to account for the status of the contrast between (9a) and (9b) under a coreferential reading of *John* and *his* (and PRO):

> (9) (a) John prefers [his winning the race].
> (b) John prefers [PRO winning the race].

Although in (9a) there is a clear preference for a reading where *John* is interpreted as disjoint in reference from *his*, it is nevertheless also possible to obtain a coreferential reading. However, this is not the case with (7), where such a reading is completely impossible.

Secondly, PRO is also available with verbs like *pensar* 'to intend':

> (10) *O Manel pensa* [PRO *ganhar a corrida*].
> 'M intends to win the race.'

On the assumption that (7) with a coreferential reading is out because of the availability of the PRO option (8), it is not clear why (6) with a coreferential reading is possible at all, given that the PRO option is also available in this case.

We thus reject the *LGB* solution for the problem presented in this section based on the Avoid Pronoun Principle.

3. Indicative versus Subjunctive Inflections

We want to propose a rather different approach to our problem. Basically, we would like to obtain a situation such that the disjoint reference reading of (7) would fall out naturally from some version of the Binding Theory alone.

The cornerstone of our proposal will be to take the binding domain of the pronominal subject in (7), but not in (6), to be the matrix clause.

Just playing with the elements that jointly make up the definition of 'governing category', several alternatives seem available to get the intended results. We will analyze and reject one that is directly based on the morphologically minimal contrast between (6) and (7): the opposition between an indicative INFL and a subjunctive INFL in the complement clause.

Let us suppose, then, that AGR in a subjunctive INFL does not qualify as a SUBJECT. Therefore, in the case of (7), the closest accessible SUBJECT to the pronoun would be AGR in the main clause. Thus the main clause would be the GC for the pronominal, within which it must be free, forcing the disjoint reference reading.

However, this approach is too strong, in that it predicts that all subjunctive complements will behave alike in the way they define the GC for an embedded subject. But, as can easily be shown, not all subjunctive INFLs behave alike in this respect.

First, factive verbal like *lamentar* 'to regret'[12] select for the subjunctive in their complement clauses. Nevertheless, they allow for a coreferential reading between the matrix subject and a pronominal in embedded subject position:

(11) *Os meus amigos lamentam que eles nunca cheguem a horas às reuniões.*
'My friends regret that they never arrive-Subj. on time to meetings.'

(11) shows that the subjunctive INFL per se cannot be the only factor responsible for the shift of GC in (7)—if our idea is correct that a shift in GC for the embedded pronominal subject is the reason for the obligatory disjoint reference reading.

Secondly, verbs of saying and epistemics in general may take a subjunctive complement whenever there is a negative or an interrogative operator-like element in the matrix clause.[13] And they still allow for a coreferential reading:

(12) (a) *O Manel não acredita que ele ganhe a corrida.*
'M doesn't believe that he win-Subj. the race.'
(b) *Que corrida é que o Manel acredita que ele ganhe?*
'Which race does M believe that he win-Subj.?'

If a subjunctive INFL didn't qualify as a SUBJECT, we would expect the coreferential reading to be out, since the GC would be the main clause, inducing obligatory disjoint reference.

Finally, there are no morphological reasons (contrary to English, for example) to take a subjunctive INFL as not qualifying as a SUBJECT. Subjunctive INFLs in EP are morphologically as visible and as rich as indicative INFLs, exhibiting the full range of paradigmatic variation for person and number. We therefore conclude that the differential choice of mood is not directly involved in the semantic differences between (6) and (7).

4. The Relevance of [± TENSE]

We would now like to suggest that the correct way to account for the obligatory disjoint reference reading of the pronominal in the embedded subject position of (7) does not lie in any improvements of the notion 'governing category' of *LGB*.

What we propose is a rather different solution which is in a way related to earlier versions of the Binding Theory. We suggest that the crucial element in determining Opacity for a pronominal in subject position is the operator TENSE in COMP.

4.1. The Motivation for [± TENSE]

It often has been observed by both traditional and generative grammarians that indicative and subjunctive complement clauses differ in the range of morphological and semantic tenses that they allow with respect to the tense specifications of the matrix clause.[14] Thus epistemic and declarative predicates, which select for the finite complement clauses with indicative mood, allow the understood time reference of their complement clauses to be completely free with respect to the time frame reference of the matrix clause. This semantic independence has a morphological correlate: almost any morphological tense may be picked up by the embedded clause while the tense of the matrix clause is kept constant:

(13) *O Manel disse/diz/dirá que a Maria chegou/chega/chegará tarde.*
'M said/says/will say that M arrived-Ind./arrives-Ind. will arrive-Ind. late.'

Another property of these predicates is that the past imperfect and the conditional tenses may be used in the complement clause to denote present or future reference if the matrix verb is [+ Past], provided that the denotation of the complement is a 'punctual' action:

(14) *A Maria disse que o Manel chegava/chegaria tarde.*
'M said that M would arrive (Past Imperf. Ind./Cond.) late.'

The semantic tense reference relations between matrix and complement clause also hold in the case in which the embedded clause is an infinitival (whether inflected or not), suggesting that the presence of the TENSE operator in COMP cuts across the distinction between finite and infinitival clauses.

Since morphological tense distinctions are now unavailable to the embedded verb, the language resorts to auxiliary verbs to carry over the temporal distinctions: [+ Past] is denoted by the auxiliary verb *ter* 'to have';[15] and [− Past] (= Present or Future), being the unmarked case, is denoted by the simple verbal form in the infinitive (but as with finite complements, periphrastic forms employing several auxiliary verbs, such as *ir* 'to go', will specifically denote a semantic future):[16]

(15) (a) *O Manel disse/diz/dirá [gostarem os meninos da Maria].*
'M said/says/will say to like-AGR the children (of) M.'
('the children to like M.')

(b) *O Manel disse/diz/dirá [terem os meninos gostado da Maria].*
'M said/says/will say to have-AGR the children liked M.'
('the children to have liked M.')

(c) *O Manel disse/diz/dirá [irem os meninos gostar da Maria].*
'M said/says/will say to go-AGR the children to like M.'
('the children are going to like M.')

Summarizing, paradigms (13)–(15) show us that with epistemic and declarative predicates the embedded clause may freely be [± Past], independently of the TENSE operator of the matrix clause. Morphologically, this means that all tense distinctions are available to the complement verb independently of the tense distinctions of the matrix verb.

We will capture these properties of epistemic and declarative predicates by postulating a semantic, operator-like element TENSE, and by specifying that these predicates select for complement clauses characterized by [+ TENSE], i.e., for complement clauses where the 'semantic tense properties' are independent from the 'semantic tense properties' of the matrix clause.

Consider now the behavior of volitional predicates (which select for subjunctive finite complements) with respect to the tense properties under study. Contrary to epistemic and declarative predicates, there are severe restrictions concerning the relation between matrix and complement clauses with respect to semantic and morphological tenses. If the matrix verb denotes present or future (i.e., is [– Past]), then the complement clause may not denote [+ Past]:

(16) **O Manel deseja que o filho fosse o melhor aluno.*
'M wishes (Pres.) that his son was (Past Subj.) the best student.'

The reverse is possible from a semantic point of view; that is, it is possible for the matrix clause to denote past tense while the complement clause denotes present or future tense. However, morphologically, the past subjunctive must be employed:

(17) (a) **O Manel desejava/desejou que o filho seja (agora) o melhor aluno.*
'M wished (Imperf./Perf.) that his son is (Pres. Subj.) now the best student.'

(b) *O Manel desejava/desejou que o filho fosse (agora) o melhor aluno.*
'M wished that his son would be (lit., was—Past Subj.) the best student.'

The generalization governing these predicates, often noted in recent as in traditional literature, appears to be that both semantically and morphologically the tense properties of the complement clause are dependent upon the tense properties of the matrix clause (which is specified for its own TENSE operator). This is the so-called 'sequence of tense' phenomenon described by many traditional grammarians:[17]

(18) (a) *O Manel deseja que o filho seja/*fosse o melhor aluno.*
'M wishes (Pres.) that his son be (Pres. Subj./*Past Subj.) the best student.'

(b) *O Manel desejava que o filho fosse/*seja o melhor aluno.*
'M wished (Past) that his son was (Past Subj./*Pres. Subj.) the best student.'

Again, these properties carry over to infinitival clauses:

(19) *O Manel deseja* [PRO *ser/*ter sido o melhor aluno*].
'M wishes to be/*to have been the best student.'

(20) *O Manel desejava* [PRO *ter sido/ser o melhor aluno*].
'M wished to have been/to be the best student.'

In the case of an infinitival clause, we find again the opposition between the presence of *ter* vs. the absence of *ter* as denoting the distinction between [+ Past] and [− Past], respectively.[18]

Use of the conditional or of any indicative tense is completely precluded with volitional predicates.[19] Thus (21) below contrasts directly with (14):

(21) **A Maria desejou que o Manel chegava/chegaria tarde.*
'M wished that M arrive (Past Imperf. Ind./Cond.) later.'

The properties of volitional predicates may be captured by specifying that they select for complement clauses without a semantic TENSE operator (i.e., that they select for complements characterized as [− TENSE]).

We now require that every morphological tense in INFL be linked to a semantic [+ TENSE] operator. In other words, tense in INFL functions as a variable-like element receiving its value from the closest TENSE operator.

In clauses selected by epistemic and declarative predicates (generally with their verb in the indicative mood), tense in INFL is linked to the TENSE operator of its own clause. In clauses selected by volitional predicates (with subjunctive mood in their verb), however, tense in INFL will have to be linked to the TENSE operator of the matrix clause, since the subjunctive clause will lack its own TENSE operator. This captures in a formal way the intuitive content of the sequence of tense phenomena.[20] Put simply, as we noted above, the tense of the complement is (at least in part) dependent upon the tense of the matrix clause.

4.2. Two Opaque Domains for Pronominals

There is a clear correlation between the presence/absence of the TENSE operator in a complement clause and the referential properties of its pro-

nominal subject. If the complement clause is a TENSED domain, coreference with a matrix subject is possible (as in [6]); if the complement clause
is an unTENSED domain, then disjoint reference is obligatory (as in [7]). In
other words, the TENSE operator, and not AGR in INFL, is creating an
opaque domain for a pronominal element in subject position (a domain
where it must be free).

When we consider subcategorized positions, however, we find that a
TENSE operator ceases to play a role in the creation of an opaque domain.
Rather, what counts now is a 'specified subject' in the sense of Chomsky
(1973, 1977):

> (22) (a) *O Manel$_i$ acredita que a Maria o$_{i/j}$ insultou.*
>   'M$_i$ believes that M insulted him$_{i/j}$.'
>   (b) *O Manel$_i$ deseja que a Maria o$_{i/j}$ insulte.*
>   'M$_i$ wishes that M insults him$_{i/j}$.'

This suggests that, as far as pronominals are concerned, there are in fact
two unrelated opaque domains: the subject of a sentence with a TENSE
operator and the c-command domain of the subject of any category.

The following binding principles (informally stated) appear then to hold
for pronominals:

> (23) (a) A pronoun is clausal subject position is free within the domain of a
>   TENSE operator.[21]
>   (b) A pronoun is free within the c-command domain of the subject of any
>   category.

It is rather unclear whether the two opaque domains can be unified in
terms of the notion 'governing category' of *LGB*.[22] Recall that this unification was made possible precisely because AGR was taken to be the inducer
of Opacity for the subject position (rather than tense). It was then possible
to define a notion of '(accessible) SUBJECT' unifying AGR and a lexical NP
subject on the basis of both being nominal elements (a SUBJECT being 'the
most prominent nominal element' in a clause). This notion was in turn the
basis for the unification of the NIC and the Opacity Condition of Chomsky
(1980) (the Tensed-S Condition/PIC and the Specified Subject Condition
of Chomsky [1973, 1977]).

If correct, our analysis shows that the notion of SUBJECT of *LGB* is not a
valid one for pronominals, i.e., that it plays no role in the definition of the
binding domains for pronominals. Our analysis rather suggests an interpretation of the Binding Theory for pronominals which is in certain respects
closer to the first versions incorporating the Specified Subject Condition
and the Tensed-S Condition of Chomsky (1973), except that what is in-

volved in our Tensed-S Condition (23a) is not the morphological tense of Chomsky (1973) but rather a semantic, operator-like TENSE in COMP.

4.3. Anaphors in Complement Subject Position

The occurrence of anaphors in complement subject position does not parallel the occurrence of pronouns in the way that the Binding Theory of *LGB* predicts.

The Binding Theory makes the very strong prediction that coreferential pronouns (with some antecedent) and anaphors (bound to that same antecedent) are in strict complementary distribution. This is illustrated in (24):

> (24) (a) *O Manel$_i$ acredita que a Maria o$_i$ insultou.*
> (b) **O Manel$_i$ acredita que a Maria se$_i$ insultou.*
> 'M$_i$ believes that M insulted him$_j$/*himself$_i$.'

On the other hand, a position where disjoint reference is required for a pronominal is predicted to accept an anaphoric element:

> (25) (a) *O Manel$_i$ insultou-o$_{j/*i}$.*
> (b) *O Manel$_i$ insultou-se$_i$.*
> 'M$_i$ insulted him$_{j/*i}$/himself$_i$.'

The *LGB* theory predicts that an anaphor should be able to occur in the subject position of a complement to a volitional predicate. But this is in fact impossible:

> (26) **O Manel deseja que si próprio ganhe a corrida.*
> 'M wishes that he himself wins the race.'

There are two possible paths that we could take in order to deal with this problem.

We could say that the Binding Theory has exactly the same principles (i.e., defines the same opaque domains) for anaphors and pronouns, but that some additional principle applies to anaphors but not to pronominals, breaking the expected parallelism and preventing an anaphor from occurring in (26). Kayne (1983) points out that the Empty Category Principle (ECP) of *LGB* (ch. 4) may apply also to lexical anaphors (in addition to applying to empty categories). Then, on the assumption that a subjunctive inflection is not a proper governor in EP, (26) is ruled out by virtue of *si próprio* 'himself' not being properly governed.[23]

Alternatively, we could encode the differential behavior of anaphors and pronouns directly into the Binding Theory. In that case, we would have to say that the binding principles that apply to anaphors are different from the ones that apply to pronominals (i.e., that the opaque domains for anaphors are different from the ones for pronouns). This is in fact the position taken by Huang (1983), on the basis of an empirical coverage completely different from the one in the present study. He suggests that the notion of SUBJECT of *LGB* should count only in the case of anaphors but not in the case of pronouns. Suppose that this is true and that, furthermore, the TENSE operator is irrelevant as far as anaphors are concerned. Then in (26), the GC for the anaphor is the complement clause, since it contains the governor of the anaphor (INFL with AGR) and an accessible SUBJECT to the anaphor (again, AGR in INFL). Since TENSE is now irrelevant, the fact that the complement clause is [− TENSE] does not affect the GC in this case. (26) is ruled out because the anaphor is not bound in its GC.

An anaphor in subcategorized position must be bound within the domain of a lexical subject. In this case, we have the expected parallelism between pronouns and anaphors, since a pronoun in this position must be free within the same domain (cf. [22]):

(27) *O Manel$_i$ acredita que a Maria$_j$ se$_{j/*i}$ insultou.*
      'M$_i$ believes that M$_j$ insulted herself$_j$ /*himself$_i$.'

(22) and (27) show that pronouns and anaphors behave in a parallel way in subcategorized positions (i.e., they behave 'well' with respect to the opposition bound/free). It is only in clausal subject position that the parallelism breaks down.[24] Slightly adapting Huang's (1983) idea, we could say that TENSE and AGR have complementary domains of Opacity inducement as far as the subject position of a clause is concerned: TENSE operates on pronouns while AGR operates on anaphors.[25]

This account gives us the observed distribution of anaphors and pronouns in the subject position of a finite complement clause: anaphors are uniformly impossible, since AGR in the complement creates an opaque domain where the anaphor has to be bound; but in the case of pronouns, both coreferences and obligatory disjoint reference are now possible, depending on whether or not the complement is [± TENSE].[26] If it is [+ TENSE], then the complement clause is a binding domain for the pronominal, where it must be free (and coreference is possible with the matrix subject); if the complement is [− TENSE], then the pronoun must search for the closest higher TENSE operator. If this is the one of the immediately dominating matrix sentence, then this clause is the binding domain for the pronoun, where it must be free. Therefore, disjoint reference is imposed with respect to the matrix subject.[27]

5. Binding Effects in Infinitival Clauses

Inflected infinitival clauses with lexical pronominal subjects should provide us with a testing ground for our hypothesis that the TENSE operator in COMP, and not AGR in INFL, is the relevant inducer of Opacity for pronominals in subject position.

Consider sentence (3) again, which we repeat here for convenience in a partial S-structure representation:

(28) *Os meninos disseram* [s̄ [COMP [+ TENSE]] [*não terem eles partido o vidro*]].
'The children said not to have-AGR (they) broken the glass.'

Dizer 'to say', a verb of saying, selects for [+ TENSE] in the COMP of its complement clause. Therefore the complement clause is the binding category for the pronoun in subject position. The pronoun is thus free in s̄ and should be able to corefer outside of it, which is the situation.

In this case, however, the alternative analysis of *LGB* makes exactly the same predictions, since INFL in the complement clause dominates AGR, which is an accessible SUBJECT to the pronoun.[28]

What we need is a matrix predicate that does not select for the TENSE operator while allowing an inflected infinitival complement. The causative predicate *deixar* 'to allow' is such a verb.[29] As the following paradigm shows, it subcategorizes for complement clauses specified as [− TENSE]:

(29) (a) *Eu deixo que o Manel compre/*comprasse o automóvel.*
'I allow (Pres.) that M buy (Pres. Subj./*Past Subj.) the car.'
('I allow M to buy/*bought the car').
   (b) *Eu deixei que o Manel comprasse/*compre o automóvel.*
'I allowed (Past) that M bought (Past Subj./*Pres. Subj.) the car.'
('I allowed M to buy/*buys the car').

That an inflected infinitival complement is possible with *deixar* is shown by the grammaticality of (30):

(30) *Eu deixei [os meninos saírem mais cedo].*
'I let the children leave-AGR earlier.'

A pronoun in the subject position of an inflected infinitival complement to *deixar* is obligatorily disjoint in reference from the matrix subject:

(31) *As meninas$_i$ deixaram [elas$_{j/*i}$ saírem mais cedo].*
'The girls$_i$ let them$_{j/*i}$ leave earlier.'

In this case, our analysis is the only one that accounts for the facts. Crucially, the embedded complement has AGR (in INFL) just like the embedded complement of (28). Therefore, if the *LGB* account was correct, the complement should be the governing category for the pronoun, the pronoun would be free in it, and coreference should be possible. Under our analysis, on the contrary, the binding category for the pronoun is the matrix clause, since this is the minimal domain with a TENSE operator including the subject pronoun. Obligatory disjoint reference is thus predicted, since the pronoun must be free in this domain. The facts in this section also argue against an account in terms of mood, for the simple reason that mood is not involved in the complement of (28) or (31).

6. The Behavior of Factive Predicates

With respect to temporal possibilities, factive predicates like *lamentar* 'to regret'[30] appear to be located in the middle of a scale which has volitionals in one extreme and epistemics/declaratives in the other. That is, tense specifications in the complement clause (both semantically and morphologically) are much less restricted than with volitionals, factive predicates select for subjunctive inflections.

The basis generalization with respect to tense properties of factives appears to be that the tense reference of the complement clause must be equal or prior in the temporal scale than the tense reference of the matrix clause. The combination [+ Past] in the matrix clause and [− Past] (= Present or Future) in the complement clause is disallowed, presumably because of the basic semantic property of factive predicates, i.e., that they presuppose the truth of the denotation of their complement clauses. Clearly, then, one can presuppose the truth of something that is happening or has happened in the past, but not of something that may (or may not) happen in the future. The relevant data are given in (32):[31]

> (32) (a) *Eu lamento que os meninos saiam/saíssem tão cedo.*
>   'I regret (Pres.) that the children leave (Pres. Subj.)/left (Past Subj.) so early.'
>   (b) *Eu lamentei que os meninos saíssem/*saiam tão cedo.*
>   'I regretted (Past) that the children left (Past Subj.)/*leave (Pres. Subj.) so early.'

Let us assume that the COMP position of complement clauses subcategorized for by factive predicates is specified for [+ TENSE]. We now expect coreference between a complement subject pronoun and the matrix subject to be permitted. This expectation is fulfilled:

> (33) *A Joana lamenta que ela chegue sempre atrasada.*
>   'J regrets that she always arrives late.'

Since factive predicates subcategorize for finite complements in the subjunctive, the possibility of coreference in (33) shows clearly that mood is not involved directly in the obligatory disjoint reference reading that we obtain with volitionals (refer back to §3).

Factive predicates also allow inflected infinitival complements. Again, coreference is possible:[32]

> (34) *A Joana lamenta* [*ela chegar sempre atrasada*].
> 'J regrets she to arrive-AGR($\emptyset$) always late.'
> 'J regrets that she always arrives late.'

The behavior of factives—which select for subjunctive mood but are specified for [+ TENSE] in their associated COMP position—provides us with an additional argument for the correctness of the analysis proposed in the preceding sections.[33]

7. Conclusion

We have postulated an abstract operator-like TENSE in the complement clause of epistemic, declarative, and factive predicates, directly capturing the freedom of tenses that they manifest with respect to the matrix clause. The complement clause to volitional predicates, on the other hand, is not specified for such an operator. If a predicate selects for [+ TENSE], it will display this operator in both finite and infinitival clauses. On the basis of the referential properties of pronouns in complement clauses, it was then shown that the TENSE operator was the crucial factor in creating an opaque domain for pronouns in subject position, rather than AGR, as far as the Binding Theory is concerned.

NOTES

[1] A shorter version of this paper was presented at the I Col.loqui Internacional de Linguistica Teorica i Llengues Romaniques, Sitges, Spain, June 1983. We are indebted to Ivonne Bordelois, Celia Jakubowicz, Tarald Taraldsen, and Janis Williamson for comments and suggestions.

[2] The rule for INFL given in LGB (p. 241) is as follows:

$$(i) \to INFL \ [[\pm \ tense], (AGR)]$$

Portuguese has the option of rewriting the INFL in [[− tense], Agr]. This is the so-called 'inflected' or 'personal' infinitive. See Raposo (1973, 1975) for a detailed study of the inflected infinitive in European Portuguese. See also Raposo (1984, forthcoming), Rouveret (1980), and Zubizarreta (1980) for an approach to the inflected infinitive in terms of the theory of Government and Binding.

[3] For an account of the inverted word order in the complement clause of (3), see Raposo (1984, forthcoming).

[4] @ in (3) refers to the complex structure [s̄ COMP [s. In *LGB*, the governing category is taken to be S and not s̄.

[5] We use capital letters to distinguish the TENSE operator from tense in INFL.

[6] Other epistemic predicates are *pensar* 'to think', *considerar* 'to consider', *supor* 'to suppose', *achar*, *calcular* 'to think'.

[7] Other verbs of saying are *declarar* 'to declare', *afirmar* 'to affirm', *acrescentar* 'to add', *confessar* 'to confess', *concluir* 'to conclude'.

[8] Other volitional predicates are *querer* 'to want', *detestar* 'to detest', *preferir* 'to prefer ', *recusar* 'to refuse', *esperar* 'to hope'.

[9] We take the basic expansion of [+ TENSE] to be [± Past] (with [− Past] = Present or Future). Den Besten (1983) and Stowell (1981, 1982) also introduce a TENSE operator. However, contrary to our approach, these authors do not consider TENSE as a selected element. In finite clauses, we take the lexical complementizer *que* 'that' as a filler of [± TENSE], and not as a filler of [− WH], as is often assumed.

[10] Null subjects will not be considered in this study, since they do not always parallel the behavior of lexical pronouns. This gives us some reason to consider that they are not [+ pronoun, − anaphor] elements, contrary to Chomsky (1982, ch. 5). Consideration of null subjects would take us too far afield. See Raposo (in preparation).

[11] *The Avoid Pronoun Principle:* Avoid Pronoun (whenever choice of PRO is possible). See *LGB* (p. 65) and Jaeggli (1980).

[12] Other factive predicates include *deplorar* 'to deplore', *censurar* 'to censure', *aprovar* 'to approve', *tolerar* 'to tolerate', *suportar* 'to stand'.

[13] These are the 'secondary subjunctives' of Jakubowicz (1983). We believe that lexically determined secondary subjunctives are involved in verbs like *duvidar* 'to doubt' and *negar* 'to deny', which were presented by Zaring (1984) as counterexamples to the analysis presented in an earlier version of this paper.

[14] For a very careful and detailed study of tense combinations (focusing on Spanish), see Luján (1979).

[15] As in Hoffman (1966) and McCawley (1971).

[16] See note 2.

[17] Besides (18), there are additional semantic combinations that can be constructed by using the auxiliary verb *ter* 'to have' in the complement clause. We won't go into these details here. The additional possibilities do not counterexemplify the generalizations presented here.

[18] Note that in (20) the bare infinitival is used to refer to [− Past] (the unmarked case). That is, if the matrix verb is [+ Past], there is no obligatory requirement that the auxiliary *ter* be used, in the case of an infinitival clause.

[19] This is readily explained on the assumption that the conditional is an indicative tense.

[20] For similar but independently developed approaches to tense phenomena, see Jakubowicz (1983) and Picallo (1984).

[21] We restrict this study to clausal occurrences of pronouns. See note 24.

[22] Consider sentences with infinitival complement clauses where S̄ deletion has applied:

(i) John $_i$ believes $_i$[$_S$ him $_{j/*i}$ to be the best student].

The existence of these sentences raises two problems for our account.

First, *believe*, being an epistemic predicate, selects for [+ TENSE] in its complement clause. If [+ TENSE] is generated in COMP and if COMP deletion is a prerequisite for S̄ deletion, then the TENSE operator must be recoverable in some way at S-structure. We assume that this is indeed the case, through the presence/absence of the auxiliary verb *to have* denoting the opposition [± Past].

Second, the binding domain for the pronominal is not the TENSED complement clause, since otherwise coreference between the pronoun and the matrix subject should be possible, which is not the case. The entire structure must be taken as the binding domain in this case, contrary to what our analysis would predict at first sight. Note, however, that this result in fact follows from a strict interpretation of our analysis. Assume, as in *LGB,* that the Binding Theory applies at S-structure. At this level of representation there is no COMP position, and therefore no TENSE operator in COMP, since S̄ deletion has applied. The closest TENSE operator is now the one of the matrix clause, which will thus be taken as the binding domain for the pronoun.

Alternatively, we could say that part of the *LGB* notion of 'governing category' is still crucial for the correct definition of the binding domains for pronouns, namely, the part requiring the binding domain to contain the element plus its governor. In (i), thus, the minimal domain containing the pronoun, its governor, and a TENSE operator is the matrix clause.

[23] Consider (i), where an anaphor occurs in the subject position of a complement to an epistemic predicate:

(i) *O Manel acredita que si próprio ganhou a corrida.
'M believes that he himself won the race.'

Even if an indicative INFL is a proper government (as in Picallo 1984), the sentence is ruled out, since now the complement clause is [+ TENSE] and the anaphor should therefore be bound in it.

[24] In addition to the cases analyzed by Huang (1983) which involve NP and not S as the governing category.

[25] In the case of NP, however, TENSE appears to be irrelevant as a necessary requirement for the creation of an opaque domain for pronouns:

> (i) *eles*$_i$ *leram* [$_{NP}$ *os livros de + eles*$_i$].
>   'They$_i$ read their$_i$ books.'

The binding domain is the object NP, since *(de) eles* may be coreferential to the matrix subject. TENSE is irrelevant here (unless we say that NPs have TENSE, in some sense).

[26] A modal verb such as *poder* 'may' seems to act as a kind of operator inducing an opaque domain even in clauses which are specified as [− TENSE]. Thus we have a contrast between (i) and (ii):

> (i)   **O Manel*$_i$ *deseja que ele*$_i$ *ganhe a corrida.*
>   'M$_i$ wishes that he$_i$ win the race.'
> (ii) *O Manel*$_i$ *deseja que ele*$_i$ *possa ganhar a corrida.*
>   'M$_i$ wishes that he$_i$ can win the race.'

The presence of the modal in (ii) substantially improves the sentence with an intended coreference reading. The modal is clearly acting as an operator fulfilling the requirements of the Binding Theory for pronouns in subject position. Additional research is needed to investigate exactly what is involved in this phenomenon, and why modal verbs line up with the TENSE operator in defining an opaque domain.

[27] In this case the higher subject also acts as a specified subject. Therefore both the Tensed-S Condition and the Specified Subject Condition conspire to induce obligatory disjoint reference.

[28] It is shown in Raposo (1984, forthcoming) that the pronoun *eles* in (28) is in subject position. In (28), we have represented the auxiliary verb *ter* and its associated AGR marker inside S. In Raposo (1984, forthcoming) it is claimed that these elements occur in COMP position at S-structure. However, this misrepresentation in (28) has no incorrect implications for the points under study.

Note that in our account, $\bar{S}$ is the binding domain for a subject pronoun, and not S (as in *LGB*), since only $\bar{S}$, but not S, includes the COMP position (with the TENSE operator).

[29] This is a marked behavior even in EP, since in subcategorized positions the unmarked case is that inflected infinitival complements are possi-

ble with predicates that subcategorize for [+ TENSE] but are disallowed with predicates that subcategorize for [− TENSE]. See Raposo (1984, forthcoming) for details.

[30] See note 11.

[31] Again, we will not consider the finer temporal possibilities that are available through the use of the auxiliary verb *ter* in the complement clause.

[32] For some reason, a coreferential reading is harder to obtain in (34) than in (33). This might be due to the peculiar categorial status of the infinitival complement in (34) under the analysis proposed in Raposo (1984, forthcoming).

[33] We might choose to analyze factive predicates in a slightly different way. Note first that with the analysis in the main text, there is no more a direct correlation between a TENSE operator in COMP and indicative inflections. Suppose that we want to preserve a one-to-one correlation between [+ TENSE] and indicative mood. We could then say that the COMP position associated with factive predicates is specified for a specific operator, call it 'Factive', which, among other properties, has the semantic temporal features described in the text. In other words, the tense properties of factives would not be associated with a TENSE operator in COMP (and factives would thus select [− TENSE] complements) but rather directly with the Factive operator. Then, selection of indicative mood vs. subjunctive mood would be regular again, depending solely upon the presence of the TENSE operator. Now, however, we have to say that the Factive operator induces Opacity, in addition to the TENSE operator. See also note 26.

REFERENCES

Chomsky, Noam. 1973. Conditions on transformations. In Roger Anderson and Paul Kiparsky (eds.), A festschrift for Morris Halle, pp. 232–86. New York: Holt, Rinehart and Winston.

———. 1977. On Wh-movement. In Peter Culicover, Thomas Wasow, and Adrian Akmajian (eds.), Formal Syntax, pp. 71–132. New York: Academic Press.

———. 1980. On binding. Linguistic Inquiry 11.1–46.

———. 1981. Lectures on government and binding. Dordrecht: Foris.

———. 1982. Some concepts and consequences of the theory of government and binding. Cambridge, MA: MIT Press.

Den Besten, Hans. 1983. On the interaction of root transformations and lexical deletive rules. In Werner Abraham (ed.), On the formal syntax of the Westgermania, pp. 47–131. Amsterdam: John Benjamins.

Dias, A. Epifânio da S. 1918. Syntaxe histórica portuguesa. Lisbon, Portugal: Livraria Clássica.

George, Leland, and Jaklin Kornfilt. 1981. Finiteness and boundedness in Turkish. In Frank Heny (ed.), Binding and filtering, pp. 105–27. London: Croom Helm.

Hoffman, T. H. 1966. Past tense replacement and the English modal auxiliary system. Langages 14.28–43.

Huang, C.T. James. 1983. A note on the Binding theory. Linguistic Inquiry 14.554–60.

Jaeggli, Osvaldo. 1980. On some phonologically-null elements in syntax. Doctoral dissertation, MIT.

Jakubowicz, Celia. 1983. Binding theory and tense in finite clauses. Unpublished paper, MIT.

Kayne, Richard. 1983. Connectedness. Linguistic Inquiry 14.223–49.

Luján, Marta. 1979. Clitic promotion and mood in Spanish verbal complements. Bloomington: Indiana University Linguistics Club.

McCawley, James. 1971. Tense and time reference in English. In Charles Fillmore and Terence Langendoen (eds.), Studies in Linguistic Semantics, pp. 97–114. New York: Holt, Rinehart and Winston.

Meireles, José A. 1972. Estruturas de complementação em Português. 'Licenciatura' dissertation, University of Lisbon.

Picallo, M. Carmen. 1984. The Infl node and the null subject parameter. Linguistic Inquiry 15.75–102.

Raposo, Eduardo. 1973. Estudos sobre o infinitivo em Português. 'Licenciatura' dissertation, University of Lisbon.

———. 1975. Uma restrição derivacional global sobre o infinitivo em Português. Boletim de Filologia 24.75–293.

———. 1984. On the inflected infinitive in European Portuguese. Paper presented at the GLOW Colloquium 1984, University of Copenhagen. To be published in Boletim de Filologia.

———. Forthcoming. Infinitival clauses in European Portuguese.

———. In preparation. On null objects and subjects in European Portuguese.

Rouveret, Alain. 1980. Sur la notion de proposition finie: Gouvernement et inversion. Langages 60.75–107.

Stowell, Tim. 1981. Origins of phrase structure. Doctoral dissertation, MIT.

———. 1982. The tense of infinitives. Linguistic Inquery 13.561–70.

Zaring, Laurie. 1984. The characterization of clause–types: Scope, obviation and independent tense. Berkeley Linguistic Society 10.

Zubizarreta, Maria Luisa. 1980. Remarks on Portuguese infinitives. Unpublished paper, MIT.

6

Ā Antecedents and Empty Subjects in Brazilian Portuguese

Dana Wheeler

Duke University

1. The following sentence-types are common to spoken Brazilian Portuguese (BP):[1]

> (1) *O brasileiro ele é muito caseiro.*
> 'The Brazilian he is a homebody.'
> (2) *Susana ela costuma chegar tarde.*
> 'Susan she normally arrives late.'
> (3) *O bom cavalheiro ele usa a perna só.*
> 'The good rider he uses his leg only.'

These sentences have in common a sentence-initial configuration consisting of an NP followed by a coreferential pronoun, with no lexical material intervening.[2] Given the assumption that the NP and pronoun are not generated under the same node, there are two possible sources for this configuration. The first is that the NP in question is the subject of S, that is

(NP, S), while its pronominal copy appears under the Inflection (INFL) node as a phonetic manifestation of the pronominal properties of verbal concordance. The second attributes subjecthood to the pronominal copy, thereby localizing the antecedent NP to the left of the subject, outside the sentence. This second potential source may be viewed as a subset of Left Dislocation, applying specifically to dislocated subjects. The two distinct structural possibilities for the above configuration are presented in (4) and (5):[3]

$$(4) \; [\; [NP_i \;] \; [pron_i \;] \; [\; \ldots \;]]$$
$$ \; S \; NP \quad \; INFL \quad \; VP$$

$$(5) \; [\; [NP_i] \; \ldots \; [\; [pron_i] \; [\ldots] \; [\ldots]]]$$
$$ \; \bar{S} \; TOP \quad \quad S \; NP \quad \; INFL \; VP$$

One might justifiably argue that both (4) and (5) are legitimate sources for the above configuration in natural language. This position was defended in Rizzi (1984). The force of Rizzi's arguments permits a shift in focus from determining the legitimacy of (4) to discerning which of the two is the correct underlying structure for the NP_i $pron_i$ configuration in a particular language.

By calling evidence from Rizzi and other factors into play, it should be a fairly straightforward proposition to determine which structure is correct for this configuration in BP. In point of fact, however, this is not the case. Not all of the diagnostics provided by Rizzi are applicable to BP, and those that are are provide unclear results. This, coupled with results obtained from examining issues pertaining solely to BP within the Romance family, led to the preliminary conclusion that neither (4) nor (5) is the correct underlying structure, strictly speaking.

The main thrust of this article is to provide arguments in favor of an underlying structure for the NP_i $pron_i$ configuration in BP that is a combination of (4) and (5). It will be argued that the configuration represents a kind of Topic construction, whose NP antecedent is generated under the TOPIC node, as in the case of Left Dislocation. Conversely, we will attempt to determine that the pronominal copy is not a resumptive in subject position but a phonetic manifestation of the pronominal properties of AGReement (AGR) in BP, which licenses an empty category in subject position. The proposed structure is presented in (6):[4]

$$(6) \; [\quad \; [NP_i] \ldots [\; [pro_i] \; [pron_i] \; [\ldots]]]$$
$$ \; \bar{S} \; TOP \quad \quad \; S \; NP \quad \; INFL \quad VP$$

2. The recent history of the study of Null Subject Languages (NSLs) can be viewed as an evolution of the intent to account formally for the observa-

tion that languages that permit a phonologically empty slot in subject position do so because their verbal inflection systems are 'rich enough' to
determine certain features of the subject.[5]

Rizzi (1982) captures this by attributing pronominal status to the verbal
inflection system itself in those languages which permit an empty subject.
Based on this claim, Rizzi develops a precise mechanism which will permit
the INFL node to license an empty pronominal in subject position. It is
argued that the AGReement component of INFL, which is a cover term for
such features as person and number, is equivalent to an abstract pronoun
in NSLs. This may be formally restated by including in AGR the feature
[pronominal], positively specified for NSLs, negatively for non-NSLs. In
more recent work, Rizzi (1984) builds on the potentially pronominal properties of AGR by proposing a further expansion of this feature when positively specified. An AGR marked [+ pronominal] has the option of
phonetically realizing this property. In the NSLs that exercise this option, a
lexical (subject) pronoun appears generated under INFL.

This latter expansion is the formal mechanism which accounts for the
distinction in NSLs between those that manifest the NP_i $pron_i$ configuration
and those that do not. In both cases, the subject position may be lexically
filled or empty; in the former case, the subject will always be followed by a
lexical pronoun.[6] This contrast is in evidence in Italian; 'standard' Italian
does not use this configuration productively, while various northern Italian
dialects do (from Rizzi 1984, sentences [1] and [3]):

(7) standard Italian (a) *Gianni parla*
                       (b) _____ *parla*
(8) northern Italian (a) *el Gianni el parla*
                       (b) _____ *el parla*

The presence or absence of a pronominal copy is in itself not directly
connected to the status of a language with respect to empty subjects, as
may be attested in French, which has some sort of very productive Left
Dislocation for subjects consisting of an NP and a subject clitic. What does
appear to be directly connected to a language's empty subject status is the
possibility of the pronominal copy appearing under AGReement.[7]
3. In this and subsequent sections, we will address the issue of the
structural possibilities for NP_i $pron_i$ configuration in Brazilian Portuguese,
an NSL.

Among the diagnostics that Rizzi provides for determining whether the
NP_i $pron_i$ configuration is a Left Dislocation or a 'Subject' structure, we find
two that are particularly relevant for BP. The first is based on the well-
attested claim that a pronoun cannot be bound by an unrestricted opera-

tor. For the purposes of this essay, let us define an 'operator' as a quantifier-like element appearing in a non-argument position which is the head of the (Ā) chain (NP, ... pronoun). Examples of operators are quantified left-dislocated phrases, and phrases in COMP that bind a pronoun in an argument position within the S. An 'unrestricted' operator is, roughly, a quantified phrase that does not contain a referential phrase; this term extends to wh-operators. In Portuguese, for example, *ninguém* 'no one', *tudo* 'everything', and *quem* 'who' are unrestricted quantifiers while *nenhuma pessoa* 'no person', *todo homem* 'all/every man', and *que pessoa* 'what/which person' are not.

The above captures the fact that in languages that possess a resumptive strategy, when the resumptive is bound to an unrestricted operator the resulting sentence is unacceptable; but if the resumptive is bound to a restricted operator, the sentence is much more acceptable:

> (9) *? *Quem$_i$ que você disse que ele$_i$ saiu?*
> 'Who did you say that he left?'
> (10) ? *Que pessóa$_i$ que você disse que ela$_i$ foi embora?*
> 'What person(f) did you say that she went away?'

With this in mind, Rizzi observes that in standard Italian and French, an unrestricted quantifier may not serve as the antecedent for a pronoun but that it may do so in northern Italian dialects: (Rizzi's sentences [12b], [14], [22b], and [20], respectively):

> (11) **Nessuno, lo conosco in questa città*
> (cf. ?? *Nessun uomo politico, lo conosco bene*)
> (12) **Personne, il n'a rien dit*
> (13) Torinese: *Gnun l'a˙dit gnent*
> 'Nobody they said nothing'
> (' = Nobody said anything')
> Trentino: *Tut l'è capita de not*
> 'Everything it happened in the night'

Rizzi attributes the difference in acceptability of (11) and (12) on the one hand, and (13) on the other, to a difference in structure. In the case of French and standard Italian, the unrestricted quantifier is under the TOPIC node, binding a pronoun generated in subject position, which accounts for the ungrammaticality of the sentences. In northern Italian, however, the unrestricted quantifier originates within the sentence in subject position, and through Quantifier Raising adjoins to S. In the resulting structure, exemplified in (14) below, the raised quantifier binds its trace in subject position; the pronoun, generated under AGR, is co-indexed with the trace but is not directly bound by the unrestricted quantifier, and the structure is grammatical:

(14) (cf. 13) [Tut$_i$ [è$_i$ [l'$_i$] [capita de not]]]
                  S   AGR

Brazilian Portuguese clearly patterns after French and standard Italian, as seen in the examples below, suggesting that the quantifier is generated under the TOPIC node:

> (15) *Ninguém (,) ele não disse nada.
>   'No one he didn't say anything.'
> (16) *Tudo (,) ele vai sair bem.
>   'Everything he is going to come out all right.'

Although we may wish to generate the quantifier outside the sentence under the TOPIC node, this does not require us to adhere to the internal sentential structure normally associated with Left Dislocations, where an overt lexical resumptive fills the argument slot in the sentence that corresponds to the dislocated phrase (in this case, [NP, S]). If the 'resumptive' pronoun were actually the phonetic reflection of AGReement, the unrestricted quantifier in the TOPIC node could still bind a pronoun in subject position, rendering the resulting sentence ungrammatical. The only difference between this structure and that of, for instance, Left Dislocations in French is that in BP, the pronoun in subject position is lexically empty.[8]

A second argument provided by Rizzi supporting the structural distinctions between these two language types involves coordinate structures. The argument is based on the observation that languages like the northern Italian dialects whose subject is accompanied by an obligatory subject pronoun must repeat this pronoun in the second conjunct of a coordinate structure, while languages patterning after French or standard Italian do not (Rizzi's sentences [39b] and [38], respectively):

> (17) la canta e la bala
> (18) elle chante et dance

Rizzi provides independent evidence that the correct structure for coordination is two conjoined sentences rather than two conjoined VPs:

> (19) [[elle$_i$ chante] et [pron$_i$ dance]]
>   S S   S

Coordination is then an instance of deletion of the coindexed pronoun in the second conjunct. Given that this is so, the question remains as to why in the case of the northern Italian dialects, the second pronoun cannot be deleted. Rizzi reduces it to a difference in structure between the two language types. In languages like French, the subject clitic is generated under the subject node, while in languages like the northern Italian cluster, it is generated under INFL.

One must then ask, is it possible for an element generated under INFL to delete in a coordinate structure? Based on evidence from small clauses which indicates that only major categories may be realized zero (deleted), Rizzi determines that the answer is negative.

BP, in this respect, again patterns after French/standard Italian in the crucial sense, as the subject pronominal may be repeated in a coordinate structure but need not obligatorily be:

> (20) *ele canta e dança*
> 'he sings and dances'
> (21) *ela deu um berro e caiu morta*
> 'she let out a yell and fell down dead'

At first glance, we could surmise from this that subject pronominal in BP is generated under the subject NP node rather than under INFL. However, it would still be possible to argue that the subject pronominal in BP is generated under INFL if coordinate structures were shown additionally to be the result of VP conjunction. There is a piece of evidence that suggests that this is so.[9] Consider the following sentence from Spanish:

> (22) *Muchas personas ganaron la carrera y bebieron cerveza.*
> 'Many people won the race and drank beer.'

The above sentence has two possible readings, given in (23) and (24) below. In (23), the quantifier *many* has scope over the entire sentence; in (24) it has scope only over the first conjunct:

> (23) For many x, x won the race and drank beer.
> (24) For many x, x won the race and *pro* drank beer.

In (24), the subject pronoun (*pro*) is not c-commanded by the quantifier; consequently, it cannot be bound by it. The *pro* then is an E-type pronoun, as defined in Evans (1980).

If (22) is logically ambiguous, it is derivable from two distinct structures. The first, corresponding to (23), conjoins two VPs, and the second, corresponding to (24), conjoins two sentences.

In BP, the evidence for two structures is clearer still. A sentence equivalent to (22) is not logically ambiguous; both conjuncts are predicated of the quantified subject. If, however, an overt subject pronominal appears in the second conjunct, it may not be bound by the quantified subject:

> (25) (= 23) *Muitas pessoas abandonaram a terra e foram para São Paulo.*
> 'Many people abandoned the land and went to São Paulo.'
> (26) (= 24) *Muitas pessoas abandonaram a terra e elas foram para SP.*

It is highly likely that coordinate structures in BP have two sources; one, conjoined VPs and the other, conjoined Ss. This line of reasoning also permits us to conjecture that if no overt subject pronominal is present in a sentence, no empty subject pronominal is either. It would be difficult to account for the lack of ambiguity in (25) otherwise. This points to two possibilities: either BP does not permit empty (third person) subjects or, if it does, those subjects must be licensed by the presence of an overt pronominal. We will consider this question further in §5.[10]

4. It must be observed that the grammar of BP possesses a structure having the properties of Left Dislocation that is productive for subjects as well as for other arguments:

> (27) *Este artigo, não vou ler ele até o Natal.*
> 'This article, I'm not going to read it(m.) until Christmas.'
> (28) *O João, você acha que ele realmente quis ir embora?*
> 'John, do you think that he really wanted to go away?'
> (29) *Monique, com quem ela teria fugido?*
> 'Monique, whom could she have fled with?' (lit. 'with whom . . .')
> (30) *Essa confusão, para mim ela é definitiva.*
> 'This confusion, for me it(f.)'s definitive.'

Sentence (28) is an instance of a subject dislocated from an embedded sentence. In (29) and (30), where the subject is dislocated from the uppermost sentence, there is material intervening between the NP and its copy. In (30), since the intervening phrase is a (possibly sentential) PP, it might still be legitimate to argue for a structure for the NP_i $pron_i$ configuration that places the NP under the subject of S. However, to do so for (29) would entail arguing independently for the placement of wh-phrases inside the sentence adjoined to the right of the subject or to INFL, an undesirable consequence. Hence, the strong claim that the configuration $NP_i \ldots pron_i$, when applied to subjects, corresponds to the structure in (4) is untenable. Either the grammar of BP includes two possible structures for this type of subject NP, or it accounts for it strictly via some form of Left Dislocation.

Left Dislocation differs from other constructions whose head is in a non-argument position in that it is a base-generated structure that does not include the binding of a variable in argument position from an operator within Ŝ (e.g., from COMP). The relation of the dislocated antecedent to the sentence has been explored as some version of a predication relation, where the sentence may be viewed as an open sentence predicated of its head (cf. Chomsky 1977).

This type of predication relation has been successfully exploited for another construction in BP, that of relative clauses (cf., in particular, Tarallo 1983). Relatives in BP do not obey the diagnostics for wh-movement, and most commonly associate an extra-sentential NP with a resumptive in-situ within the sentence. For the most part, they conform to the observation, common to languages that have a productive resumptive strategy, that a resumptive appears in wh-constructions when the gap that they fill is far away from their antecedent, that is, that they are blocked in 'short movement' and do not appear in the sentence directly dominated by their antecedent.

There is one common exception to this in BP. Tarallo (personal communication) has observed that the use of a resumptive for subject position is markedly increased in short movement in Relative Clauses when they are presentational:[11]

(31) ... *analisam fenômenos semânticos que eles são chamados intencionais.*
      '... they analyze semantic phenomena that they are called intentional.'
(32) *Tem um Prefeito de Goiânia que ele iniciou este sistema.*
      'There's a Mayor of Goiania that he initiated this system.'
(33) *Vou levar você para uma pessoa que ela é anarquista.*
      'I'm going to take you to a person that she is an anarchist.'

This type of RC may be viewed as a sort of condensed Typic construction. Topics are traditionally defined as focused material that is the given, or not new information (cf. Chafe 1976). In the sentences above, the material is introduced in the presentational format, the NP head of the relative presented as the object (the common slot for introducing new material), and the relativized S predicated of the head is the same form as the sentence predicted of the left-dislocated subject (subject resumptive, VP). Thus this type of RD and a Left Dislocation have the same syntactic form and the same semantic function.[12]

In sum, BP presents three instances of the NP_i $pron_i$ configuration: 'true' Left Dislocations, as in (29) and (30), presentational RCs, as in (31) to (33), and the 'Subject' type of sentences, of the kind presented in (1) to (3). For the first two types, the grammar of BP independently requires a coreference relation between a subject pronoun within the sentence and an antecedent NP in a non-argument position outside S. Via Rizzi's first diagnostic, we have established that the NP antecedent for the 'Subject' constructions is outside the sentence.

An argument that has been presented in support of the existence of a separate structure for the 'Subject' constructions is that the NP_i $pron_i$ configuration appears with startling frequency in BP, possibly more so than do comparable configurations where the NP is not the subject (cf. Pontes 1981). It is also argued that this configuration appears as much as its 'regular' counterpart, the lexically filled subject without a corresponding pronominal (cf. Galves 1983).

There is, however, an argument along these lines that to a certain extent diminishes the force of the above suggestion. While it is true that this configuration appears more often than other Left Dislocations, its appearance is generally an indication of some sort of topic marking. Informally speaking, the usage of this configuration serves, like a topic marker, to focus the given. This is concretely exemplified by the fact that the NP is often accompanied by a demonstrative, cleft marker, or transitional phrase:[13]

> (34) *Essa indústria Fiat, ela é nacional?*
>   'This Fiat company, is she national?'
> (35) *É que o experiençador ele é codificado.*
>   'It's that the experiencer it(m.) is codified.'
> (36) ... *então o Camões ele usa uma inversão muito marcada.*
>   'then Camões he uses a very marked inversion.'

The appearance of this configuration is greatly reduced in embedded contexts, which suggests that it may be a root phenomenon (cf. Emonds 1976). That this is so is further indicated by the fact that it may not appear in an embedded sentence whose verb is in the subjunctive or personal infinitive:[14]

> (37) ??*Aí eu disse que o João ele fosse embora.*
>   'Then I told John to go (subj.) away.'
>   (cf. *Aí eu disse que o João ele foi embora.*)
> (38) *Mamãe pediu para os meninos eles pararem de berrar.*
>   'Mother asked for the boys they to stop(PI) yelling.'
>   (cf. *Mamãe pediu para os meninos pararem de berrar.*)
> (39) *Os homens eles levantarem cedo me incomoda.*
>   Lit. 'The men they to get up(PI) early bothers me.'
>   'The men's getting up early ...'
>   (cf. *Os homens levantarem cedo me incomoda.*)

In each of the above sentences, the appearance of the subjunctive/ personal infinitive is triggered by the subcategorization requirements of the main verb (including [39], where *incomodar* is a type of ergative requiring the verb of its sentential NP to be in the subjunctive).

In recent work, Picallo (1984) explores the precise nature of this relation. She argues that the domains in which the binding conditions apply are determined by operators whose scope delimit them; further, that this delineation creates domains that are islands, or opaque. One type of operator creating an opaque context is TENSE, which has scope over the sentence. Based on the observation that the binding conditions for pronominals apply differently between a main and embedded sentence depending on the mood of the embedded verb, Picallo argues that in the case of subjunctives (and the personal infinitive in Portuguese), TENSE in the embedded sentence is unspecified, and receives its time frame specification from the TENSE specification in the sentence that contains it. In these cases, the embedded sentence is transparent to the main sentence, as the operator which has scope over the embedded sentence is in the main sentence.

Given the above, an explanation for the ungrammaticality of (37) to (39) presents itself. In each case, the sentences are acceptable if no pronominal copy follows the subject of the embedded sentence. This suggests that the NP_i $pron_i$ configuration may itself be some type of operator having scope over the embedded sentence, thus creating an interpretive island blocking further operations between the main sentence and its embedded clause. In this case, TENSE in the embedded sentence would be prevented from receiving a time frame specification from higher up, leaving the embedded sentence an incomplete proposition.

If the NP antecedent were a dislocated subject generated under TOPIC, it would in fact be a type of operator. Recall that the relation between a dislocated NP and its pronominal copy is one of prediction; this type of relation is known to form interpretive islands, or opaque domains.[15] Thus TENSE in the higher sentence is blocked from having scope over the embedded sentence in (37) to (39) because, in each case, the dislocated subject of the embedded sentence has caused it to become an island.

From the evidence presented thus far, it is clear that the NP_i $pron_i$ configuration shares many of the properties of Left Dislocation. If we argue that it is a subset of Left Dislocation, two related questions remain: (1) how do we account for the relative frequency of this configuration as opposed to other types of Left Dislocation? and (2) should it be disassociated completely from the 'Subject' configuration? By addressing the first, we may begin to speculate on the second.

5. One of the most productive typologies studied for natural languages divides them into the two categories of discourse-oriented versus subject-oriented.

BP is increasingly identified by linguists from various disciplines as a language that is, if not already strictly discourse-oriented, well on its way to becoming one.[16] Although this issue will not be explored here, it suffices to look briefly at three properties noted in Huang (1984) that distinguish discourse-oriented languages from sentence-oriented languages.[17] The first is 'Topic NP deletion', which operates across discourse to delete the topic of a sentence under identity with a topic in a preceding sentence. The second, proposed by Huang and defined as the underlying property from which the other three fall out, is that discourse-oriented languages possess a zero-topic, a lexically empty topic that licenses an empty object. Both of these properties may be successfully argued for in BP, and the latter may extend to other empty (non-subject) arguments as well (cf. Wheeler 1985).

The third property, proposed in Li and Thompson (1976), divides languages into the categories of 'topic prominent' or 'subject prominent'. They further divide the subject/topic typology to provide for languages in middle states, in an attempt to characterize languages in transition from one type to the other. One of the properties of languages in this middle state is that a blurring of the formal distinctions between subject and topic occurs, and the concepts as separate entities lose force. If in a given language it is clear that topic configurations cannot be derived from more basic intrasentential forms (e.g., subjects), and that they appear with some frequency, it is argued that the language is at least no longer strictly subject prominent.

Let us approach the NP_i $pron_i$ configuration as a subset of Left Dislocation from the context of BP as a middle-state language on its way to topic prominence.

A more formalized way to capture this blurring between subject and topic might be to 'blur' the separate structural properties attributed to each by combining them. This is precisely what the structure presented for the NP_i $pron_i$ configuration in (6) proposes to do; it is neither strictly a 'Subject' construction nor a Left Dislocation, reflecting the idea that subjects may be moving into topics and that topics may in the process be semantically and syntactically more constrained.[18]

Up to this point, we have addressed almost exclusively the question of the placement of the NP antecedent, leaving aside the role of its pronominal copy. We have claimed that the antecedent is generated outside and to the left of the sentence; this alone does not qualify it as a Left Dislocation. Very little hinges at this point on the exact status of the NP antecedent; it suffices to have demonstrated that it is generated outside the sentence and to the left of COMP, and that it has topic-like properties. The antecedent NP has been termed a left-dislocated NP throughout the course of this article, given that it displays similarities to dislocations in other languages or to properties that are associated with dislocations.

If one of the strict properties of a Left Dislocation is that its antecedent is coreferential with a resumptive pronoun in its corresponding argument slot within the sentence, then we may wish to say that the construction discussed here is not a strict Left Dislocation. However, very little seems to hinge directly on that pronoun being lexical; it may also be phonetically empty and still qualify as a pronoun, as is the case of *pro*, the empty pronominal whose appearance is generally but not exclusively confined to the subject slot of NSLs. Assume that the NP antecedent *is* coreferential with a pronoun in subject position: that pronoun may be a *pro*.[19]

This brings us back to the second question regarding disassociating the NP_i $pron_i$ configuration from the 'Subject' structure. Given the status of BP as a middle-state between subject and topic languages, excluding the 'Subject' structure altogether is undesirable. The principal characteristic of the 'Subject' structure is that the subject pronoun is generated not under (NP, S), but under INFL, as a phonetic reflection of its pronominal properties. If we retain this characteristic for BP, we accomplish two things: the NP_i $pron_i$ configuration is not completely cut off from the 'Subject' structure, and we have a solution for the shaky status of BP as an NSL.

It is well known that verbal inflection in BP is in some sense diminished,[20] and that the entire system of concordance is in a state of flux, especially with regard to third person. It is also common knowledge that BP differs from other Romance NSLs in that third person overt subject pronouns are neither contrastive nor emphatic, and appear with a much higher degree of frequency. These tendencies have led to the speculation that if BP still is a NSL, it will not be so for long (cf. do Nascimento 1984) for a principled treatment of the properties associated with NSLs and their relation to BP).[21] Two concrete ways of describing this transitional state are: (a) BP is currently an NSL in first and second person but not in third (cf. Moreira 1983); or (b) it is an NSL across the board, but in third person, the impoverished inflectional system needs an extra push. Exploring the latter possibility, if we assume that the ubiquitous third person overt subject pronoun is actually generated under INFL, we do not have to give up the idea that BP still falls under the rubric of the NSL family.

To my knowledge, the most comprehensive proposal in favor of generating the overt pronominal under AGR was offered by Galves (1983). Using the NP_i $pron_i$ configuration as the empirical framework for her hypothesis, Galves accounts for the discrepancies between BP and Continental Portuguese (CP) in a series of apparently unrelated phenomena by reducing the distinctions to a parametrized concept of AGR. The argument, somewhat telescoped here, proceeds as follows: given that AGR has a pronominal capacity in NSLs, it also possesses the property of being referential. This property, however, is parametrized: in CP, AGR is referential, while in BP, it is non-referential, that is, it has lost the property of independent reference. It is due to this factor that BP permits the NP_i $pron_i$ configuration but CP does not; in BP, reference is attributed to AGR only through the presence of an overt pronominal realized under it, and only then may the subject node be co-indexed with it.

Galves' explanation is based on treating the NP_i $pron_i$ configuration as strictly a 'Subject' phenomenon. She takes the reasonable position that, due to BP's impoverished inflectional system, although a phonetic pronominal under INFL *must* be present when the subject is lexically empty, it may also be present even if the subject is overt. While it accounts in a principled manner for the discrepancies between BP and other Romance NSLs, a treatment of this kind fails to take into account the syntactic and semantic properties that the NP antecedent has in common with dislocated phrases.

The approach described herein has the advantage of accounting for BP within the context not only of NSLs but also of (potentially) discourse-oriented languages. It argues for two syntactic sources for a 'Subject' NP, either as a type of focused element or as (NP, S). If the NP is focused, it is co-indexed with an empty pronominal under (NP, S). This captures the intuitively satisfying claim that while the abstract pronominal feature of AGR licenses an empty subject in first and second person, in third person it only licenses an empty subject if this abstract feature is phonetically realized.

There are, then, three possibilities for third person declaratives:

(40) [pro]   [ele$_i$]   [jantou]   = *ele jantou* 'he dined'
     NP   INFL   VP

(41) [Maria]   [-overt]   [jantou]   = *Maria jantou*
     NP   INFL   VP

(42) [Maria]   [[[pro$_i$]   [ela$_i$]   [jantou]]   = *Maria ela jantou*
     TOP   Š S NP   INFL VP

In (40), the empty subject is licensed by the phonetic pronoun under AGR. In (41), the subject is overt and the phonetic pronoun is unnecessary. And in (42) the NP in TOPIC is co-indexed with the empty subject pronoun, which is licensed by the phonetic pronoun under AGR.[22]

6. This has been a preliminary investigation into the possibility of structurally synchretizing certain aspects of the grammar of BP with certain of its semantic and transitional peculiarities. BP appears to be occupying some middle ground between topic and subject languages on the one hand, and NSLs and non-NSLs on the other. By proposing that it possesses a structural idiosyncrasy that is half-topic, half-subject, and incorporating in the process a modified version of Galves' treatment of empty subjects, we formally capture the state of flux the language is in.

The act of proposing a 'combined' structure for the NP$_i$ pron$_i$ configuration in BP in no way undermines Rizzi's proposal for the parametrized status of subject clitics in Romance, as his arguments may be interpreted as dividing into two categories—one set determining the placement of the pronominal, the other determining the locale of its antecedent. We have then adapted this to the singular properties of Brazilian Portuguese, a language that occasionally appears to have little in common with the rest of the Romance family.

NOTES

[1] I wish to thank D. Koike, M. Montalbetti, and C. Picallo for their support, linguistic and moral.

[2] With the exception of certain sentential adverbs, such as *também* 'also' or *realmente* 'really'.

[3] In (4) and (5), the mechanism of subscripting is used solely to indicate some inexplicit notion of coreference between the pronominal and its antecedent. The relation between two coreferential NPs that does not fall under the conditions of the Binding Theory is generally expressed via co-superscripting (cf. Chomsky 1981); we will assume that this is so in the case of (4), and leave aside the question of (5).

[4] Again, co-subscripting of the three elements simply indicates coreferentiality, and in no way indicates that the relation is between the two sets of NPs (TOP, [NP, S]) and ([NP, S], AGR) is the same. Nor do we make any claims with respect to the explicit nature of the relation among the three. That the two sets of relations are distinct is obvious; one distinction is mentioned in note 21, where it is argued that the pronoun under AGR, and not the NP antecedent, licenses the ec in the subject position.

[5] Cf. Taraldsen (1978) for the first treatment of this issue within the framework of Binding.

[6] Independent evidence related to inversion indicates that the northern Italian dialects are NSLs. This rules out the alternate hypothesis that the subject slot in these languages must be filled by a lexical item and may be doubly filled by NP-scl.

[7] Impoverished verbal inflection systems are not a factor in determining whether in a given language the configuration is a subject or a Left Dislocation. In French, which possesses a relatively minimal system, the configuration is a Left Dislocation; in the northern Italian dialects, whose inflectional system also gives some evidence of being diminished, the configuration is a subject.

[8] In BP, the difference in acceptability between binding a pronoun by a restricted quantifier or an unrestricted quantifier is an across-the-board phenomenon, applying to relatives, questions, dislocations, and tough constructions. This is presumably related to the referential or non-referential status of these two quantifier types.

[9] I am grateful to M. Montalbetti for suggesting this line of reasoning, and for discussion of the Spanish data.

[10] This leaves us with no immediate explanation for the obligatory presence of the subject clitic in languages like the northern Italian dialects. A possible solution might lie in the direction of (a) or (b):

(a) Languages vary with regard to permitting VP conjuncts in coordination;

(b) Languages of this type do permit VP conjunction, but these pronominals, being clitics, are in fact inside the VP. This reduces the distinction between these languages and BP to the fact that the pronouns are clitics in the former but stressed forms in the latter.

[11] This is not the case in a non-presentational RC:

(i) *Vi a mulher que ela estava saindo do banco.*
'I saw the woman that she was leaving the bank.'

[12] The structural difference between the two reduces to an empty (Left Dislocations) versus a filled (RCs) COMP. This may have to do with the fact that in Romance, an embedded tensed sentence must be preceded by a lexically filled COMP.

[13] Some of the data in this article were taken from the Projeto de Estudo Conjunto e Coordenação da Norma Lingüística Urbana Culta da Cidade de São Paulo (NURC—SP), 1970–73, financed by FAPESP.

[14] Cf. Moreira (1983: 243), who notes that this configuration may not appear in infinitival relatives when the infinitive is inflected, or in gerundive sentential subjects.

[15] Cf., for instance, Williams (1980).

[16] BP is a language that provides a field day for linguists working on language variation or change. Most speakers who have more than a sixth grade education give evidence of possessing two fully operative grammars. These overlap enough to make the elicitation of accurate data judgments a tortuous process for all involved, and often reduce valid theoretical disagreements to quibbles over the acceptability/appropriateness of the data in question.

[17] Huang also notes a fourth property: in a discourse-oriented language, an anaphor may be discourse-bound. BP deviates, at least superficially, from discourse-oriented languages in this respect.

[18] This is reflected in the fact that as often as not no distinct pause (represented orthographically by a comma) is heard between the topic and its pronoun in BP.

[19] The theoretical consequences entailed in the differences between lexically overt and empty resumptives will not be taken up here; cf. Wheeler

(1985).

[20] For example, there is no distinction between second and third person plural or singular. In 'substandard' BP, the entire paradigm is in the process of going over to third person singular forms.

[21] do Nascimento argues that BP is still an NSL, but that the most salient property associated with this parameter—free inversion—is no longer operative.

[22] That it is the pronoun under AGR doing the licensing of the empty subject, and not the NP under TOPIC, is deduced from the following:

> (i) *A Maria$_i$ achou e$_i$* (empty object)
> (ii) *A Maria$_i$ achei e$_i$* (topicalized or scrambled object)
> (iii) **A Maria (,) achou* (with focus intonation)

(iii) is derived from two structures; in (iv), it is the focused object, and in (v), the focused subject. Either reading is ungrammatical:

> (iv) *Maria$_i$ e$_j$ achou e$_i$*
> (v) *Maria$_j$ e$_j$ achou e$_i$*

Although the ungrammaticality of (iv) could be explained by the lack of any overt NP locally determining the content of the empty subject, the ungrammaticality of (v) demonstrates that something else must be the cause. If the subject ec must be licensed by a phonetic pronominal in INFL, then the ungrammaticality of (v) as well as (iv) is explained.

It is interesting to note that the grammatical equivalent of (iii) where Maria is coreferential with the subject involves two TOPICs, one for the subject and one for the empty object (cf. Huang 1984):

> (vi) [e$_i$]   [Maria$_j$]   [pro$_j$]   [ela$_j$]   [achou e$_i$]
>   TOP TOP   NP   AGR   VP

If this is the correct structure, it means that BP, like Japanese and Chinese, takes double TOPICs. An obvious extension of this analysis would apply it to certain types of RCs whose head is a subject. For the validity of this proposal, cf. Wheeler (1987).

REFERENCES

Chafe, William. 1976. Givenness, contrastiveness, definiteness, subjects, topics and point of view. In Charles Li (ed.), Subject and topic, pp. 25–56. New York: Academic Press.

Chomsky, Noam. 1977. On Wh-movement. In Peter Culicover, Thomas Wasow, and Adrian Akmajian (eds.), Formal syntax, pp. 71–132. New

York: Academic Press.

———. 1981. Lectures on government and binding. Dordrecht: Foris.

do Nascimento, Milton. 1984. Sur la postposition du sujet dans le Portugais du Brésil. Doctoral dissertation, Université de Paris VIII.

Emonds, Joseph. 1976. A transformational approach to English syntax. New York: Academic Press.

Evans, Gareth. 1980. Pronouns. Linguistic Inquiry 11(2).337–62.

Galves, Charlotte. 1983. Algumas diferenças entre o Português de Portugal e Português do Brasil e a teoria de 'Regência e Vinculação'. Unpublished manuscript. UNICAMP, Brazil. Paper presented at Syntax Conference, UNICAMP, February 1983.

Huang, C. T. James. 1984. On the distribution and reference of empty pronouns. Linguistic Inquiry 15(4).531–74.

Li, Charles, and Sandra Thompson. 1976. Subject and topic: A new typology of language. In Charles Li (ed.), Subject and topic, pp. 457–89. New York: Academic Press.

Moreira da Silva, Samuel. 1983. Études sur la symetrie et l'asymetrie subjet/object dans le Portugais du Brésil. Doctoral dissertation, Université de Paris VIII.

Picallo, M. Carmen. 1984. Opaque domains. Doctoral dissertation, City University of New York.

Pontes, Eunice. 1981. Da importância do tópico em Português. Anais do V Encontro Nacional de Lingüística, Vol. 2. Rio de Janeiro: PUC/RJ.

Rizzi, Luigi. 1982. Negation, Wh-movement and the null subject parameter. In Luigi Rizzi (ed.), Issues in Italian syntax, pp. 117–84. Dordrecht: Foris.

———. 1984. On the status of subject clitics in Romance. Paper presented at LSRL XIV, Los Angeles, February 1984.

Taraldsen, Knud T. 1978. On the NIC, vacuous quantification, and the that-trace filter. Unpublished manuscript, MIT.

Tarallo, Fernando. 1983. Relativization strategies in Brazilian Portuguese. Doctoral dissertation, University of Pennsylvania.

Wheeler, Dana. 1987. The grammar of empty arguments in Brazilian Portuguese. Doctoral dissertation, UCLA.

Williams, Edwin. 1980. Predication. Linguistic Inquiry 11(1).208–38.

Section IV–Pragmatics

7
Tópico e Ordem Vocabular

Maria Luiza Braga
Universidade Federal Fluminense, R.J.

1. Introdução

O trabalho que ora apresentamos é parte de um projeto mais amplo em que pretendemos analisar topicalizações (daqui por diante TOPs), deslocamentos para a esquerda e aquelas construções em que um SN aparece na posição mais à esquerda de uma oração e é, posteriormente, repetido no corpo da mesma oração. Aqui nos restringimos a topicalizações visto que até o presente momento encontramos apenas 1 caso de deslocamento para a esquerda e 5 casos da outra construção referida acima.

Para se caracterizar uma determinada construção como TOP, utilizamos a definição proposta por Prince (1980):

$$[\quad [\quad\quad X_1] \quad [... \quad \cdot[\quad\quad X_2 \quad] \quad ...] \quad]$$

S   SN   S   SN

em que X_1 e X_2 precisam ser coreferenciais; X_1 precisa ser não vocativo e X_2 precisa ser uma lacuna.

Embora TOPs possam envolver distintas funções sintáticas, neste trabalho nos limitamos a topicalizações de objeto direto. Nosso objetivo é analisar este tipo particular e, uma vez compreendidas suas características e funções, estender nossa análise às outras funções sintáticas de forma a obter uma visão global do funcionamento da regra de TOP.

Até o presente momento analisamos TOPs e orações não marcadas que ocorreram no discurso oral emitido por 9 dos 48 falantes adultos entrevistados pelos membros do Projeto Censo da Variação Lingüística do Rio de Janeiro. No que se segue nos referimos a 3 das 11 variáveis utilizadas para descrever e caracterizar TOPs, oferecemos explicações para os resultados encontrados e tentamos analisar as funções que as mesmas desempenham no discurso. Desnecessário dizer que nossas conclusões têm um caráter preliminar, considerado o número reduzido de TOPs analisadas até o presente.

2. Variáveis

2.1. O primeiro grupo de fatores selecionado pelo VARBRUL foi o denominado *presença/ausência de sujeito*. Este grupo compreendia 3 categorias:

(a) a proposição referente ao SN topicalizado teria sujeito inexistente ou omitido. Exemplos:

(0) Braço, quebrei em seis lugares (14 131)
(1) ... que aqui divertimento, há muito (15 104)

(b) a proposição referente ao SN topicalizado teria sujeito explícito com dimensão não superior a 5 sílabas. Exemplos:

(2) Elas por Elas, *eu* vejo de relance (35 121)
(3) Pos-operatório, *todo mundo* tem (11 136)

Como os exemplos acima indicam, não distinguimos sujeitos pronominais de sujeitos constituídos por SNs plenos.

(c) a proposição referente ao SN topicalizado teria sujeito explícito com dimensão superior a 5 sílabas. Em nosso corpus não encontramos nenhum exemplo que satisfizesse esta condição.

Obtivemos os seguintes resultados:

Tabela 1

	n	Perc.	Prob.
Sujeito oculto ou inexistente	19/172	11,0%	.26
Sujeito explícito	66/171	39,0%	.74

Os números acima indicam que topicalizações de objeto direto tendem a ocorrer em orações com sujeito explícito. A análise das 19 topicalizações que não seguem esta tendência mostra que as mesmas apresentam a seguinte distribuição:

Quadro 1

Orações sem sujeito explícito

indeterminação do agente	sujeito inexistente	sujeito oculto (la. pessoa)

∅	partícula se		ter existencial	haver existencial

| 1 | 2 | 6 | 1 | 9 |

Se excluirmos as 7 topicalizações cujo predicado é constituído pelo verbo existencial *ter* ou *haver*, observaremos que a grande maioria dos casos restantes envolvem a primeira pessoa do singular como sujeito. Ora, nestas circunstâncias, a omissão do sujeito não provoca nenhum problema de processamento ou interpretação visto que a informação sobre o agente expressa-se através da desinência verbal (8 ocorrências de primeira pessoa de singular do presente do indicativo e 1 de perfeito do indicativo). O que nos surpreendeu agradávelmente foi a ocorrência da partícula *se*, o que julgávamos improvável no tipo de discurso que estamos analisando. Em que pese o número reduzido de ocorrência desta partícula e o caráter preliminar de nossa pesquisa, acreditamos que esta presença explica-se por um processo que visa impedir a ocorrência de ambigüidade: o falante, prevendo que o desvio da ordem não-marcada poderá provocar interpretações inadequadas do seu enunciado, utiliza uma marca explícita de indeterminação do sujeito, indicando, assim, que o SN mais à esquerda não deverá ser interpretado como sujeito. Compare

(4)   O dinheiro, ainda, se ganha outro (05 018)
      com
(4') O dinheiro ainda ganha outro,
oração cuja aceitabilidade nos parece duvidosa.

Que o falante seja capaz de antecipar e prevenir interpretações ambíguas tem sido referido por vários autores. Assim, Chafe (1976) alude ao fato de que a pronominalização poderá ser evitada se o falante prever que a mesma causará ambigüidade. Oliveira e Silva (1982), ao estudar a variação entre *seu/dele*, mostram que a escolha da forma possessiva *dele* se processa com antecedência relativamente grande para se evitar a ambigüidade que a escolha da forma *seu* causaria.

A análise das 66 topicalizações restantes revela que 38 delas envolvem sujeitos de primeira pessoa do singular e as demais 28, sujeitos pronominais de terceira pessoa ou SNs plenos. Este último grupo é particularmente interessante. Se omitirmos o sujeito das topicalizações deste grupo, ou (a) mudaremos a regência verbal, ou (b) alteraremos radicalmente o significado do enunciado, ou (c) obteremos orações cuja aceitabilidade é questionável. A segunda possibilidade é particularmente forte quando o SN mais à esquerda tem o traço [+ hum] ou pode ser assim interpretado. Considere os exemplos abaixo:

(5)   ... mas *dinheiro* mesmo, ele não tinha (05 164)

(5')   mas *dinheiro* mesmo, não tinha

(6)   E *os amigos* assim cê vai ajudar? (25 103)

(6')   E os amigos assim vai ajudar?

(7)   *Carne* ninguém pode quase comer (05 066)

(7')   ? Carne não pode quase comer

Resta um pequeno grupo de topicalizações cujo sujeito pronominal de terceira pessoa ou sujeito constituído por SN pleno poderia ser omitido desde que a pausa, o acento tônico e a curva entonacional se acentuasse. Observe os exemplos abaixo:

(8)   E *tudo de ruim que tem nessa* vida, aqueles cara já fizeram
        (21 144)

(8')   E tudo de ruim que tem nessa vida, já fizeram

(9)   ... *tudo que eu quero*, eles me dão (24 01)

(9')   tudo que eu quero, me dão

A explicação para a preservação do sujeito nas orações topicalizadas é aquela fornecida para a ocorrência da partícula *se*: o sujeito é mantido para que se evitem ambigüidades. É provável, todavia, que outros aspectos contribuam para a conservação do sujeito das orações topicalizadas. Assim, a omissão de sujeito parece mais aceitável naqueles casos em que há um elemento interferente entre o SN topicalizado e a proposição a ele referente. Observe os exemplos abaixo:

(10)   *Vontade*, eu tenho (25 064)

(11)   *Vontade*, eu (não) tenho não (25 081)

(12) *Esses*, eu vejo (11 198)

(13) *Essa*, eu (não) sei fazer (35 140)

Enquanto em (11) e (13) o sujeito pode ser omitido sem causar estranheza, a sua omissão em (10) e (12) parece possível apenas se se intensificar a sílaba tônica do SN topicalizado e se se tornar mais marcada a curva entonacional da oração inteira. Levantamos estes aspectos aqui para lembrar que a omissão ou preservação do sujeito em orações topicalizadas é matéria delicada e envolve a atuação de aspectos distintos.

Lira (1982) mostrou que, no discurso oral, diferentemente do referido pelas gramáticas tradicionais, sujeitos pronominais tendem a ser mais freqüentes do que sujeito zero. A diferença percentual é de 12,0. Seus números são apresentados abaixo:

Tabela 2

	n	%
Suj. pronominal	5024	56
Suj. zero	3900	44
TOTAL	8924	100

Freqüência de Sujeitos Pronominais e Zero.[1]

No caso das topicalizações as diferenças percentuais e probabilísticas são muito mais acentuadas, conforme mostramos anteriormente, e esta exacerbação parece-nos relevante: ela indicaria que topicalizações distinguem-se de orações não-marcadas pelo desvio da ordem das palavras, pelo tipo de informação transmitido, e também pelo nível de preservação de sujeito.

Finalmente, este grupo de fatores sugere uma indagação de ordem metodológica: o mesmo condiciona a regra da TOP ou é por ela condicionado? Em outras palavras, o falante pode topicalizar um SN porque a proposição a ele referente apresenta sujeito explícito ou o falante preserva o sujeito da proposição porque topicalizou um de seus constituintes pós-verbais? A resposta a tal pergunta implica em analisar os condicionamentos que determinam a omissão dos sujeitos quer nas topicalizações quer nas orações não-marcadas e em verificar se eles permanecem os mesmos ou se modificam de acordo com a mudança na ordem das palavras. Todavia a questão fica aqui lançada pois parece-nos pertinente uma vez que se relaciona à aplicação da metodologia da teoria da variação a fenômenos sintáticos e discursivos. Lavandera e Naro (comunicação pessoal) têm questionado a possibilidade de tal aplicação e aqui gostaríamos de lembrar que tal problema merece considerações cuidadosas.

2.2. Referir-mos-emos, agora, ao *status informacional do referente*. Para caracterizar o tipo de informação transmitido por um referente, utilizamos as 3 categorias propostas por Prince (1979): *evocado, novo* e *inferível*. Um referente será considerado *evocado* se já mencionado no discurso anterior (textualmente evocado) ou se presente no contexto físico em que se desenvolve o discurso em questão (contextualmente evocado). Um referente será considerado *novo* se está sendo mencionado pela primeira vez no discurso. Referentes novos se subdividem em *totalmente novos* e *novos não-usados*. Os últimos dizem respeito àquelas entidades que estão sendo mencionadas pela primeira vez, mas que se supõe sejam familiares ao ouvinte. *Totalmente novas* são aquelas entidades que o ouvinte terá de 'criar' a partir do texto. A terceira categoria inclui os *inferíveis*, entidades dedutíveis de outras entidades já evocadas ou mesmo inferíveis.[2]

Introduzimos duas modificações no modelo referido acima:

(a) conservamos, apenas, as categorias básicas—*evocado, novo, inferível*—ignorando as posteriores subdivisões;

(b) as categorias *novo* e *evocado* foram subdivididas de forma a captar o caráter genérico ou específico do referente. A nossa versão do modelo de Prince consta, pois, de 5 categorias exemplificadas a seguir:

Novo específico:

(14) Mas a minha situação agora não dá, no momento não dá para mim me divertir, porque eu tenho que tomar conta do bar com meu marido. O bar, sem eu lá, não é nada, n'é? E *meus filhos*, tenho que olhar, são dois pequenininhos. Eu não tenho carro, n'é? Eu não tenho carro. E para mim ... (10 002)

Novo genérico:

(15) Às vez eu ('quando vou') no mercado com ele, eu fico tonta! Tanta coisa que eu não sei por onde começar. E é ... E a ... O custo de vida está muito alto mesmo. Alto. *Carne*, ninguém pode quase comer mais, n'é? (05 066)

Velho específico:

(16) E: ... fala aí um pouco, por exemplo, sobre seu ... seu irmão, um dos seus irmãos.
     F: Tem um que eu adoro! *O mais novo*, eu adoro! Fora de série, o garoto. (21 001)

Velho genérico:

(17) F: Dinheiro não é muito, que eu nunca ando com muito dinheiro,

só o necessário e mais algum ... Ele pra me assaltar tem que
ser antes de eu fazer as compras (riso).

E: Põe uma plaquinha: 'Já fiz as compras'.

F: Porque depois já ... aí já está ... Só, se ele carregar as compras.

E: É. Mas isso também acontece, n'é?

F: Pois é. Então, *dinheiro*, não carrego muito. (11 131)

Inferível:

(18) F: Falou que tem que operar, já estou lá no dia seguinte (riso).
Não tenho medo não.

E: Caramba, quanta operação! E nenhuma delas você teve compli-
cação, assim? Não?

F: Não, graças a Deus. Não tive não. Não tive não.
Não tem lembrança desagradável nenhuma em relação a elas?

F: Não, não. Correu tudo bem, n'é? *Pós-operatório*, todo mundo
tem. (11 136)

Obtivemos os seguintes resultados para esta variável:[3]

Tabela 3

	n	Perc.	Prob.
Inferível	23/47	49,0	.73
Velho específico	16/36	44,0	.61
Velho genérico	30/110	27,0	.45
Novo específico	05/36	14,0	.25
Novo genérico	09/108	08,0	.18

Status Informacional do Referente.

A Tabela 3 constitui um exemplo de uma bela hierarquia de fatores:
topicalização de objetos diretos tendem a envolver, principalmente, entidades inferíveis e, raramente, entidades novas. Ocupando posição interme-
diária, encontramos os referentes que transmitem informação velha.
Chamamos atenção para o fato de que a probabilidade de ocorrência de
entidades específicas em topicalizações de objeto direto é sempre superior
à de entidades genéricas, para ambas categorias: *evocado* e *novo*.

Prince (1981), entre outros, utiliza o critério de tipo de informação
transmitido por um SN mais à esquerda de uma oração para distinguir
TOPs de 'Focus-movement'. Restringindo-se às duas primeiras regras, uma
das diferenças seria que, para uma determinada construção ser considerada
como TOP, o seu SN mais à esquerda precisa ser referencial, isto é, precisa
representar uma entidade que já tenha sido evocada no discurso ou que
esteja numa relação de conjunto com alguma outra entidade já evocada ou

que seja inferível do discurso. Assim (19b') é aceitável mas não (20b'):

(19) A: You want to see Stardust Memories?
     B: I saw Stardust Memories yesterday.
     B': Stardust Memories I saw Ø yesterday.
(20) A: Why are you laughing?
     B: I saw Stardust Memories yesterday. It was very funny.
     B': Stardust Memories I saw Ø yesterday. It was very funny.

Já no caso de 'Focus-Movement', o SN mais à esquerda precisa representar atributos ou valores de atributos:

(21) They just bought a dog. *Fido* they named it.
(22) This is a student who went here two years. *Five semesters* she was here.

Conforme explicamos anteriormente, nossas categorias para classificar o status informacional de um referente divergem em parte das de Prince e estamos interessados em regras distintas de 'Focus-Movement'. Apesar destas diferenças, parece-nos muito relevante que, também em português, a grande maioria de objetos diretos topicalizados envolva entidades inferíveis ou evocadas. A ordenação das categorias específico/genérico, por outro lado, sugere que, além de inferíveis ou evocadas, as entidades topicalizadas deverão ser facilmente identificáveis e localizáveis pelo ouvinte.

O comportamento desta variável explica-se ao levarmos em conta as funções que TOPs desempenham no discurso. Todavia é provável que aspectos relacionados à ordem não-marcada das palavras em português contribuam para a tendência de referentes inferíveis e evocados ocorrerem mais freqüentemente em TOPs do que referentes novos. Observações informais mostram que a ordem não-marcada das palavras em português tende a ser Suj V OD OI e também que informação nova tende a ser expressa pelo OD. Ora uma topicalização de OD envolvendo informação nova constituirá um duplo desvio: desvio da ordem não-marcada e desvio da tendência de informação velha preceder informação nova (Halliday 1967). Daí a estranheza de TOPs envolvendo referentes novos e a tendência para se privilegiar entidades inferíveis ou evocados. Convém lembrar que esta estranheza causada pela presença de entidades novas na posição mais à esquerda da oração já havia sido referida também por Pontes (1980) ao estudar construções de tópico em português.

2.3. O terceiro e último grupo de fatores a ser considerado aqui relaciona-se ao *caráter definido do SN topicalizado*. Para caracterizar este aspecto, utilizamos os determinantes explícitos que precediam o N do SN em questão. Trabalhamos com 3 categorias:

(a) [+ def]: o N era precedido por artigo definido, pronome posses-
sivo, ou demonstrativo.

(23) Agora *esse Júlio Iglésias*, eu também queria ir assistir
(05 159)

(b) [− def]: o N era precedido por artigo ou pronome indefinido.

(24) Mas pelo menos *uma orientação*, eu dou (10 079)

(c) [outros]: o N era precedido por Ø.

(25) *Pudim de leite condensado*, cê num sabe fazer? (11 017)

Obtivemos os seguintes resultados para esta variável:

Tabela 4

	n	Perc.	Prob.
[+ def]	39/120	32,0	.62
[− def]	11/82	13,0	.29
[outros]	35/141	25,0	.58

Caráter Definido do SN.

Inicialmente pareceu-nos que os resultados acima mencionados se expli-
cariam por uma interação com a variável *status informacional do referente*, isto é, pensávamos que haveria uma correlação entre o traço [+ def]
e referentes evocados e entre o traço [− def] e referentes novos. Naro
(comunicação pessoal) tem alertado para a possibilidade da interação dos
fatores, ponto crucial para a teoria da variação uma vez que o cálculo das
probabilidades pressupõe a independência dos fatores. Para verificar se os
números da Tabela 4 estavam correlacionados ao status informacional do
referente, distribuimo-los pelas categorias *inferível, evocado específico,
evocado genérico, novo específico, novo genérico*. Obtivemos os seguintes
resultados:

Tabela 5

	[+ def]	[− def]	[outros]
Inferível	12/25: 48,0%	04/25: 16,0%	09/25: 36,0%
Evoc. específico	12/16: 75,0%	02/16: 12,5%	02/16: 12,5%
Evoc. genérico	09/30: 30,0%	04/30: 13,5%	17/30: 56.5%
Novo específico	04/05: 80,0%		01/05: 20,0%
Novo genérico	02/09: 22,0%	01/09: 11,0%	06/09: 67,0%

Distribuição de Entidades Inferíveis, Evocadas e Novas Segundo
o Seu Caráter Definido.

Os dados acima mostram que não há interação entre tipo de informação
transmitido por um referente e a presença ou ausência do traço [+ def]. A
presença deste traço parece ser determinada pela maior ou menor necessi-

dade de especificação de um referente e não de seu caráter novo ou velho.

O quadro acima mostra também que a especificidade e a genericidade não se circunscrevem a um único tipo de determinante. Estas duas noções podem se exprimir quer através do traço [+ def], quer através do traço [− def], quer através de ∅, combinado com os demais elementos do contexto lingüístico em que o referente ocorreu.

3. Topicalizações e Discurso

Nesta secçao nos referiremos a alguns dos fatores discursivos que podem levar à topicalização de um SN. Em nosso corpus, topicalizações são freqüentemente usadas quando um falante quer destacar um elemento de um conjunto. Observe o exemplo abaixo:

(26) E: Que desastre que o senhor teve?

F: Eu bati . . . bati com o carro, num . . . poste.

E: E aí foi . . . me quebrei todo, quase que perdi a perna. Cê tá vendo aí, ó? Aqui fez . . . só aqui tem seis operações aqui, nessa perna. Quebrei a tíbia, o perônio, entendeu? *Braço*, quebrei em seis lugares, tá bom? Aqui fez três, aqui tem nove! Olha! (14 131)

Topicalizações com esta função representam 19,0% de nossos dados e todas apresentam a mesma estrutura: um tópico está sendo considerado, o falante está enumerando seus constituintes e, a uma certa altura, topicaliza 1 deles.

TOPs também foram utilizadas para se retornar a um tópico ou aspecto de tópico mencionado imediatamente antes. A grande maioria destas topicalizações envolvem a presença de um demonstrativo revelando a consciência que o falante tem da proximidade do tema. A combinação destes dois aspectos—o uso do demonstrativo e desvio da ordem não-marcada— sugere que estas topicalizações foram utilizadas para reforçar aquele tópico sob consideração. Observe o exemplo abaixo:

(27) Então ali eu acho que devia existir o . . . o . . . (ininteligível) cozinheiro como existe, não é isso? Você vai no exército, você vai lá, é o cozinheiro, n'é? Nos hotéis tod . . . A mulher mais é para ajudar! Cortar batata ou lavar louça, n'é? Serviço mais leve. Eu acho que *esses serviços brutos*, assim, a mulher não devia exercer, não. (14 123)

Topicalizações com esta função constituem o grupo mais numeroso: representam 22,5% do total.

Há um terceiro grupo cuja função é bastante intrigante: a uma consideração geral segue-se uma topicalização que constitui uma atenuação, uma quebra das expectativas sugeridas pelo enunciado anterior. Muitas das topicalizações com esta função apresentam uma alternância entre negativo/afirmativo, isto é, se o enunciado é negativo, a TOP será positiva e vice-versa. Considere (28) e (29):

(28) Eu sou segundo casamento com esse. Tem essas duas crianças, que, aqui, ninguém sabe da minha vida. Que eu moro aqui ... Se você me perguntar o nome desse vizinho aí do lado eu não sei. Conheço, mas *nome* não sei. (10 097)

(29) ... se for olhar bem tanta coisa, num tem nada bom aqui nessa, nessa terra. O presidente ... T'aí, gosto desse presidente nosso. Eu gosto muito dele. Eu gosto porque eu acho que ele ... ele tem muita vontade de fazer muita coisa, mas a ... o pessoal todo tem que ajudar, n'é? Que se não ajudar, ele sozinho não pode fazer grande coisa. *Vontade*, ele tem. (05 061)

Além disso, no trecho de discurso que precede topicalizações com esta função, alguns aspectos não são explicitados, cabendo ao ouvinte preencher as lacunas. Isso é evidente em (29): o falante considera a situação calamitosa do país, evoca o presidente e depois atenua a responsabilidade dele lembrando que, apesar de não poder fazer nada, 'vontade ele tem'.

Visto que muitas destas topicalizações são precedidas por uma conjunção adversativa ou admitiriam a sua explicitação, uma análise superficial poderia considerá-la como TOPs com função contrastiva, interpretação de que discordamos. Alguns autores (Chafe 1976) têm argumentado que topicalizações são utilizadas basicamente para exprimir contraste, ponto de vista rejeitado por Prince (1981) e Pontes (1982). Estas autoras argumentam que esta função é apenas uma dentre as várias que podem ser desempenhadas por TOPs e que a mesma tende a ocorrer nas enumerações. Ao analisar TOPs no crioulo caboverdeano, observamos que um grande número delas apresentava função contrastiva. Na ocasião, observamos, também, que um paralelismo superficial, isto é, repetição do mesmo verbo, explicitação dos referentes em questão, presença de conectivos adversativos reforçava a interpretação contrastiva atribuída àquelas TOPs. Na ocasião, impusemos como condição para considerar uma TOP como contrastiva que o número de candidatos que se opunham ao referente do SN topicalizado fosse delimitável. A se manter o mesmo critério para o português, veremos que o número de TOPs com função contrastiva é relativamente baixo: em nosso corpus, elas representam 9,5%. (30) é um exemplo:

(30) Agora: *garoto*, aqui tem demais. *Garota* não tem muito não
(24 007)

Topicalizações podem também ocorrer em resposta a uma questão proposta por um dos interlocutores, como (31) exemplifica:

(31) E: Voĉe não tem vontade de passar carnaval, assim, na Bahia, em
outro lugar?
F: Vontade, eu tenho (25 064)

Embora tenhamos nos referido a 'resposta e questão', o estímulo apresentado pelo falante pode se encontrar num enunciado declarativo como mostra (32):

(32) E: E além de Sétimo Sentido, a senhora está vendo ...
F: Ah, e *as outras*, eu não vejo assim de ficar sentada, prestando
muita atenção, não. (35 121)

Nossa interpretação é que, ao fazer uma pergunta, um dos interlocutores propõe um determinado tópico à consideração do outro que retoma, enuncia e, então, predica a respeito daquele tópico particular. Tal explicação aplica-se também aos casos de declarações semelhantes a (32). É como se o falante interrompesse seu enunciado e convidasse o outro interlocutor a completá-lo. TOPs com esta função representam 16,5% de nossos dados. É interessante lembrar que Pontes (1982) refere-se a diálogos como locais apropriados para a ocorrência de construções com tópico.

Finalmente, TOPs podem se seguir umas às outras, como se a ocorrência de uma primeira topicalização determinasse a ocorrência da segunda:

(33) E: Bota tempero, uma manteiguinha, um claybom, ovos ... Mistura tudo e põe pra assar, fica ó!
F: É? Vou fazer porque aí já com pouco bacalhau, n'é?
E: Fica mais fácil.
F: É. *Essa*, eu nunca fiz, não. *Purê de forno*, assim, eu gosto de
fazer.

A existência deste tipo de condicionamento já havia sido referida por Labov e Weiner (1979) que mostravam que paralelismo de estrutura superficial é um fator poderoso na determinação da escolha de uma construção ativa ou passiva.

A consideração dos aspectos mencionados acima auxilia a compreensão dos resultados da Tabela 3, qual seja, que TOPs tendem a envolver, principalmente, referentes inferíveis ou evocados. Se lembrarmos que TOPs são utilizadas, básicamente, para destacar um elemento de um conjunto, para atenuar uma afirmação anterior, ou para predicar sobre um elemento já introduzido no discurso, compreenderemos porque seus referentes topicalizados tendem a ser inferíveis ou evocados.

4. Conclusão

Neste trabalho nos referimos a 3 variáveis que condicionam a ocorrência de TOPs no discurso semi-coloquial oral, mostramos algumas das funções que podem ser desempenhadas por esta construção e também como certos contextos podem favorecer o aparecimento de uma construção topicalizada. Gostariamos de terminar lembrando que o âmbito das funções discursivas de TOPs merece cuidadosas investigações e que se TOPs, por um lado, podem auxiliar na caracterização dos tipos de discurso, por outro lado, a compreensão de suas caracteristicas e funções pressupõe uma teoria global do discurso.

NOTAS

[1] Dados de 30 falantes, 15 minutos de gravação de cada um.

[2] Para maiores informações e exemplificações destas categorias e suas outras subdivisões, remetemos o leitor ao artigo de Prince (1979) e à reanálise do mesmo feita por Braga (1982) e Oliveira e Silva (1982).

[3] Desta tabela foram excluídos 2 dados préviamente classificados como *inferíveis resumidores*. O número de dados para esta categoria era tão reduzido que qualquer generalização sobre a mesma seria temerária.

REFERÊNCIAS

Braga, Maria Luiza. 1982. Left dislocations and topicalizations in Capeverdean Creole. Doctoral dissertation, University of Pennsylvania.

Chafe, Wallace. 1976. Giveness, contrastiveness, definiteness, subjects, topics and point of view. In Charles Li (ed.), Subject and topic, pp. 25–56. New York: Academic Press.

Halliday, Michael A. K. 1976. Notes on transitivity and theme in English. Journal of Linguistics 4.179-215.

Labov, William and John Weiner. 1977. Constraints on the agentless passive. Mimeo, University of Pennsylvania.

Lira, Solange de Azambuja. 1982. Nominal, pronominal, and zero subject in Brazilian Portuguese. Doctoral dissertation, University of Pennsylvania.

Oliveira e Silva, Gisele M. 1982. Estudo da regularidade na variação dos possessivos no Português do Rio de Janeiro. Doctoral dissertation, Universidade Federal do Rio de Janeiro.

Pontes, Eunice 1980. Da importância do tópico em Português. Artigo apresentado no V Encontro Nacional de Lingüística, PUC/RJ.

————. 1981. Topicalização e deslocamento à esquerda. Artigo apresentado no VI Encontro Nacional de Lingüística, PUC/RJ.

Prince, Ellen F. 1979. On the given/new distinction. Paper from the Fifteenth Regional Meeting, Chicago Linguistic Society 15.267–78.

Prince, Ellen F. 1980. A functional syntax approach to text analysis: Left dislocation and topicalization. Paper presented at the Symposium on Approaches to Text Analysis, University of Chicago.

8

Brazilian Portuguese Directives and a Hierarchy of Strategies for Politeness

Dale April Koike
University of Texas at Austin

1. Introduction[1]

The social relationship between speaker S and hearer H in a context of communication is reflected in the language used. This is demonstrated in directives, or the ways in which S utilizes language to express the desire that H act on his or her utterance. Directives may take the form of commands, requests, questions, suggestions, etc. (Bach and Harnish 1979:47). The purpose of this study is:

(1) To illustrate that the forms of directives in Brazilian Portuguese cor-

relate with a combination of factors related to politeness; i.e., (a) the relationship between S and H, and how that relationship can be altered linguistically; (b) the force of the directive; and (c) the options with which H can respond to the directive; and

(2) To suggest the existence of a base form of the directive, to which peripheral structures can be added or strategies employed to alter its force in a hierarchical order of more to less force, and to suggest a theory of acquisition of this hierarchy, based on Macedo's application of a markedness theory to pidginization (1986).

Some studies involving directives, such as those by Austin (1962) and Searle (1969), focus on the force (i.e., 'illocutionary force') with which meaning is conveyed through variation in structure. Haverkate believes that the various forms of directives and their force in Spanish depend on the 'psycho-social relations' between S and H (1979:1). R. Lakoff discusses speech acts that reflect S's attitudes toward the social context of the act: i.e., S's relationship and feelings toward H, the importance of the information to be conveyed and the formality of the act, and the effect S wishes to achieve via the utterance (1973:293). Such attitudes and feelings affect the form of the utterance in the case of directives, in which there is communication between S and H about a matter directly affecting H, and in which S must make judgments about the relationship between the two parties in the expression of the directive. Brown and Levinson present the idea of 'face' or a self-image that every individual wants to claim for him/herself, and that S is constantly aware of his or her self-image and that of the hearer in verbal interaction. Speech acts that can threaten one's face are orders, requests, suggestions, and advice. Interrelated with these speech acts are the variables of power, distance, and rank between S and H.[2] For example, Brown and Levinson postulate that most people will use strategies in expressing a serious directive that pose the least risk to face with strangers of higher social positions than themselves and 'will choose ways of doing face-threatening acts that minimize those threats' (1978:66–88).

The notions of 'strategies', variation in linguistic form, and the force with which the directive is conveyed are related to the politeness that S wishes to convey to H. R. Lakoff defines three rules of politeness, which are: (1) Don't impose; (2) Give options; and (3) Make A feel good—be friendly (1973:298). This study will take the position that the selection of a particular strategy or device in the communication of a directive in Brazilian Portuguese involves three dimensions of politeness:

(a) S's relationship with H, and how it can be changed through linguistic means;

(b) The desired illocutionary force of the directive; and

(c) The options left to H with which to respond to the directive.

2. Data Collection and Informants

In order to gather data on directives used by educated Brazilians in giving orders in three different types of relationships between S and H, 45 native informants of the city of Rio de Janeiro were interviewed by the investigator. All participants had completed at least a high school education, and their ages ranged from 18 to 60. The 24 female and 21 male informants were mostly from lower middle to upper middle class socioeconomic backgrounds. Interviews were conducted at the informants' homes or places of work.

The investigator asked informants in individual tape-recorded interviews to pretend they were in a situation in which a person X of social ranking or relationship Y came to their house and sat in a chair reserved for their very strict father. They were to tell X (embodied in the investigator) that he or she could not sit there. Person X represented three different relationships to S: (1) a stranger of a much higher social ranking than S; (2) a person of approximately the same social ranking as the informant, and who was considered to be a good friend; and (3) a child he or she knew well. In each case, a specific person was named to represent X; e.g., the governor of the state, a close friend, or a particular child.

3. Variation in the Form of the Directive

According to the data collected from the interviews, the directives expressed across the three registers could be classified and ranked in one of the following illocutionary forms: orders and assertions, requests, suggestions, hints, and avoidance of giving the required directive.[3] They are defined and exemplified below and in Figure 1.

3.1. ORDERS AND ASSERTIONS, where S expresses the directive explicitly in what I call the 'base form'. I will return to this notion later. S assumes that directness is acceptable to H, since S is definitely in a position of real power with respect to H, and that this is sufficient reason for H to carry out the action (Bach and Harnish 1979:47). However, as my data will indicate, S can also assume that directness is acceptable when there are feelings of social proximity or solidarity with H.[4] H could respond negatively to the orders and assertions but would be directly confronting authority or the feelings of solidarity, and would then have to face the consequences; e.g.:

124

Orders/Assertions

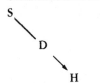

Suggestions

Requests

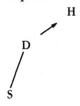

S = speaker
H = hearer
D = directive
X = communication X

Hints

Avoidance

Figure 1. Relationship between S and H in Directives.

Sai daqui.
'Get out of here.'

Olha, meu filho, não pode sentar aí não, porque essa é a cadeira do vovô; ninguém senta
'Look my son, you can't sit there, because that's grandpa's chair; no one sits there.'

3.2. *Suggestions,* in which S appears to include H in the decision-making process of carrying out the command, or states an opinion that indirectly expresses the directive. Due to the implicit strength of the force of the directive, S does not have many options with which to respond other than compliance, without appearing uncooperative. S can be in any position of real power in relation to H, but assumes a higher position through the use of suggestions; e.g.:

Olha, A, vamos sentar nessa outra aqui, que papai está querendo sentar nesta cadeira
'Look, A, let's sit in that other (chair) here, since Dad is wanting to sit in this chair.'
Eu acho melhor você sentar aqui
'I think it would be better for you to sit here.'

3.3. *Requests,* or ways of asking H to comply with the directive. S assumes a position of less linguistic power and authority than that of H. H has more options with which to respond than with orders, since H is in the higher position and is being asked to do the action of his/her own will; e.g.:

Dá para você se mudar?
'Is it all right for you to move?'
Poderia sentar-se em outro local?
'Could you sit in another place?'

3.4. *Hints,* or ways in which S makes an allusion to the action desired, but never expresses directly what that action is. S can be in any position of power in relation to H, but is probably on the same level or in a lower position, since S does not want to be direct. Among other responses, H has the option of completely ignoring the directive by pretending not to understand the hint without causing an affront to S; e.g.:

Você roubou a trono do papai, você está usando o trono! (laughter)
'You stole Dad's throne, you're using his throne!'

3.5. *Avoidance of the directive* and/or the problem, through some form of diversion or the invention of another story, or ignoring the problem completely; e.g.:

*Boneca, vamos fazer uma coisa. Vamos aqui dentro com titio, que
titio vai mostrar umas coisas para você.*
'Doll, let's do something. Let's go inside with uncle, because uncle is
going to show you some things.'

3.6. NO RESPONSE, or being unable or unwilling to deal with the situation.

The difference in these options and the corresponding variation in force
is based on variation in the three dimensions of a directive mentioned
earlier; i.e., S's relationship to H, the directness in illocutionary force with
which the directive is conveyed, and the options left to H with which to
respond to the directive.[5]

4. Base Form of the Directive

To account for the variation in force and form, we may turn to some
ideas put forth in a study by Macedo on the role of core grammar in pidgin
development (1986). In this study, he states that one principle of language
acquisition is that there is a preference for the selection of unmarked or
least marked structures because they are more accessible and more easily
acquired. He bases his theory on Eckman's theory of markedness, which is:
"A phenomenon A in some language is more marked than B if the presence
of B in a language implies the presence of B, but the presence of B does not
imply the presence of A" (1977:329).

As evidence to support his claim, he shows how the relative pronouns
que, de que, sobre quem, do qual, and *cujo* were all collapsed into a single
unmarked form *qui* in Capeverdean creole. That is, *que, de que, sobre
quem, do qual,* and *cujo* all imply the presence of the form *qui,* but the
reverse is not true, so the latter is considered the unmarked or the least
marked form while all of the former are marked or more marked.

Although Macedo is dealing with syntax in his study, the ideas of markedness can be applied to pragmatic rules to explain a hierarchy of force of
the directives, according to a kind of continuum of politeness. We can
posit the existence of a base form or least marked form of the directive, or
the idea of [+ directive], which in colloquial Brazilian Portuguese is most
commonly expressed as a direct order in the present indicative verb form
(e.g., *Senta aí.* 'Sit there' or *Não senta aí.* 'Don't sit there'), as seen in Table
1 and Figure 2.[6]

Table 1
Frequency of Various Elements of
Directives According to the Form of Directive

		Ord/Assert	Sug	Req	Hints	Avoid
	informants n:	(55)	(16)	(38)	(16)	(9)
A.	Vocative	25	9	20	2	4
B.	Terms of endearment	6	2	0	0	2
C.	Present indicative	44	7	10	-	-
D.	Subjunctive	6	2	3	-	0
E.	Conditional	0	0	6	-	0
F.	Cond/imperf. subjunctive	0	0	10	-	0
G.	Impersonal expression	0	3	0	-	0
H.	Jokes/laughter	3	0	0	-	0
I.	Slang	8	2	3	2	0
J.	Tag quest	6	3	1	3	2
K.	Kinship terms	9	0	0	1	1
L.	Nós	2	6	0	-	3
M.	Explain	24	9	29	9	1
N.	Ask for favor	3	2	12	0	3
O.	Beg forgiveness	2	2	11	1	0
P.	Don't be offended	1	2	5	0	0

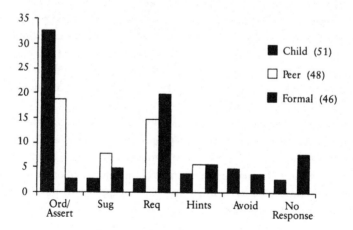

Figure 2: Directives Given by Well Educated
Respondents

It is the least polite form, and to this base, one can add or superimpose elements to dilute or soften the force of the directive by modifying one or more of the three dimensions of a directive discussed earlier. Thus the order *Senta aí* spoken to a peer could easily be turned into a request, for example, by the addition of a tag question '*tá?* (i.e., *Senta aí, tá?* 'Sit there, OK?') which alters the force of the order by putting S in a theoretically subordinate position to H by asking H to comply with the directive instead of ordering him or her to do so. H now has the option to refuse without as much confrontation to S as with orders, since H would not be challenging S's position of authority (Brown and Levinson 1978:74–75). After the base form of the direct order, the directive second in terms of strength of force is a suggestion which, as stated in §3.2, cannot easily be refused by H, since S assumes a position of greater linguistic power. The directive is indirectly expressed through syntactic options such as the use of the *nós* 'we' pronoun and/or corresponding verb inflection (e.g., *Vamos sentar ali* 'Let's sit there'), or strategies such as stating an opinion that the hearer should carry out the directive (e.g., *Melhor você sentar ali* 'Better for you to sit there').

The next strongest directive is the request, in which the directive is indirectly expressed and S is in an inferior position to H. For this reason, its force is weaker than in suggestions. It is usually expressed in the data in a question format accompanied by an explanation but also appears with the performative verb expressed (e.g., *Pediria para o senhor se mudar* 'I would (like to) ask you to move').[7]

Hints are next in the continuum of force, since the base form is the underlying basis for the directive, but the directive is not overtly expressed at all. Instead, S uses discourse strategies which revolve around the directive, and S relies on H understanding through shared cultural and linguistic knowledge.[8] Of course, there is greater risk that H will not understand that implicit directive, or will ignore it.[9] Finally, complete avoidance of the directive is last in the continuum.[10]

Now that we have examined a hierarchy of the directives in the data, we can turn to the concept of learnability proposed in Macedo's study. Regarding the preference for the form *qui* in Capeverdean creole, he claims that this form was more learnable because it was the unmarked or least marked form. If the same idea of 'learnability' can be applied to directives and pragmatic rules that govern their forms, then the base-form directive would be that which is acquired first, and the options by which one can soften its force would be acquired later as one gains experience with the language and strategies for politeness. We would expect to see the base form used most in addressing children, in children's speech, and perhaps in the speech of adults who have not acquired the more marked or more polite forms. We would also expect to see the more marked forms in situations where more politeness is required; i.e., the formal register.

5. Evidence from the Data

5.1. 'CHILD REGISTER'. As evidence for the base-form directive and the acquisition of other forms, the data in Table 2 and in Figure 3 show that the most commonly used directive form in the register employed by adults with children is the direct command, given in the present indicative verb form. In data from Wherritt, and from my own informal observations of young children (approximately 2 to 6 years old), children also most commonly utilize the base form in giving directives, e.g.:

> *Dá um pouquinho p'r' esse.*
> 'Give a little to this one.'
> *Mamãe, põe esse.*
> 'Mother, put this one on.'
> *Toma.*
> 'Take it.'
> *Me dá cor de rosa, me dá.*
> 'Give me a pink one, give me.'
> (Wherritt 1983:116)

This suggests that the base form is the first to be acquired. Studies in child language acquisition in English also support this hypothesis. Read and Cherry (1977), citing evidence from a study by Garvey (1975), state that although direct, indirect, and inferred request forms are in the linguistic repertoire of children 3 to 6 years old, the majority of the forms are direct. They suggest that this is logical, since there is little reason for the children not to use the more direct form with their peers or very familiar adults, with whom they are almost always in contact. They also state that children learn to soften their requests as they acquire notions of politeness (1977:490, 499).

As further evidence for this base form of the directive and its order in acquisition, we may look at data from 12 adult native speakers of Rio de Janeiro exposed to no more than eight years of formal education who participated in the same experiment.[11] The results in Table 3 show that most of these speakers rely on use of the base form in speaking to a child or a peer; in the formal register, most informants use either orders or requests, or avoid the problem. The directive is lessened in force mainly through the use of the vocative (e.g., *Ô A, levanta da cadeira* 'O A, get up from the chair', or simply H's name or *ô, ó,* or *olha*), explanations, asking

Table 2
Linguistic Options and Strategies in Expressing
Directive According to Register
Less Educated Respondents

	Child	Peer	Formal
informants n:	(11)	(10)	(9)

A. Forms of Directive

Orders/assertions	12	8	3
Suggestions	0	2	1
Requests	0	0	3
Hints	1	1	1
Avoidance	2	2	2
No Response	1	2	3

B. Forms of Address

Vocatives (or name or ô, ó, olha)	9	9	4
Você	3	5	1
O senhor/excelência	0	0	2
Tu/te	0	1	0
Terms of endearment/nicknames	3	0	0

C. Verb Tenses

Present Indicative	10	8	4
Imperfect Indicative	0	0	0
Subjunctive	1	0	1
Conditional	0	0	1
Conditional/imperfect subjunctive	0	0	1
Será que	0	0	0
Dá para	0	0	0
Impersonal (e.g., ser melhor você)	0	0	0

D. Attempts at Solidarity

Jokes/laughter	0	0	0
Slang	0	1	0
Tag questions	2	3	2
Criticism of situation	0	1	1
Kinship terms	5	0	0
Nós/a gente	3	2	0

E. Other Strategies

Explanations	5	9	7
Asking for favor	0	1	3
Thanking for understanding	0	0	1
Begging forgiveness	0	2	3
Asking not to be offended	0	3	2
Warning of sanctions	3	4	2
Belittling request	0	0	0

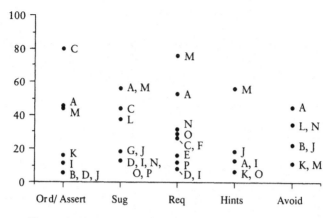

Figure 3: Percentage of Frequency of Some Elements of
Directives According to the Form of the Directive (see Table 1)

for forgiveness, and asking for favors. Some respondents avoid the situation
by offering another diversion. We see that although many of these speakers
produce more polite forms, nearly one-third of the directives used are
more direct, in a situation where one would expect the most indirect and
polite forms. This is in contrast to the directives employed by more educated speakers, in which 18% are requests and suggestions. We also see that
almost all of these less-educated speakers do not use the syntactic options
which the more educated employ to soften their directives (e.g., condi-
tional/imperfect subjunctive, as in *Pediria que você se sentasse ali* 'I would
ask that you sit there'), showing that they probably have not acquired these
syntactic options through exposure to the formal register or formal education. Instead, they use strategies to soften directives that emphasize their
lower power and/or status position in asking the imposition (e.g., asking for
favors, etc.). In other words, they achieve the same illocutionary effects
through different means.[12]

Table 1 and Figure 2 also show that, in this child register employed by
well-educated adults, the order or assertion is most commonly softened
with the lexical options of the vocative, explanations, or some term of
kinship or endearment (e.g., *Sai daí, molequinho* 'Get out of there, you
rascal'). As Brown and Levinson note, the use of 'in-group address forms'
has the effect of turning the command into a request (p. 113). Slang expressions (e.g., *Sai daí, molequinho, que eu vou te dar um esporro dan-
ado* 'Get out of there, you rascal, because I'm going to give you a damned
beating') or tag questions often accompany the directive (e.g., *'tá?'* 'All
right?'), both of which build a feeling of solidarity with H.[13]

Table 3
Linguistic Options and Strategies in Expressing
Directive According to Register—
Well Educated Respondents

	Child	Peer	Formal
informants n:	(42)	(45)	(37)
A. Forms of Address			
Vocatives (or name or ô, ó, *olha*)	15	28	17
Você	12	23	1
O *senhor/excelência*	0	0	19
Tu/te	2	0	0
Terms of endearment/nicknames	8	2	0
B. Verb Tenses			
Present Indicative	30	22	9
Imperfect Indicative	2	2	1
Subjunctive	4	4	4
Conditional	0	3	3
Conditional/imperfect subjunctive	0	3	7
Será que	1	2	1
Dá para	1	2	1
Impersonal (e.g., *ser melhor você*)	0	0	1
C. Attempts at Solidarity			
Jokes/laughter	0	5	4
Slang	5	9	2
Tag questions	7	5	3
Criticism of situation	0	7	3
Kinship terms	11	0	0
Nós/a gente	7	4	0
D. Other Strategies			
Explanations	17	33	22
Asking for favor	3	4	13
Thanking for understanding	0	0	3
Begging forgiveness	1	9	6
Asking not to be offended	1	3	4
Warning of sanctions	5	6	0
Belittling request	1	0	0

5.2. 'PEER REGISTER'. In the formal 'peer register' used with a friend of the same social rank and status, the most commonly employed directives are the base form of a direct order, or requests (see Figure 3). As in the child register, orders are softened through the lexical options of the vocative and slang expressions, and an explanation is almost always given along with the directive (see Table 2). However, in this register there is also more syntactic diversity in the requests: i.e., the formulation of the directive through a question (e.g., *Pode sentar em outra cadeira?* 'Can you sit in another chair?'), which also includes the frozen expressions of *dá para* and *será que* in question format (e.g., *Dá para você sentar nesta cadeira?* 'Is it all right for you to sit in this chair?'; *Mas será que você poderia sentar na outra cadeira?* 'But is it possible that you could sit in the other chair?'); the imperfect indicative or the conditional form, usually involving the verb *poder* 'to be able, can' (e.g., *Podia sair daí?* 'Could you get up from there?'; *Poderia sentar-se em outro local?* 'Could you sit in another place?'); and the scattered use of the present subjunctive structure (e.g., *Tenho que pedir a você que saia desta cadeira* 'I have to ask you to get up from that chair') or the conditional/imperfect subjunctive structure (e.g., *Eu pediria que você sentasse em outra cadeira* 'I would [like to] ask you to sit in another chair') (see Table 2 and Figure 2). As stated earlier, the question format softens the directive by turning it into a request, and affects the position of S with respect to H and H's options to respond. The other structures, such as the conditional/imperfect subjunctive, express the performative verb, e.g., *eu pediria que ...* 'I would (like to) ask you ...' According to Fraser, the expression of 'would like to' implies that the 'speaker is seeking the hearer's permission for this state of affairs', which immediately makes the utterance more polite, since S is subordinate to H (1975:202–204). The other verb tenses besides the present indicative, such as the conditional *poderia* or the imperfect indicative *podia*, remove the directive from the present time in these contexts, which creates a quality of politeness through a weakening of direct force (Koike 1989). In addition, the use of the verb *poder* in a question allows the directive to take the form of a request, since S is asking H if he or she is willing to do the action through the use of this verb.

In the informal peer register, much of the softening of the directive is done through other strategies to build solidarity with H (see Table 2). This is accomplished through the use of jokes and laughter (e.g., *Você sabe que esta cadeira é do chefe da tribu, e ele é uma pessoa muito sistemática, muito cheia de coisa, e ele 'tá para chegar aí* 'You know that this chair belongs to the chief of the tribe, and he is a very strict person, full of quirks, and he is about to arrive'), slang (e.g., *Meu pai não gosta, e tal, e depois ele dá uma bronca em mim, sabe como é que é* 'My dad doesn't like it, and then he'll give it to me, you know how it is'), tag questions (e.g., *tá, n'é?* 'right?'; *sabe?* 'you know?'), and S's own criticism of the request or situation (e.g., *Ô H, não senta aí, que o velho não gosta. O velho 'tá gamado nisso.* 'O H, don't sit there, because the old man doesn't like it. The old man has a thing about it'). The latter option shifts the blame of S's imposition on H onto the shoulders of the third party who caused the situation to be a problem, thus allowing S to save face, and also allows S and H to share a certain bond in criticizing or ridiculing the request. Some informants also include a warning of the consequences or sanctions (e.g., *Se tiver alguem sentado nela, Deus me livre, tampa seus ouvidos, sai de perto, porque* ... 'If there is someone sitting there, God help me, cover your ears, get out of there, because ...'), which serves the purpose of reinforcing the urgency of the directive and the request for action, but also reinforces the idea that the directive is actually coming from a third party and not from S. Other strategies sometimes used in the peer register to soften the force of the directive and to put S in a position subordinate to H are to ask forgiveness of H before or after issuing the directive (e.g., *Você me desculpa* 'You will forgive me') or to ask H not to take offense (e.g., *Não leva a mal* 'Don't take it wrong').

5.3. FORMAL REGISTER. The data from the register used in a more formal situation with a stranger of much higher rank and social status in Figure 3 show that most informants employ requests, while some respondents use suggestions and hints. Explanations accompany most directives, as shown in Table 2. Aside from the present indicative tense, several informants utilize the conditional/imperfect subjunctive structure, largely in requests. The other verb tenses used in the peer register are employed here in nearly the same frequencies.

The most frequent lexical options are the vocative or simply *ô, ó,* or *olha,* or the person's name, and the subject pronoun of respect *o senhor.* We also see in this register many more strategies that inform H that S recognizes t'iat the directive is an imposition, especially given S's inferior social or power position in relation to H. S must ask H to carry out the action as a favor to S. For this reason, the expressions *por favor, ter a bondade,* and *por gentileza* are used by several informants.[14] Other strategies which also accomplish the same effect are thanking H for understanding (e.g., *Se o senhor pudesse levantar e sentar em qualquer uma outra, eu agradeceria muito a gentileza e a compreensão, n'é* 'If you could get up and sit in any other, I would appreciate very much the courtesy and understanding'), asking H for understanding (e.g., *O senhor me acompanha* 'You understand'), asking H not to take offense (e.g., *Não vai ficar chateado* 'Don't be upset'), and letting H know that it is very difficult for S to be asking this imposition (e.g., *Não sei como lhe pedir para se levantar desta cadeira* 'I don't know how to ask you to get up from this chair'). These strategies are not used as much in speaking with a peer, and are very seldom employed with children. This indicates that when S is in a subordinate position with respect to H due to real circumstances and did not place him or herself there through linguistic strategies, S must underscore his or her inferior position with strategies to indicate respect and acknowledgment that S is making a great imposition on H.

One strategy used by several respondents in the formal and child registers but very little in the peer register was the avoidance of the problem by inventing another story to stimulate H to move from the chair, or luring H away with an enticement, utilized mostly with children (see Figure 3). In speaking to children, it is often easier to deal with the situation by inventing another story or a diversion, and children would probably not perceive the real motive. I believe that there is 'story-invention' in the formal register because S has two choices: either to give the directive, trying to soften it in the most polite way to fit the occasion, or not to give it. In not giving it, S can make up another story as another attempt to get the desired results, or forget about the problem completely. In fact, several informants who willingly gave directives in the child and peer registers found it too difficult to do in the formal register.

6. Summary

From the data gathered in this study, we see the following:[15]

(1) In all three registers, the form of the directive is determined by the relationship between S and H and corresponding strategies for more or less politeness in a hierarchical order of more to less force. In the forms of the directive used across the three registers, orders/assertions are employed most in the child register, while orders/assertions and requests are the most common directive in the peer register. In the formal register, most informants utilize requests. It appears that the data support the proposed hierarchy of politeness in directives, since the least marked base form is used most in situations where politeness is not as essential to the communication, and the more marked form of requests is employed where politeness is an essential factor in the interaction. I believe that hints, the more marked form in our hierarchy, are not preferred in the formal context because they are much more ambiguous and S runs a greater risk of the directive not being accomplished. The vacillation in the peer register between the more and less polite forms may be due to factors such as S's personality and degree of familiarity with H, which would influence S to choose either a more or less direct form of the directive. We also see in this vacillation some clues as to which position of linguistic power S wishes to assume with respect to H.

(2) The base form of the directive is used by nearly all informants in speaking to a child. The directive is most often softened through explanations and lexical options such as the vocative or the use of H's name, or simply the use of *ô*, *ó*, or *olha*. In the peer register, most respondents employ the base form or requests. Strategies most often utilized to soften the directive are: (a) attempts to establish solidarity with H through the use of slang, tag questions, jokes, and S's own criticism of the situation; (b) hints and suggestions about the directive, instead of direct expression of it; (c) asking H to forgive the imposition or not to take offense; and (d) giving warnings of sanctions, to remove the responsibility from S onto the person who caused the situation to be a problem, and to emphasize the need for cooperation.

(3) Directives in the formal register are communicated primarily through requests, which are more marked for politeness in the hierarchy. Other strategies used are asking forgiveness from H for the imposition and/or asking H not to take offense at the directive, which are strategies that emphasize S's inferior position to H and recognition of the great imposition on H, given the social distance between the two parties. Requests illustrate more syntactic diversity in the use of other tenses and structures besides the present indicative tense, such as the conditional/imperfect subjunctive structure. The data indicate that, in the formal register, the more educated respondents conform more closely to syntactic norms prescribed for formality and politeness (e.g., conditional/imperfect subjunctive) learned through formal education and exposure to the formal register, instead of strategies such as those for solidarity, seen in the peer register.[16]

(4) Returning to Eckman's theory of markedness applied by Macedo to language acquisition and pidginization, we see evidence from data in Brazilian Portuguese that lends support to such an application in pragmatics. That is, the least politeness-marked base form of the directive manifested in orders and assertions is seen largely in the speech of educated adults to children, in children's speech, and in the speech of many less-educated speakers of Brazilian Portuguese. This seems to indicate that the least marked directive forms are used when the context does not require politeness (i.e., with adults to children) and is the first to be acquired, as seen in children's speech, while more politeness-marked forms expressed in more elaborate syntactic structures (e.g., conditional/imperfect subjunctive structure) are acquired through increased experience with the language and social interaction that defines and shapes communicative competence. Thus the data suggest that formal education teaches one to be implicit and more polite through syntactic options rather than rely on

lexical strategies such as asking for favors or begging forgiveness for the imposition.

NOTES

[1] I would like to thank Dana Wheeler and Donaldo Macedo for their helpful comments and suggestions in the development of this paper, and Hissao and Anete Arita and Eulália Fernandes for their assistance in finding informants. The research discussed here was supported by a development grant from North Carolina State University.

[2] I will refer to 'power' in two different senses: 'real power' in which real life rank or status plays a part (e.g., a boss to his or her secretary), and 'linguistic power', which denotes the control that one has in the context of the communication, regardless of real power status.

[3] This paper will not discuss intonation, which certainly is an important factor in expressing directives.

[4] In other words, an order is not necessarily a reflection of a real power hierarchy.

[5] I wish to emphasize again that these forms of the directive do not necessarily correspond to a hierarchy of real life power between S and H. Thus someone in a higher real life position (e.g., a director of a company) may choose to assume a lower position of control with respect to H (e.g., an office boy) by using a request.

[6] In taking the position that the base form directive is the base for requests, hints, suggestions, etc., I am rejecting the proposition that a sentence such as 'Can you pass the salt, please?' can be understood as a question regarding H's salt-passing abilities, given a certain context of asking for salt (Bach and Harnish 1979:173, 180–85). Haverkate (1979:1) also states that the forms of directives in Spanish (e.g., requests, orders, etc.) are variants of the same act, which is the 'impositive act'.

[7] We can say that some requests are stronger than others. For example, the statement format with an expressed performative verb (e.g., *Pediria para o senhor* 'I would ask you') is stronger than the question format (e.g., *Poderia se mudar?* 'Could you move?') since H has more options in the latter.

The most variation in verb tenses appears in requests, as shown in Figure 2 and Table 1. This is discussed in §5.3.

[8] Searle (1979:31–32) states that in 'indirect speech acts, the speaker communicates to the hearer more than he actually says by relying on their mutually-shared background information, both linguistic and non-linguistic, together with the general powers of rationality and inference on the

part of the hearer.' In suggestions, and even more so in hints, S relies on H inferring the directive from the utterance(s). The more H is called on to infer, the weaker the force and the more freedom H has with which to respond.

[9] As shown in Figure 2, all directives are usually preceded by the vocative except for hints, which indicates that perhaps the informants view its force as so weak that it is not expressed as a true directive. Hints are usually accompanied by tag questions which are checks for agreement and comprehension. That is, it seems that S needs constant confirmation to see if H is following the line of the communication to make sure that the directive underlying the hint will be grasped by H.

[10] The variables shown in Figure 2 for 'avoidance directives' are mostly those for cases in which S gives a directive to do an action other than the one required.

[11] All participants had completed no more than eight years of formal education, and their ages ranged from 17 to 61. The 4 females and 8 males were from lower class backgrounds.

[12] I am certainly not implying that less-educated adult speakers communicate like children, but simply that they use different strategies than the more educated. Adults have a much broader and more perfect awareness of expectations in social interactions which children do not have, such as the notion of politeness and in what situations it is expected. Also, adults can manipulate strategies which are available to them to a greater degree than children.

[13] The directives in Brazilian Portuguese are revealing of the many attention-calling devices in the language. The vocative (*Ó, A,* or *Olha A,* or *Ô A*), or simply the person's name or the use of *ô, ó,* or *olha,* calls the person to attend to the message and also has the effect of personalizing the proposition. It is also used as a device to signal a change in the discourse from the previous topic to a command. Other devices include commands to listen or pay attention (e.g., *Escuta* 'Listen' or *Vem cá* 'Hey' [lit., 'Come here']) and tag questions (e.g., *'Tá ouvindo?* 'Are you hearing?' *viu?* 'Did you see?' *ouviu?* 'Did you hear?' *n'é?* 'right?' *sabe?* 'you know?' *'tá?* 'ok?' *entendeu?* 'Did you understand?') which elicit some reaction (most often agreement or a sign of comprehension) on the part of H.

[14] It is interesting to note that in teaching children to soften their demands in the base form directive, parents nearly always teach *por favor* 'please'. However, the results show that this form is most used in formal situations, indicating that *por favor* is marked for formality and politeness, putting S in a definitely subordinate position to H.

[15] Of course, given that this study is limited to the analysis of one directive in three hypothetical registers, the linguistic options and strategies listed are far from exhaustive of the possibilities existent in the language. For this reason, the conclusions are also limited in scope.

[16] There are indications that the base form directive, which has the most illocutionary force, may be softened through the use of new semantic meanings for certain verbs. For example, instead of ordering a newspaper in a base form, such as *Me dá um jornal* 'Give me a paper', it is also popular to say *Me ve um jornal* 'Give (lit., 'see') me a paper', which is less forceful due to the use of a verb which is not associated with a demand.

REFERENCES

Austin, J. 1962. How to do things with words. Cambridge, MA: Harvard University Press.

Bach, Kent, and Robert M. Harnish. 1979. Linguistic communication and speech acts. Cambridge, MA: MIT Press.

Brown, Penelope, and Stephen Levinson. 1978. Universals in language usage: Politeness phenomena. In Esther Goody (ed.), Questions and politeness: Strategies in social interaction, pp. 56–310. Cambridge: Cambridge University Press.

Brown, R., and A. Gilman. 1972. The pronouns of power and solidarity. In Pier Paolo Giglioli (ed.), Language and social context, pp. 252–82. London: Penguin Books.

Eckman, Fred R. 1977. Markedness and the contrastive analysis hypothesis. Language Learning 27(2).315–30.

Fraser, Bruce. 1975. Hedged performatives. In Peter Cole and Jerry L. Morgan (eds.), Syntax and semantics: Speech acts, Vol. 3, pp. 187–210. New York: Academic Press.

Garvey, Catherine. 1975. Requests and responses in children's speech. Journal of Child Language 2.41–63.

Haverkate, Henk. 1979. Impositive sentences in Spanish. Amsterdam: North Holland Linguistic Series.

Koike, Dale. 1984. Linguistic variation in register and Spanish directives. Paper presented at LSRL XIV, Los Angeles, February 1984.

———. 1989. Requests and the role of deixis in politeness. Journal of pragmatics 13.187–202.

Lakoff, Robin. 1973. The logic of politeness; or, Minding your p's and q's. Papers from the Ninth Regional Meeting, Chicago Linguistic Society 9.292–305.

Macedo, Donaldo. 1986. The role of core grammar in pidgin development. Language Learning 36(1).65–75.

Read, Barbara, and Louise Cherry. 1977. Children's spontaneous directive use in elicited situations. Papers from the Thirteenth Regional Meeting, Chicago Linguistic Society 13.489–502.

Rutherford, William. 1982. Markedness in second language acquisition. Language Learning 32(1).85–108.

Sadock, Jerrold M. 1974. Toward a linguistic theory of speech acts. New York: Academic Press.

Searle, John. 1969. Speech acts: An essay in the philosophy of language. Cambridge: Cambridge University Press.

————. 1979. Expression and meaning. Cambridge: Cambridge University Press.

Wherritt, Irene. 1983. Directives in Brazilian Portuguese: Mother-child interaction. In John Bergen and Garland Bills (eds.), Spanish and Portuguese in social context, pp. 105–118. Washington, D.C.: Georgetown University Press.

Section V
Text and Discourse Analysis

9

The Definite Article in Portuguese: A Discourse Oriented Approach

Célia Mendonça

Universidade Federal da Paraíba

1. Purpose

The purpose of this paper is to offer an analysis of the definite article in texts. It is my view that texts usually contain explicit elements that enable the hearer or reader to construct appropriate contexts for them. One such element is the article. In this sense, the article is a tool used by the speaker or writer to signal an assessment of the hearer's or reader's knowledge and probable expectations.

2. Methodology

It is a well-known fact that in any communicative situation—be it oral or written—individuals necessarily make familiarity inferences about what they hear or read. That is, they expect to see connections between what they hear or read and things they have experienced before, which are, in this sense, known to them. These inferences are shared, or at least they are assumed by the speaker or writer to be shared with the hearer or reader.

It is this kind of familiarity inference that has often been discussed under the notion *shared knowledge*—a notion claimed to be relevant to definiteness, as well as to comprehension in general. Prince (1979) proposes the term *Assumed Familiarity*, and shows, by analyzing a naturally occurring oral narrative, that it represents a range of discrete types of information, which includes what she labels as *unused, inferable,* and *evoked* entities, or referents.

An unused entity is a referent that is introduced into a piece of discourse for the first time, but the speaker assumes it is familiar to the hearer on the basis of the situational environment that the speaker assumes they share. An *inferable* entity is a referent that is mentioned in a text for the first time, but is not entirely new to the hearer in the sense that it can be inferred from other items in the text. An *evoked* entity is a referent that, having first been introduced into a text, recurs at different places, and as such is said to be evoked by the hearer.

This analysis will be based on Prince's framework, and will take as its starting point the understanding of the hearer or reader. In other words, the elements or items of a given piece of discourse will be analyzed not in terms of their forms, but rather in terms of what is somehow felt to be familiar to the hearer or reader. It happens that all such elements identified here can be formally realized by means of the definite article.

The analysis will concentrate on written texts, more specifically, vignettes, i.e., short literary sketches, by contemporary Brazilian writers.[1] The reasons for choosing such texts are the following: (1) this kind of literary genre is very common in Brazilian literature; (2) these texts are good examples of linguistic communicative interactions, with the writer on the one side, who wants to impart some information to a receiver, i.e., the reader(s); (3) these vignettes usually portray everyday life situations in which fictitious characters are advanced as real and engage in conversations, expressed in the form of dialogues or quotes.

Several points need to be mentioned in connection with the analysis. First, in analyzing these texts it is important to take into consideration two different kinds of communicative interaction—one between the writer and the reader(s), the other between the characters themselves as they talk to one another. Given this distinction, the quote should be also seen as a text, embedded into a larger one, but, nevertheless, autonomous in itself. Thus the analysis is under both perspectives; on the one hand, that of the reader(s), and, on the other hand, that of the hearer(s) in the quotes.

Second, it is common in these texts for the writer to introduce fictitious referents and expect the reader to know the particular entities mentioned. In creating this atmosphere of pseudo-familiarity, the writer presumes the reader's familiarity with these specific fictitious referents. This is very common in the opening sentences of narratives, as in the text presented here.

Third, these texts usually contain material that, in the last analysis, is a figment of the writer's imagination—material about which one cannot share knowledge in the completely conventional sense. Furthermore, readers may simply not know certain kinds of facts, but may still be able to understand the text at some level. For example, the reader does not, in fact, have to know the place *o Rio de Janeiro* [2], introduced at the beginning of the text, in order to understand it. The reader need only acknowledge that the writer is acting as if the reader is familiar with it.

Finally, although the analysis concentrates on single NPs (i.e., those consisting of the article plus a noun), it may be extended to include both pre- and post-modified NPs (i.e., those in which other elements precede or follow the noun; e.g., NPs consisting of a relative clause, a prepositional phrase, a pre/postposed adjective). In many such cases, however, the occurrence of the article is further determined by factors other than those discussed here, such as semantic and/or syntactic properties of the lexical units attached to the noun. Also excluded from the analysis are idiomatic expressions in which the definite article occurs.

3. The Analysis

To illustrate my analysis, I have chosen the text 'A Cabra e Francisco' ('The Goat and Francisco')—one of the vignettes in a collection by the contemporary Brazilian writer Carlos Drummond de Andrade (1981).

In this text, the writer imaginatively creates a story in which a little she-goat unexpectedly shows up in a hospital in Rio in the middle of the night, being operated on by the doorman after he finds out that she has a bullet lodged in her neck. Throughout the incident, the doorman talks to the goat as if she were human, until to his amazement he notices that the goat herself can speak, having indeed conversed with him. In short, the story centers upon these two characters—the goat and the doorman.

For ease of reference, I will consider first those referents which can be identified on the basis of linguistic facts; i.e., their recognition by the hearer or reader is dependent on circumstances within the discourse itself. Then I will analyze those referents which the hearer or reader can supposedly identify on the basis of extra-linguistic facts that surround the discourse. Within the former group are both those referents that I have described as evoked and inferable. Within the latter are those described as unused referents.[2]

3.1. EVOKED REFERENTS. Let us first consider evoked referents. The familiarity shared by speaker/hearer or writer/reader in what concerns these items comes from the fact that either the referent is potentially visible in the situation of utterance, in which case it is situationally evoked, or the referent has already been mentioned in the text. In this case, it is textually evoked.

Situationally evoked referents in the text are *o hospital* [12] and *o Miguel Couto* [28]. They are situationally evoked in the sense that, within this particular text (the conversation between the doorman and the goat), they are potentially visible for both speaker and hearer. In other words, their identification is dependent on what the hearer can immediately perceive rather than on what has been previously mentioned. Both referents are expressed by NPs preceded by a definite article.

Textually evoked referents are any subsequent mentions of referents previously introduced into the discourse. Thus *a cabra* [4], [9], [20], [26], [37], *o animal* [5], [23], and *o bichinho* [21] are all subsequent mentions of the goat previously introduced into the discourse by means of the NP *uma cabrinha malhada* ('a little spotted she-goat') in the first paragraph.

In the same way, *o homem* [8] and *o porteiro* [24] are both subsequent mentions of *o porteiro* [3] (the doorman), a referent introduced in the opening paragraph. Also *a Lapa* [31] and *o Miguel Couto* [32] are second mentions of the previously introduced referents *a Lapa* [30] and *o Miguel Couto* [28]. And *o hospital* [18] is a subsequent mention of *o hospital* [1], introduced at the beginning of the text. All these referents stand in a coreferential relationship with an antecedent, and their identification by the hearer or reader is based on the previous linguistic context. Formally, they are all expressed by NPs preceded by the definite article.

One can see that in many of these cases the subsequent mention of the referent is lexically different from the first mention, although it is capable of the same reference. Thus *uma cabrinha malhada* is referred to again not only by means of the NP *a cabra* [4], [9], [20], [26], [37], but also by means of the NPs *o animal* [5], [23], and *o bichinho* [21]. The latter are identified by the reader on the basis of his/her knowledge of the language, more specifically, knowledge of a class inclusion relationship between *uma cabrinha malhada* and *o animal* [5], [23], as well as between *uma cabrinha malhada* and *o bichinho* [21]. There is in each case a relationship of hyponymy between these terms; that is, one in which o *animal* [5], and o *bichinho* [21] are superordinate terms. Similarly, there is a class inclusion relationship between o *homem* [8] and its antecedent o *porteiro* [3].

All these instances illustrate the fact that coreferentiality is indeed a semantic phenomenon. As pointed out by Halliday and Hasan (1976:62), anaphoric reference items refer to meaning, not to the forms that have gone before.

3.2. INFERABLE REFERENTS. There are other items in the text whose identification by the hearer or reader is also determined by the linguistic environment; i.e., by what has been previously mentioned. However, unlike those referents analyzed as evoked, they do not stand in coreferential relationship with an antecedent; rather, they are inferred from items previously mentioned. Within this group are those referents described here as inferables. This is the case, for example, of o *porteiro* [3], first mentioned in the text, which is related to the referent o *hospital* [1], introduced at the beginning of the text. One can say that such a referent has brought up a particular frame for the reader, a 'hospital' frame as it were, which has implicitly introduced the subsequent items o *porteiro* [3], as well as os *doutores* [15], a *sala de cirurgia* [16], and a *farmácia* [17], later mentioned in the text. The identification of these referents on the part of the reader is determined by some sort of associative relation between these items and the previously mentioned referent o *hospital* [1]. Furthermore, the item o *porteiro* [3] leads the reader to infer yet another frame—namely, one consisting of items usually associated with people, say, a 'human being' frame of which items like o *braço* [6], a *mão* [34], o *lado* [36] are seen as natural and expected parts. In fact, the degree of associative relation between, on the one hand, o *braço* [6], a *mão* [34], o *lado* [36] and, on the other, o *porteiro* [3] is quite high, given that the mention of a person immediately brings into consideration all his/her body parts.[3]

It is also likely that the first-mention o *porteiro* [3] brings up for the reader a different sort of frame, namely, one concerning the physical aspects of the activity undertaken by people such as doormen.[4] Thus the subsequent-mention a *cadeira* [11] can be inferred from the first-mention o *porteiro* [3] plus the knowledge that it is common for doormen to have a place to sit (at least, in some cultures). Other inferable referents in the text are o *cheiro* [7], o *pescoço* [14], os *olhos* [35], as *barbas* [38], all of them associatively related to the initially introduced referent uma *cabrinha malhada*. Again, as in the case of evoked referents, all these referents are formally realized by NPs with the definite article.

3.3. UNUSED REFERENTS. Let us now consider those referents which the hearer or reader can supposedly identify on the basis of his/her knowledge of extra-linguistic facts that surround the discourse, i.e., those referents here described as unused. Again, they are also expressed by NPs with the definite article.

In the text, the referents expressed by the NPs *o Rio de Janeiro* [2], *o Icó* [25], *a Lapa* [30], *o hospital Veterinário* [29], as well as *o dia* [13], [19], *a noite* [22], *o céu* [41], and also *as cabras* [33], and *a cabra* [40] (that is, goats in general) are not present in the situation of utterance; they are not potentially visible referents, nor have they been mentioned in the text before. Nevertheless, they can presumably be identified by the hearer/reader on the basis of the extra-linguistic context.

Thus in the case of *o Rio de Janeiro* [2], *o Icó* [25], *a Lapa* [30], and *o Hospital Veterinário* [29], it is knowledge of the existence of places such as cities, suburbs, and hospitals, respectively, that underlies the identification of these referents on the part of the hearer/reader. This does not necessarily mean that the hearer/reader has specific knowledge of these referents, but rather that the writer is acting as if the reader knows about them. This acknowledgement is based on some general knowledge that things like cities, suburbs, and hospitals exist. They are, therefore, part of the universe of discourse shared by both speaker/writer and the hearer/reader.

In the case of *o dia* [13], [19], and *a noite* [22], these are referents identified by the hearer/reader on the basis of some general knowledge concerning time division, as conventionally established in western cultures. We can mention, in passing, that these referents are the so-called unique referents, whose identification is always made on extra-linguistic grounds no matter what the situation. The referent *o céu* [41] can also be viewed as a unique referent, whose identification by the hearer/reader is made on knowledge of certain religious beliefs or creeds—knowledge presumably shared by both the speaker/writer and hearer/reader. An interesting aspect to be noted here is that the abstract concept *heaven* is an extension of the concrete referent *sky*, both being expressed by the same form, *o céu*. As discussed in Chafe (1972:52), these unique referents can be regarded as known sets which have but one member. Thus if the hearer/reader knows, say, the concept *céu* ('sky'), he or she cannot help but know which member of the set is being discussed, since there is only one.

Similar to these 'uniques' are the referents expressed by the NPs *as cabras* [33] and *a cabra* [40], mentioned in the text. Since they refer in a unique way to a set or class, it is knowledge of the existence of such sets or classes that underlies the identification of these generic referents on the part of the hearer/reader. This is directly related to the fact that generic concepts, as discussed in Du Bois (1980:226), are directly available in the speech situation. Therefore, they are not processed via the mediation of some prior mention; rather, they are directly processed. In this sense, then, the speaker/writer may presuppose that the hearer/reader is familiar with these sets, or is informed about them.

3.4. *Further Distinctions.* Let us examine now some other referents in the text which are also expressed by NPs with the definite article. At the beginning of the text, the NP *o hospital* [1] expresses a referent which is introduced to the reader for the first time. There is nothing in the linguistic or the extra-linguistic context that may lead the writer to assume that the reader is familiar with the introduced referent. Nevertheless, he uses the definite article. In doing so, the writer pretends that there is a context in which just one particular hospital exists, and assumes that the reader should know the particular entity mentioned. In this sense, such a referent is not altogether different from those discussed under the label *unused.* It differs only in that the reader's presupposed familiarity is based on an invented rather than a genuine context. In isolation, a sentence like *o hospital como o Rio de Janeiro dorme* would not make much sense, and would very likely provoke a wh-question on the part of the hearer, such as *que hospital?* 'what hospital?' In the context of the narrative, however, it makes perfect sense. It is evident that this sort of first-mention reference is an example of a well-known type of literary device, whose effect is to place the reader immediately within a context which the writer creates.

Examples such as this one point to the fact that the concepts of existence and uniqueness that underlie the use of the definite article should not be considered in absolute terms. Existence in such cases can only be defined in terms of various 'possible worlds', and uniqueness is always relative to a given communicative situation.

At the end of the text, there is a referent expressed by an NP consisting of the definite article plus a proper name, i.e., *o Ariano Suassuna* [39]. This is another instance of an unused referent. The speaker/writer presupposes the hearer/reader's familiarity with such a referent, as evidenced by the fact that there is no further explanation by the speaker/writer concerning this item. Given the uniqueness feature inherent in proper names (a proper name usually designating a single, determined entity), one would not expect the definite article to occur with a proper name. It occurs, however, in the above-mentioned NP, viz. *o Ariano Suassuna* [39]. In pragmatic terms, this phenomenon may be seen as a strategy used by the speaker/

writer to signal closer familiarity with the referent. That is, in addition to the uniqueness boundary already present in the proper name itself, the speaker/writer imposes yet another boundary, a close-to-self boundary, as it were (Acton 1977). Thus in mentioning *o Ariano Suassuna*, the speaker/ writer invites the hearer/reader to share a closer degree of familiarity with the referent.

There are two other items in the text that deserve additional comments, namely, *a razão* [10] and *o diálogo* [27]. They are both first-mentions, but the reader is able to identify them on the basis of what has been previously mentioned. Thus in the case of *a razão* [10], it is introduced into the text after the doorman has explained to the goat why she is not allowed into the building. The entity expressed by the NP *a razão* [10] refers to this expla- nation, being also inferred from the previously mentioned event of the goat who is forced to leave the building. Similarly, the NP *o diálogo* [27] refers to the conversation held by the doorman and the goat, and in this sense it can be said to be an evoked entity. Lyons (1977:672) discusses a similar example to show that 'a potential referent is salient in the universe of discourse, even though it is not present in the situation of utterance and has not been mentioned previously by either the speaker or the addressee.' Such cases illustrate the fact that anaphoric items need not relate to mean- ings introduced through a direct reference, but may refer to meanings introduced indirectly, as in the case of *a razão* [10] and *o diálogo* [27].

4. Implications

The analysis presented here has several bearings on the study of the linguistic phenomenon in general. First, it permits a generalization of ana- phora as a process which involves not only linguistic but also extra-linguis- tic facts. In this sense, an item is anaphoric not only when it stands in a coreferential relationship with some item previously mentioned, as in the case of evoked referents, but also when it refers to some knowledge which the speaker/writer assumes that the hearer/reader shares with him/her on the basis of their experiential background. In other words, it refers to something which is, as pointed out by Lyons (1977:672), 'in the intersub- jective experience of common memory of speaker and addressee'—some- thing which has been, as it were, previously established in the universe of discourse common to both. It is this broader view of anaphora that under- lies the introduction of unused referents into discourse.

The second aspect of the analysis is the generalization of notions like existence, referentiality, uniqueness, specificity, and genericness, which underlie the use of the definite article, as belonging to a larger class of distinctions—namely, that of familiarity inferences on the part of the hearer/reader. By taking into consideration these familiarity inferences, one is able to account for both the specific and nonspecific uses of the definite article in a unified way, and to bring under the right perspective both the uniqueness and inclusiveness features of the definite article, which most analyses solely based on semantic distinctions claim to be essential characteristics. Thus it is clear in the text that in the case of, for example, *a cadeira* [11], *a sala de cirurgia* [16], *a farmácia* [17], and *o braço* [6], *a mão* [34], the reference is neither specific nor unique. The hospital may certainly have more than one chair, operating room, or pharmacy, and the doorman should have both his hands and arms, since it has not been mentioned otherwise. In such cases, the items introduced by the definite article are not linked to an actual referent, nor to a verbal description, but to a conceptual representation. In other words, the writer's reference is to a type rather than to an individual thing. In this sense, the choice of, say, a particular chair, operating room, pharmacy, etc., is immaterial. What is at issue here is the establishment of a link to the concepts *chair, operating room, pharmacy,* as part of the relevant frame, namely, the 'hospital' frame.

One sees, then, the relevance of the notion *frame* in the analysis of the definite article. This brings us to the third aspect of the analysis—the need in linguistics for a more complex notion of *frame* in order to account for the several kinds of inference underlying the process of decoding on the part of the hearer/reader. In this connection, a distinction is made between, on the one hand, inference determined by facts that are basically linguistic (i.e., having to do with the inherent properties of the meaning of the word) and, on the other hand, inference determined by extra-linguistic facts in which culture certainly plays a decisive role. In the first case are those *inferables* whose degree of associative relationship with the entity from which they are inferred is very high. A case in point is *possession relations*, in particular, those defined as *inalienables*. For example, the referents expressed by the NPs *o braço* [6] and *a mão* [34] are inferred from the referent *o porteiro*, plus the fact that humans are known, among other things, to have both hands and arms. Putting it still another way, one can say that the mention of *o porteiro* [3] has foregrounded a frame for the reader in which items like *o braço* and *a mão* are taken for granted.

In the second case are those inferables for which this associative relationship is rather loose. Thus the entity expressed by the NP *a cadeira* [11] can also be inferred from *o porteiro* [3] through the foregrounding of another frame, one concerning the activities usually associated with doormen. However, the degree of inference here is much weaker than in the case of *o braço* and *a mão*. And it is less determined by some semantic properties of the trigger, i.e., the referent that triggers these associations, than by other facts in which cultural expectations come into play. Thus whereas it is most likely for human beings to have hands and arms, having a chair to sit upon is a contingent rather than an inherent property of being a doorman. One can see, then, that the notion *frame* and its underlying associative relations are very much dependent on probabilities. This does not mean just the *possibility* that a particular thing exists in a frame, but, as pointed out by Rhodes (1981), the *probability* of finding a frame with such a characteristic—a situation which in the last analysis is very much tied up with cultural facts.

Finally, the analysis hints at the old and much debated issue of how language and culture are intertwined, the former being in many instances a reflection of the latter. In this connection, one may want to inquire into the facts that determine the use of the definite article with abstract nouns, a phenomenon typical of the Portuguese language (and, in fact, of Romance languages in general) as opposed to other languages such as English. In English these nouns are characterized by the absence of the article, as in *o amor* 'love', *a alegria* 'joy', *a riqueza* 'wealth', *a paz* 'peace', *a felicidade* 'happiness', etc. The Greco-Roman tradition of personifying such abstract concepts in the forms of gods made them concrete entities, which became a part of the public record of these cultures. According to Rhodes (1981), the public record includes all those things in a society on which people's interactions are based, the things that make up their common universe of discourse. As part of this common universe, these entities constitute information shared by the members of these communities. Therefore, it is no surprise that the languages that have flourished under the Greco-Roman tradition still reflect such distinctions.

To conclude, I would like to acknowledge the fact that this analysis is to a certain extent subjective. It is my view, however, that psycholinguistic experimentation can both provide this kind of analysis with greater objectivity and shed more light on the processes that involve the hearer/reader's understanding and comprehension.

NOTES

[1] Since the article in Portuguese is not restricted to written prose, it is my belief that the analysis presented here can be generalized to account for the occurrence of the article in both written and oral texts. This is not to deny that there are certainly different degrees of formality between the oral and written language, which may affect the use of the article. This fact,

however, does not invalidate the generalizations made here.

[2] These referents are fully discussed in connection with the definite article in Lacerda (1983).

[3] Downing (1980:93) points out that 'these parts are seen as affiliated to their wholes, and this affiliation is expressed by the use of possessives, and by the use of the definite articles which can be appropriately used only because the whole has already been mentioned setting up the expectation that the part also exists.'

[4]Jones (1980:46) discusses the fact that the frames of a person's knowledge are related to one another in different and complex ways. Furthermore, 'the possibility that frames may be members of more than one class of frames indicates one aspect of the incredible complexity of knowledge structures.'

Appendix

A Cabra e Francisco

de

Carlos Drummond de Andrade

Madrugada. [1] *O hospital*, como [2] *o Rio de Janeiro*, dorme. [3] *O porteiro* vê diante de si *uma cabrinha malhada*, pensa que está sonhando.

—Bom palpite. Veio mesmo na hora. Ando com tanta prestação atrasada, meu Deus.

[4] *A cabra* olha-o fixamente.

—Está bem, filhinha. Agora pode ir passear. Depois você volta sim?

Ela não se mexe, séria.

—Vai, cabrinha, vai. Seja camarada. Preciso sonhar outras coisas. É a única hora em que sou dono de tudo, entende?

[5] *O animal* chega-se mais para perto dele, roça-lhe [6] *o braço*. Sentindo-lhe [7] *o cheiro*, [8] *o homem* percebe que é de verdade, e recua.

—Essa, não! Que é que você veio fazer aqui, criatura? Dê o fora, vamos.

Repele-a com jeito manso, porém [9] *a cabra* não se mexe, encarando-o sempre.

—Aiaiai! Bonito. Desculpe, mas a senhora tem de sair com urgência, isto aqui é um estabelecimento público. (Achando pouco satisfatória [10] *a razão*.) Bem, se é público devia ser para todos, mas você compreende ... (Empurra-a docemente para fore, a volta [11] *à cadeira*.)

—O quê? Voltou? Mas isso é hora de me visitar, filha? Está sem sono? Que é que há? Gosto muito de criação, mas aqui [12] *no hospital*, antes [13] *do dia* clarear . . .(Acaricia-lhe [14] *o pescoço.*)Que é isso! Você está molhada? Essa coisa pegajosa . . . O que: sangue?! Por que não me disse logo cabrinha de Deus? Por que ficou me olhando assim feito boba? Tem razão: eu é que não entendi, devia ter morado logo. E como vai ser? [15] *Os doutores* daqui são um estouro, mas cabra é diferente, não sei se eles topam, sabe de uma coisa? Eu mesmo vou te operar!

Corre [16] *à sala de cirurgia*, toma um bisturi, uma pinça [17], *à farmácia*, pega mercúrio-cromo, sulfa e gaze; e num canto [18] *do hospital* assistido por dois serventes, enquanto [19] *o dia* vai nascendo, extrai do pescoço [20] *da cabra* uma bala de calibre 22, ali cravada quando [21] *o bichinho*, ignorando os costumes cariocas [22] *da noite*, passava perto de uns homens que conversavam à porta de um bar.

[23] *O animal* deixa-se operar com a maior serenidade. Seus olhos envolvem [24] *o porteiro* numa carícia agradecida.

—Marcolina. Dou-lhe este nome em lembrança de uma cabra que tive quando garoto, [25] *no Icó*. Está satisfeita, Marcolina?

—Muito, Francisco.

Sem reparar que [26] *a cabra* aceitara [27] *o diálogo*, e sabia o seu nome, Francisco continuou:

—Como foi que você teve idéia de vir [28] *ao Miguel Couto*? [29] *O Hospital Veterinário* é [30] *na Lapa*.

—Eu sei, Francisco. Mas você não trabalha [31] *na Lapa*, trabalha [32] *no Miguel Couto*.

—E daí?

—Daí, preferi ficar por aqui mesmo e me entregar a seus cuidados.

—Você me conhecia?

—Não posso explicar mais do que isso, Francisco. [33] *As cabras* não sabem muito sobre essas coisas. Sei que estou bem a seu lado, que você salvou. Obrigada, Francisco.

E lambendo-lhe afetuosamente [34] *a mão*, correu [35] *os olhos* para dormir. Bem que precisava.

Aí Francisco levou um susto, saltou para [36] *o lado*.

—Que negócio é esse: cabra falando? Nunca vi coisa igual na minha vida. E logo comigo, meu pai do céu!

[37] *A cabra* descerrou um olho sonolento, e por cima [38] *das barbas* parecia esboçar um sorriso:

—Pois você não se chama Francisco, não tem o nome do santo que mais gostava de animais neste mundo? Que tem isso, trocar umas palavrinhas com você? Olhe, amanhã vou pedir [39] *ao Ariano Suassuna* que escreva um auto [40] d*a cabra*, em que você vai para [41] *o céu*, ouviu?

The Goat and Francisco

It was early morning. [1] *The hospital*, like (the rest of) [2] (*the*) *Rio de Janeiro*, was asleep. [3] *The doorman* saw *a little spotted she-goat* in front of him; he thought he was dreaming:

"Good idea. It came just in time. I am so behind in my payments, my goodness."

[4] *The goat* just stared at him.

"All right, little one. You can go now. You'll come back later, OK?"

She didn't move, (she just stood there) looking serious.

"Go away, little goat, go away. Be a pal. I need to dream of other things. This is the only time that (I feel) I own everything, understand?"

[5] *The animal* came closer to him and touched [6] *his* (*the*) *arm*. [7] *Her* (*the*) *smell* told [8] *the man* that she was real. He took a step back.

"Hey! What on earth are you doing here? Get moving, right away!"

He pushed her gently, but [9] *the goat* wouldn't budge; she just kept staring at him.

"Hey! I'm sorry but you have to leave immediately; this is a public building. (He does not find that a good reason—lit.: He does not think [10] *the reason* satisfactory.) Well, if it is public, it should be for everybody, but you know ..." (He pushed her gently out, and returned to [11] *his* (*the*) *chair.*)

"What? Again? But isn't there a better time to come and visit me, dear? What's the matter? Can't you sleep? I like farm animals, but here in [12] *the hospital*, before daybreak (lit.: [13] *the day* gets light) ... (He strokes [14] *her* (*the*) *neck.*) What is this? Are you wet? What's this sticky stuff.. Oh, blood?! Why didn't you tell me, little thing? Why did you keep looking at me like a dope. You're right! It was me who didn't understand; I should have realized immediately. But what are we going to do? [15] *The doctors* here are the greatest, but goats are another matter. I don't know if they'd agree to it. You know what? I'll operate on you myself!"

He rushed to [16] *the operating room*, got a scalpel and a pair of tweezers. He went to [17] *the pharmacy* and got some antiseptic, sulfas, and gauze; and in a corner of [18] *the hospital*, aided by two janitors, while [19] *the sun* rose, he extracted a twenty-two caliber bullet from [20] *the goat's* neck, which lodged there when [21] *the little thing*, unaware of nighttime habits of the big city (lit.: the 'carioca' habits of [22] *the night*), was passing some men who were talking in front of the door of a saloon.

[23] *The animal* submitted quietly to the operation, her eyes fixed on [24] *the doorman* with an expression of gratitude.

"Marcolina, I give you this name in memory of a goat I had when I was a boy in [25] (*the*) *Icó*. Are you happy Marcolina?"

"Very much, Francisco."

Without noticing that [26] *the goat* had responded to [27] *his* (*the*) *question*, and that she knew his name, Francisco continued:

"What gave you the idea of coming to [28] (*the*) *Miguel Couto*? [29] The Veterinary Hospital is in [30] (*the*) *Lapa*."

"I know, Francisco. But you don't work in [31] (*the*) *Lapa*, you work in [32] (*the*) *Miguel Couto*."

"So?"

"So I decided to stay here and have you take care of me."

"Did you know me?"

"I cannot explain more than that, Francisco. [33] (*The*) *goats* do not know much about such things. I only know that I feel good by your side, and that you saved my life. Thank you, Francisco."

And licking [34] *his* (*the*) *hand* gently, she closed [35] *her* (*the*) *eyes* and went to sleep. She certainly needed it.

Then Francisco realized with a big start what had just happened and jumped back (lit.: to [36] *the side*):

"What the hell is this? (A) talking goat? I've never seen such a thing in my entire life. And (talking) to me, my goodness!"

[37] *The goat* opened a sleepy eye, and seemed to smile over [38] *her* (*the*) *whiskers*:

"But aren't you Francisco? Don't you have the name of the saint who best loved animals in this world? Is there anything wrong in exchanging a few words with you? You know, tomorrow I'm going to ask [39] (*the*) *Ariano Suassuna* to write a play about goats (lit.: [40] *the goat*) in which you go to [41] (*the*) *heaven*, all right?"

Referents Identified in the Text
according to the Analysis Here Presented

Referents	Evoked	Inferable	Unused
[1] o hospital			+
[2] o Rio de Janeiro			+
[3] o porteiro		+	
[4] a cabra	+		
[5] o animal	+		
[6] o braço		+	
[7] o cheiro		+	
[8] o homem	+		
[9] a cabra	+		
[10] a razão		+	
[11] a cadeira		+	
[12] o hospital	+		
[13] o dia			+
[14] o pescoço		+	
[15] os doutores		+	
[16] a sala de cirurgia		+	
[17] a farmácia		+	
[18] o hospital	+		
[19] o dia			+
[20] a cabra	+		
[21] o bichinho	+		
[22] a noite			+
[23] o animal	+		
[24] o porteiro	+		
[25] o Icó			+
[26] a cabra	+		
[27] o diálogo	+		
[28] o Miguel Couto	+		
[29] o Hospital Veterinário			+
[30] a Lapa			+
[31] a Lapa	+		
[32] o Miguel Couto	+		
[33] as cabras (gen.)			+
[34] a mão		+	

Referents	Evoked	Inferable	Unused
[35] *os olhos*		+	
[36] *o lado*		+	
[37] *a cabra*	+		
[38] *as barbas*		+	
[39] *o Ariano Suassuna*			+
[40] *a cabra* (gen.)			+
[41] *o céu*			+

REFERENCES

Acton, William. 1977. A conceptual framework for teaching articles in English. Unpublished manuscript, University of Michigan.

Chafe, Wallace. 1972. Discourse structure and human knowledge. In Roy O. Freedle and John B. Carrol (eds.), Language comprehension and the acquisition of knowledge, pp. 41–69. New York: Halsted.

Downing, Pamela. 1980. Factors influencing lexical choice in narrative. In Wallace L. Chafe (ed.), The pear stories: Cognitive, cultural and linguistic aspects of narrative production, pp. 89–126. New Jersey: Ablex.

Drummond de Andrade, Carlos. 1981. Cadeira de balanço. 13 ed. Rio de Janeiro: José Olympio.

Du Bois, John W. 1980. Beyond definiteness: The trace of identity in discourse. In Wallace L. Chafe (ed.), The pear stories: cognitive, cultural and linguistic aspects of narrative production, pp. 203–76. New Jersey: Ablex.

Halliday, Michael A. K., and R. Hasan. 1976. Cohesion in English. London: Longman.

Jones, Larry B. 1980. Pragmatic aspects of English text structure. Doctoral dissertation, University of Texas at Arlington.

Lacerda, Célia M. 1983. The article in Brazilian Portuguese narrative discourse. Doctoral dissertation, University of Michigan.

Lyons, John. 1977. Semantics. Vol. 2. Cambridge: Cambridge University Press.

Prince, Ellen F. 1979. On the given/new distinction. Papers from the Regional Meeting, Chicago Linguistic Society 15, 267–276.

Rhodes, Richard. 1981. Discourse workshop, held at Ann Arbor, Michigan.

10

Our December

Haj Ross

MIT

We all know that the power of a great poem is not that we felt that person expressed himself well. We don't think that. What we think is 'How deeply I am touched.' That's our level of response. And the great poet docs not express his or herself, he expresses *all* of our selves. And to express *all* of ourselves, you have to go beyond your own self like Dogen, the Zen master, said, 'We study the self to forget the self. And when you forget the self, you become *one* with all things.'

> Gary Snyder,
> *The Real Work* (p. 65)

I propose that we go on a journey of the exploration of meaning together.[1] The text that will launch us is a fairly modern one—a poem by the contemporary writer Carlos Drummond de Andrade, a poet from the state of Brasil that lies north and west of Rio de Janeiro—Minas Gerais. The title of the poem is 'Interpretação de Dezembro'—interpretation of December. On one level, the poem concerns the meaning that Drummond finds in *his* December—the collection of all of the Decembers he has lived through in his native state. But if you find, as I do, that you are personally moved by Drummond's 'Interpretação', then we may ask you how this has happened. How has the poet gone beyond himself to express all of ourselves? How has he become one with all things?

More importantly (for the true poem is not *about* something, it *is* something), we must seek to understand how Drummond's journey beyond his self has taken us beyond ourselves, has helped *us* to become one with all things.

Our understanding need not be limited to our intellect; indeed, no journey beyond the self can remain bounded by *any* one type of mental activity. But we can start with our intellect, start with the form of the poem, see how far this can take us.

Before we look at the text, let me try to provide an important context—the notion of a year in a tropical country in the Southern Hemisphere. For those of us whose lives have been largely or entirely lived in the Northern Hemisphere, it requires a large mental leap to place ourselves in a bio rhythm which I at least find very strange. For the Brasilian December corresponds most closely to our Northern June, at least in countries like the United States, where the school year ends in June. June, July, and August are our traditional months of vacation, or relaxation, of gathering ourselves to recommence the yearly cycle again in September. In Brasil, as in the United States, the time of vacation, of going to the beach, is the hottest season of the year, when the days are the longest—but midsummer comes just four days before Christmas, ten days before New Year's. In the second month of the new year, the hottest month of the tropical summer, February, will be held the great festival of Brasil, which dominates the psyche of the Brasilian—*carnaval*. In December, as the old year ends, the people relax, dress more lightly, go to parties, begin to prepare themselves for the four days of carnival. Costumes are made, new songs written; there is a quickening of the pulses, of the blood. It is a time to take things lightly, to laugh. As carnival approaches, less and less 'of importance' will get done. It is a time to celebrate—until March, the beginning of the new school year, the month of the equinox, when the days get shorter and shorter, and people move slower, to the depths of winter—June 21.

Another thing that is difficult for us to grasp is the relative unimportance of spring and fall. These seasons exist, technically; there are words for them in the language, but our identification of spring with the beginning of an annual growing cycle, through the time of blossoming and growth (summer), to an annual harvest, and preparing for the rigors of a cold winter is largely absent from the Brasilian mind. In the tropical climate, most plants grow all year round, and the difference between winter and summer is between merely very warm (70°–90°) in winter to blazing hot (over 100°) in summer. Thus in Brasilian consciousness, the year is more bipolar than it is in the Northern Hemisphere. March to September, the darker part of the year, is a time of dormancy, of moving slowly, while the other six months are a time of increasing movement and joy, culminating in the great explosive and fusional pageant of *carnaval*.

For Drummond, then, December will be a time of looking back, of taking stock, of seeing what has been done, a time of recommitment. A time of relief, of celebration of the traditional joy of Christmas and the New Year, a time of looking forward.

INTERPRETAÇÃO DE DEZEMBRO[2]

Carlos Drummond de Andrade

A   1 É talvéz o menino   (It)-is maybe the boy
      2 suspenso na memória.   suspended in memory.
      3 Duas velas acesas   Two candles lit
      4 no fundo do quarto.   at-the back of-the room
      5 E o rosto judaico   And the Jewish face
      6 na estampa, talvéz.   on-the print, perhaps.

B   1 O cheiro do fogão   The smell of-the stove
      2 vário a cada panela.   different for each pot.
      3 São pés caminhando   (They)-are feet walking
      4 na neve, no sertão   on-the snow, in-the desert
      5 ou na imaginação.   or in-the imagination.

C   1 A boneca partida   The doll broken
      2 antes de brincada,   before played (with),
      3 e também uma roda   also a wheel
      4 rodando no jardim,   turning in-the garden,
      5 e o trem de ferro   and the train (of iron)
      6 passando sobre mim   passing over me
      7 tão leve: não me esmaga, so lightly: (it) (does) not crush me
      8 antes me recorda.   (it) reminds me.

D   1 É a carta escrita   (It)-is the letter written
    2 com letras difíceis,   with difficult words,
    3 posta num correio   put in-a post-office
    4 sem selo e censura.   without stamp and censorship
    5 A janela aberta   The open window
    6 onde se debruçam   where (refl) lean-over
    7 olhos caminhantes,   walking eyes,
    8 olhos que te pedem   eyes that ask you
    9 e não sabes dar.   and (you do) not know (how)
                                         to-give (it to them).

E   1 O velho dormindo   The old man sleeping
    2 na cadeira imprópria.   in-the inappropriate chair.
    3 O jornal rasgado.   The newspaper torn.
    4 O cão farejando.   The dog sniffing.
    5 A barata andando.   The roach crawling.
    6 O bolo cheirando.   The cake smelling.
    7 O vento soprando.   The wind blowing.
    8 E o relógio inerte.   And the $inert_2$ $clock_1$.

F   1 O cântico de missa   The hymn of mass
    2 mais do que abafado,   more than subdued,
    3 numa rua branca   in-a $white_2$ $street_1$
    4 o vestido branco   the $white_2$ $dress_1$
    5 revoando ao frio.   fluttering in-the cold.
    6 O doce escondido,   The $hidden_2$ $candy_1$,
    7 o livro probido,   the $forbidden_2$ $book_1$,
    8 o banho frustrado,   the $frustrated_2$ $bath_1$,
    9 o sonho do baile   the dream of the ball
    10 sobre chão de água   on (a) floor of water
    11 ou aquela viagem   or that trip
    12 ao sem-fim do tempo   to-the without-end of time
    13 lá onde não chega   there where (does) not reach
    14 a lei dos mais velhos.   the law of-the elders.

G   1 É o isolamento   (It)-is the isolation
    2 em frente às castanhas,   in front (of) the nuts
    3 a zona de pasmo   the zone of surprise
    4 na bola de som,   in-the ball of sound
    5 a mancha de vinho   the stain of wine
    6 na toalha bêbada,   on the drunk tablecloth,
    7 desgosto de quinhentas   sorrow of five hundred

8 bocas engolindo	mouths swallowing
9 falsos caramelos	false candies
10 ainda orvalhados	still bedewed
11 do pranto das ruas.	by-the crying of-the streets.

H   1 A cabana oca — The hollow$_2$ hut$_1$
2 na terra sem música. — in-the land without music.
3 O silêncio interessado — The silence interested
4 no país das formigas. — in-the country of-the ants.
5 Sono de lagartos — Sleep of alligators
6 que não ouvem o sino. — that (do) not hear the bell.
7 Conversa de peixes — Talk of fish
8 sobre coisas líquidas. — about liquid$_2$ things$_1$.
9 São casos de aranha — (They) are stories of spider(s)
10 em luta com mosquitos. — in fight(s) with mosquitos.
11 Manchas na madeira — Stains on-the wood
12 cortada e apodrecida. — chopped and rotten.
13 Usura de pedra — Meanness of-the stone
14 em lento solilóquio. — in slow monologue.
15 A mina de mica — A mine of mica
16 e esse caramujo. — and this snail.
17 A noite natural — The night natural
18 e não encantada. — and not enchanted.
19 Algo irredutível — Something irreducible
20 ao sopro das lendas — to-the blowing of-the tales
21 mas incorporado — but incorporated
22 ao coração do mito. — to-the heart of-the myth.

I   1 É o menino em nós — (It)-is the boy in us
2 ou fora de nós — or outside of us
3 recolhendo o mito. — gathering the myth.

◎

The most important metaphor in this poem, using the type of metaphorical 'equations' which constitute the formal core of the algebra of metaphorical connectedness sketched in George Lakoff and Mark Johnson's clear and penetrating *Metaphors We Live By*, is 'a life is a year.'

Thus we speak of *the seasons of a person's life*—or *a May-December wedding*. Just as the Brasilians take stock of their year in December, so anyone is free to see this moment as the *dezembro da vida*—the most important, final, framing 'month' of their life. Indeed, this is a poetic vision that finds expression in the poetries of many cultures, possibly all.

> who knows how short their life is?
> who is so wise as to know for certain
> that after this breath that they let out,
> they will draw yet one more breath in?

Thus many poets, like the Samurai warriors who likened their lives to the falling cherry blossoms, live a stance toward life which is wonderfully expressed by a great Indian chief on the day of the battle in which he died:

> today is a good day to die, for all the things
> that are important to me are with me.

So Drummond, in looking for *uma interpretação* of **his** *dezembro*, in finding how his life coheres, has meaning, is not suggesting to us to place importance in the particulars of his life, many of which are too private to communicate fully;

> (indeed, are we not to take their often surreal character as an indication that these images are just variables, place-holders if you like, for the kinds of dreams and fantastic fantasies which any of us will find in our own unconscious life?)

rather, he is a living example of the only stance toward life which 'makes sense', as we say, of his life.

And so we may say, as we can of Brecht's paean of the sorrow, but joy, of the life of political struggle 'An die Nachgeborenen' ('To those who will be born after me'), that this poem is *true* of Drummond, is *part* of his true stance toward life.

I am aware that in saying this I am using a sense of *true* which is far removed from the way logicians and most formal thinkers about semantics choose to refer to truth. These scholars would limit the meaning of true to the relationship of a formal expression, like a string of symbols, or words, and a situation, or model, or world. They might see my usage of true as 'only' metaphor.

Yet each one of us is ultimately responsible for the way we choose to define our terms. We can choose to have a concept of truth which is only one of correspondence—or we can choose to view our lives, in Gandhi's words, as experiments in truth. And we can choose the truths we wish to live.

In Gary Snyder's permanent words,

> The true poem is walking that edge between what can be said and
> that which cannot be said.

The Real Work (p. 21)

Thus I see the study of poetry as being of focal importance to the adequacy
of our most basic notions of formal semantics. Not only are all current formal
approaches to the study of meaning not *preparing* for the day when it will be
time to talk about how meanings—in particular, stances toward life—are
conveyed by the formal structures we find in poetry, but I see formal
semanticists as hoping, by a campaign of silence, that poetry and the problem
posed by its interpretation will simply vanish.

My proposal, which I find inescapable, since I am in love with the beauty of
formal patterns *and* with the transformative power of a great poem, is to look
at poems both with the tightest type of formal machinery for analysis *and* with
the most precise subjective accounts of *the experience* of poetic power.

> If I read a book and it makes my whole body
> so cold no fire can ever warm me, I know that
> it is poetry. If I feel physically as if
> the top of my head were taken off, I know that
> it is poetry. Is there any other way?

Emily Dickinson

I want to know *where* a poem moves one, *how fast* it happens, how long the
feelings last, and so on. I am hampered in my seeking to establish a fusion
between form and meaning by the unavailability of any precise and common
set of terms to describe the obvious and universal fact of poetic power. But we
have to make the best start we can, for otherwise we will be left with a too
limited theory of meaning.

Let us start with the form of this poem. The first thing that strikes us is the
absence of main clauses. Except for four occurrences of the main verb *é* 'is', and

two of *são* 'are', there are no clearly indicated main clauses (the paired verbs *esmaga* 'crush'–*recorda* 'remind' probably are meant to be ambiguously subordinate and independent, and there is a bit of that flavor for the last line of strophe D as well: *e não sabes dar* 'and [which?] you do not know how to give').

How are the six unquestionably main clause occurrences of the copula arranged with respect to the stanzaic structure of the poem? Let us examine a superficial structure in (1), and give *a poetic deep structure* in (2).

(1)	A	(6 lines)	Begins with *é*
	B	(5 lines)	Last sentence begins with *são*
	C	(8 lines)	No copula
	D	(9 lines)	Begins with *é*
	E	(8 lines)	No copula
	F	(14 lines)	No copula
	G	(11 lines)	Begins with *é*
	H	(22 lines)	(Ninth line begins with *são*)
	I	(3 lines)	Begins with *é*

(2)   (a) *Tripartitioning*   (b) *Halving*

I.	A (6)	k	*é*	initial
	B (5)	k−1	*são*	final
	C (8)	k+2	ø	

	A	*é*	initial
	B	*são*	final
	C	ø	
	D	*é*	initial

II.	D (9)	m	*é*	
	E (8)	m−1	ø	
	F (14)	m+5	ø	

┌E   5 present participles
│   1 past participles

III.	G (11)	n	*é*	initial
	H1 (10)	n−1	*são*	final
	H2 (12)	n+1	ø	

└F   1 present participle
5 { 4 past participles and
    1 de-participial noun
    vestido

IV.	I (3)	n	*é*	initial

	G	*é*	initial
	H1	*são*	final
	H2	ø	
	I	*é*	initial

There is only one important difference between (1) and (2)—the number of stanzas. I am arguing that the longest stanza of the poem, H, should be viewed as consisting of two halves: H1, the first 10 lines; and H2, the last 12 lines. I have argued similarly that Frost's 34-line poem 'Out, Out—' is to be seen as consisting of four 'hidden', or deep stanzas, of 9, 9, 8, and 8 lines (cf. Ross 1981). Let us see what the postulation of a 'hidden' stanza-break in the middle of H will buy us.

The poem's 10 deep verses are divided into four sections by the 4 é's. The line structure of the first 3 parts is as shown:

(3) (a) | I | II | III |
|---|---|---|
| 6 lines | 9 lines | 11 lines |
| 5 lines | 8 lines | 10 lines |
| 8 lines | 14 lines | 12 lines |

Thus in these three 'thirds' of the poem, the first of their 3 stanzas have one more line than their second stanzas, and their last stanzas have more lines than their first stanzas. The formula is

$$\boxed{\begin{array}{l} X \\ X-1 \\ X+Y \end{array}}$$

This basic tripartite grouping of three groups of three *stanzas* is followed by a 3-*line* stanza, whose first line has one more word than its second line, in partial consonance with the boxed pattern above. In other words, splitting H into H1 and H2 'makes sense' of the distribution of é, and begins to make sense of the distribution of lines per stanza. I take these symmetries, visible only by splitting H into H1 and H2, as one argument for the correctness of the deep structure in (2a).

The poem can, however, equally well as seen as divided into two 5-stanza halves. The first 4 and last 4 stanzas agree in having the repeated distribution of the copula shown below:

(3) (b) | é | initial |
|---|---|
| são | final |
| ø | |
| é | initial |

Between these two groups of four are two copula-less stanzas exhibiting an antisymmetric distribution of present participles versus past participial forms: 5-1/1-5.

I think that the having sectioning of (2b) can be supported most compellingly be examining another traditional source of poetic structure—the pattern of lexical repetitions.

$$\bigcirc \quad \bigcirc$$

For while the first thing that strikes one about the structure of this poem is surely the lack of main clauses of action—all of the clearly independent clauses are copular—the second thing must surely be the fact that while this poem is quite long, its 86 lines contain very few occurrences of repeated content words. We know from other poems how powerful a device for structuration is provided by the repeating of whole verses (so-called refrains), or whole lines ('Quoth the raven: nevermore') or even just phrases ('A horse! A horse! My kingdom for a horse!').

This is not to say that the reduced clause structure of the poem is unimportant—on the contrary, it is precisely because the clauses are so few and far between that the positioning of the four *é*'s and two *são*'s is such an important indicator of the (twin) deep structure of the poem.

And what I want to argue now is that the same is true of the sparse, but tellingly positioned, instances of lexical repetition. In (4), I have displayed the way this repetition interacts with the halving sectioning of (2b).

The dominant fact of this network of repetition is of course the repetition of *menino* 'boy'.[3] It is also the longest span for any repetition, extending from line A.1 to line I.1, a distance of 83 lines. It is also the most all encompassing repetition, with one exception; namely, the repetition that ends the poem—*mito* 'myth'. The arc from $_1$*menino* to, $_{84}$*menino* encloses all other paired words. It is, by the way, extremely relevant that there are no terms repeated more than twice—this is a poem of pairings.

This predominance of pairing, and the theme of the poem—the December of recollection, of appraisal—leads me to see the sonata form—A-B-A—as the major structural figure that this poem manifests. Memory is seen, in the metaphorical system fossilized in the morphological prefix *re-*, as a return; the use of this morpheme is particularly luxuriant in English (re-member, re-call, re-mind, re-collect), but it is visible in Brasilian, too: *re-cordar*. Etymologically, the stem of this verb, *cord-*, is the Latin noun *cor*, 'heart'. Thus memory was seen as a calling to heart, in Roman times. I doubt that this image is alive for the typical speaker of Portuguese however. We say in English: *I called to mind how it was to be a child*. The image is that the scenes of childhood are 'out' of our conscious mind, but that they are sentient enough to obey a summons, so that when we 'call' to them, they obey us and return.

(4)

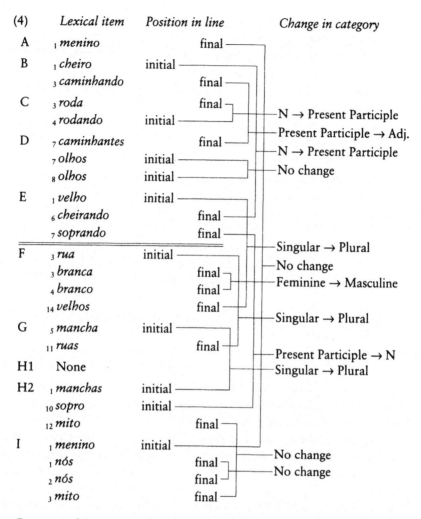

	Lexical item	Position in line	Change in category
A	₁ *menino*	final	
B	₁ *cheiro*	initial	
	₃ *caminhando*	final	
C	₃ *roda*	final	
	₄ *rodando*	initial	N → Present Participle
			Present Participle → Adj.
D	₇ *caminhantes*	final	N → Present Participle
	₇ *olhos*	initial	No change
	₈ *olhos*	initial	
E	₁ *velho*	initial	
	₆ *cheirando*	final	
	₇ *soprando*	final	
F	₃ *rua*	initial	Singular → Plural
	₃ *branca*	final	No change
	₄ *branco*	final	Feminine → Masculine
	₁₄ *velhos*	final	
G	₅ *mancha*	initial	Singular → Plural
	₁₁ *ruas*	final	
			Present Participle → N
H1	None		Singular → Plural
H2	₁ *manchas*	initial	
	₁₀ *sopro*	initial	
	₁₂ *mito*	final	
I	₁ *menino*	initial	
	₁ *nós*	final	No change
	₂ *nós*	final	No change
	₃ *mito*	final	

Drummond is concerned with illuminating this process. Implicit in the poem is the idea that there is in him a mythic boy and that re-membering is rebecoming that boy. This is how we first understand the first modifier in the poem: *suspenso na memória* 'suspended in memory' suggests that one's memory is a bit like a museum. The use of the preposition *em* 'in' (here in the allomorph *n-*) suggests that memory has an interior, has contents. One thing that Drummond's memory contains is a boy, suspended—in suspended animation. What follows is a series of images from a possible childhood—two candles burning in a bedroom; the framed picture of Christ—a typical part of most country homes in Brasil. And then come the smells of childhood, mixing and intertwining, different from each pot. And this intertwining of smells is now a metaphor for the way the early memories mix and interact, with the way imagination blends in with 'reality'.

So as we begin to read this poem, once we have heard that its title concerns the interpretation of the final month, when we start with the verb *é* '(it)-is', we may assume that the subject of this copula is the head noun of the title: *interpretação*. So we hear Drummond as saying that the interpretation is (possibly) the boy within him, who is suspended, lifeless, in the museum of his memory.

But as the poem proceeds through its images, often hard to interpret or surreal (e.g., *usura da pedra* 'the meanness of the stone'), we return to a boy, in line I.1—but one line after the first mention of *o mito*—the myth. And then Drummond gives us a new view of memory, with the final occurrence of *é*.

> É o menino em nós
> ou fora de nós
> recolhendo o mito.

Here there is a boy no longer in suspended animation; here there is an actor—the subject of a volitional predicate of gathering. The root verb *colher* means 'harvest'—the poem's final verb suggests that its agentive subject is engaged in a project of construction, of assembly. This verb, like its translation 'gather', typically occurs with a plural object. This metaphorically imposes a view of myth as an assemblage, a collage of disparate elements which are somehow to be fitted together to make a larger entity. Thus the many images of this poem arc the parts of an organic whole. And Drummond has dropped the uncertainty that the double occurrence of *talvéz* 'perhaps' conveys—once at the beginning of the first sentence A, once at the end of the last sentence. But the boy who was the object of the verb *suspender* in A, and who was meta-phorically seen as within the poet, has become alive, and has a life of his own (*fora de nós* 'outside of us'), as well as in us, and is now the agent of the last verb of the poem: *recolhendo*.

And the person of the poem has changed, too. The poem's nouns are all third person, with the exception of the three references to the first person singular at the end of C,

> passando sobre *mim*   'passing over me
> tão leve; não *me* esmaga   so lightly: not me it-crushes
> antes *me* recorda   rather me it-reminds'

and the two references to the second person at the end of D (the verb *sabes* has a second person singular inflection).

| olhos que *te* pedem | 'eyes that you they-ask |
| e não sabes dar | and not you-know (how) to-give' |

Thus the poem goes from referring to the poet in the first person singular, to including him in a generalized second person singular (perhaps the most accurate translation in English would use 'one': 'eyes that ask something of one, and one doesn't know how to give it to them'), to speaking of all of us, in the last verse.

And concurrent with that change in person is the change from a static, suspended boy within Drummond to an active gathering boy, who is the child within all of us and simultaneously outside us.

So it is far too simplistic to ascribe to this poem the structural figure A-B-A— the 'second' A is no mere copy of the first. This re-calling, re-harvesting, has had a great impact on Drummond, and on us. Just as this voyage into his mythic past changes Drummond's perception of memory, and of his relationship to the boy that he believed to live suspended within him, it changes ours. In Gary Snyder's words, Drummond has gone beyond his own self to express all of our selves.

This voyage of discovery is a necessary trip, but not necessarily a smooth one. While A is very well-behaved structurally, in that it consists of three two-line sentences, and has no grammatical surprises, or surreal flashes, B is not so predictable. First of all, it introduces the first three-line sentence, with a bang: *são* 'are' (third plural). What is the subject of this plural verb? Implicit in the adjective *vário* 'various' is the notion that there are many smells coming from the stove, but there is no way that the implied subject of *são* can comfortably, placidly, refer to these smells. And even if they could be the subject of *são*, its object is *pés* 'feet'. How can smells be feet? Only in the land of metaphor.

But it is clear that we are in a strange land as we proceed with the line after *caminhando* in B: snow is not a normal experience in Brasil, let alone in December. Whatever they are (and the poem never erases our uncertainty) that are feet walking, they walk in a land of wild contrasts—snow, desert (*sertão* has the connotation of the burning heat of the Sahara), and, finally, the bang that the first three-line sentence ends with—these feet walk in the imagination.

If B has departed from the grammatical and imagistic tranquility of A, C represents an even more radical departure; again, as in B, both at the beginning and at the end of its last (and also first) sentence. The word *brincada* derails the syntax of Brasilian. It is the feminine singular form of the past participle of the verb *brincar* 'to play', being used, since it is the object of the compound preposition *antes de* 'before', as a noun. However, while some feminine past participles have a use as nouns (for example, *querida*, the past participle of *querer* 'to want', means 'darling [woman]'), there is no such use for *brincada*. Also, just as we require 'with' to precede toys that are the object of the English verb *play* (cf. **I played my yoyo*), so *brincar* would require *com* 'with', and the combination of verb plus preposition never allows passives in Brasilian: there is no passive sentence corresponding to *This yoyo must not be played with!* Thus the first clause of C ends with a bucket of syntactic ice water in the face.

And the last line of C is another: *recordar*, a slightly poetic, formal, verb, has only a reflexive use, with personal objects—it can never have a subject like *o trem de ferro* with a first person object, *me*. Thus the coming of the train, an event around which life would revolve in the kind of Brasilian country village Drummond's *menino* might have grown up in (I have heard that village girls would bathe and put on pretty clothes to prepare for the arrival of the train), has a disruptive effect on the poet: he lets the train roll over him, metaphorically, and the train 'remembers him'.

I should also note that the structure of the discourse itself is rent at this point in the poem. The colon after *tão leve* 'so lightly' in line C.7 is the only sentence-closing line-internal punctuation in the poem (there are two internal commas—one before the important word *talvéz* in line A.6, and one after *na neve*, in line B.4, which rhymes with *tão leve* and is in the corresponding place in the previous verse), and is the only case in the poem in which a clause ends in mid-line. What is the syntactic status of the *esmaga-recorda* construction that follows this colon? Is it a subordinate clause, being semantically subordinate to *tão* 'so', like the *that*-clause in a *so-that* construction? Or is it a main clause? I think Drummond intends this to be an irresolvable ambiguity. The extent to which the reader of *antes de brincada* and *me recorda* has to jettison the traditionally conceived normality of Brasilian grammar in order to fight their way to an interpretation is matched by the necessity of jettisoning the distinction between main and dependent proposition in syntax, a cornerstone of grammatical structure.

○

Let me recapitulate. I have been demonstrating how the poem begins its voyage of interpretation with a boy suspended in memory, and ends with a boy whom we contain and who contains us. This voyage goes through a space in which time is no longer relevant. Thus E ends with a reference to the inert clock, and F ends with the reference to a voyage to a place where time itself has been suspended, and where the law of the adult world—that events happen in sequence, that the sense of events is this sequence or the causal laws inferred to underlie it—does not penetrate. This land of memory is not a land of clauses, where subjects impose their wills upon objects. It is a land of nouns of all kinds—sights, smells, sounds, tactile experiences, all jumbled together, a land with no clear demarcation of main and subordinate clauses, a land where dream and reality fuse and become inseparable.

The voyage begins gradually, but by D, the feet which metaphorically walk in the imagination have given way to personified eyes—eyes that lean out over windowsills, that walk, that ask us for something, something we cannot give. And when we return from this land, we are differently the same.

Thus I would suggest that rather than saying that the main structural figure of the poem is the simple A-B-A of the sonata, we should see the figure as that of (5).

(5)   A B A'

Armed with this abstract concept, let us now reexamine the network of repetitions displayed in (4). The predominant fact that emerges is that most of the words that repeat are repeated with a difference either in grammatical category or in position within the line they occupy. This point is made most clearly by the first repeated pair in the poem: *roda/rodando* in C, which exhibits, in adjacent lines, a change of both types. The next completed pair is formed by *caminhantes*, an adjectival form with a meaning that is almost identical to that of the other member of its pair, *caminhando*. There is a morphosyntactic difference—the first form, being highly verbal, does not agree in number and gender with the masculine plural *pés* 'feet' which it modifies, while *caminhantes* agrees with the masculine plural *olhos* 'eyes' in number.

I note in passing that there are five body parts mentioned in the poem: *rosto* in A, *pés* in B, *olhos* (twice) in D, *bocas* in G, *coração* in H. All occur as the first lexical items in their lines. The first and last are singulars, the middle three are plurals. The first two plurals—*pés* and *olhos*—are highlighted by virtue of the fact that they are followed by the highly salient repetition of two derivatives of the verbal root *caminh*—'walk'. The third, *bocas*, is also followed in its line by a quadrisyllabic present participle—*engolindo* 'swallowing'. The three plural nouns support the tripartitioning diagrammed in (2a): each three-stanza third of the poem contains one plural reference to a body part.

The next pair of words we encounter are the two occurrences of *olhos*, at the beginning of lines D.7 and D.8. Except for the two *mitos*, in the last four lines of the poems, the two occurrences of *olhos* constitute the only lexical repetition with no change in category or position. However, on a higher level, the fact that in the first half of the poem the only pair of such unchanging lexical repeaters is line-*initial*, while the corresponding pair in the second half is line-*final* contributes to the theme of difference within sameness which the pattern of repetition seems concerned with developing.

Following the two occurrences of *olhos*, we come to the pair *velho–velhos*, which differ in position and number. They are also located in an important way for the hypothesis of (2b)—that the poem exhibits a halving structure. For in the structure of (2b), there are two central stanzas, E and F, which share the properties of being copula-less and of each exhibiting a striking number of line-final participles, present participles in E, past in F. As we see, the pair of *velho–velhos* serves to bracket this participial center of the poem.

As we proceed through stanza E, we come to two adjacent lines, E.6 and E.7, which are highlighted by the pattern of repetition. The present participle *cheirando* is the line-final 'repetition' of the line-initial masculine singular noun *cheiro*; the present participle *soprando* is the line-final precursor of the line-initial masculine singular noun *sopro*. The A-B-B-A structure of these two pairs thus takes us on a kind of journey, from nominality, through verbality (or at least participiality), and back to normality. This noun-participle-participle-noun substructure runs from the seventh line from the beginning of the poem to the sixth line from its end, *almost* an identical distance, which may be significant—I do not know. The 75-line span of the A-B-B-A structure is roughly coextensive with the 83-line span of the two occurrences of *menino*, but since the first *menino* is 6 lines before *cheiro*, and the last *menino* is not 6 lines but 3 after *sopro*, I am not sure that there is any fact of structural relevance for our understanding of the poem in the rough coextensiveness of these two spans.

I see greater importance in the meaning of the noun phrase in the line that immediately follows *cheirando* and *soprando*: *o relógio inerte* 'the inert clock'. Here, at the dead center of the poem, time has stopped. The laws of this land of the imagination are not oriented around an even flow of time. If there were a sequentiality to the images that Drummond presents to us, the poem could have been written in normal tense clauses, whose relations of temporal succession or inclusion could have been indicated by the tense system of the verbs in question. But instead, there is *a simultaneity of presence* of the images conveyed by the poem's noun phrases. Hence the inert clock, which is an image in consonance not only with the timelessness of the imagination, but also with the slowness of the pace of small-town life. This theme of timelessness is taken up again at the end of F—where there is a reference to 'that voyage to the endlessness of time'.

In the second half of the poem, we encounter first the pair *rua–ruas*. I call *rua* in F.3 initial, even though it is preceded by two syllables, because these syllables are a non-lexical preposition and article combination. Then we find the line-adjacent pair *branca* (fem.)–*branco* (masc.) 'white', both line-final, in lines F.3 and F.4. In the first half, there are two repetitions on adjacent lines: *roda/rodando*, and *olhos/olhos*, both of whose second occurrences are line-initial. The two corresponding adjacent line pairs in the second half both have their second occurrences line-final. The parallel is less than perfect, however, for while all adjacent repeating forms are line-final in the second half, only three of the four in the first half are line-initial. Still, the fact that the four line-adjacent pairs are as follows:

(6)   *Line-initial*   *Line-final*
                                          roda

      rodando

      olhos
      olhos

---
                                          branca
                                          branco

                                          nós
                                          nós

with the first pair in each half exhibiting the final vowels *o–a*, and the second pair being identical and nominal (and ending in [s]), may constitute enough of a pattern to be perceptible poetically.

There is one more connection between the two pairs *olhos–olhos* and *branca–branco*. Note that while the first pair is in D, the stanza opening in the middle third of the tripartitioning in (2a), the second pair is in F, the stanza closing this third. The first occurrence of *olhos*, in line D.7, is followed by the second repetition of a form of *caminh-*, and is thus linked to stanza B, part of the first third of the poem. Correspondingly, the first occurrence of the pair in *branc-*, namely *branca*, in line F.3, is preceded by *rua*, which is repeated in G, a stanza in the last third of (2a). Thus the distribution of the poem's two inner line-adjacent repetitions contributes to the tripartitioning of the poem.

The next second-half repetition is the pair *mancha* (fem. sing.)–*manchas* (fem. plur.), both line-initial. The span of this repetition is 17 lines, which corresponds exactly to the span of the pair *caminhando–caminhantes* in the first half. Significantly, I believe, these two 17-line repetitions go from the second to the fourth of the five stanzas in each half (under the hypothesis that the printed stanza H is to be segmented into H1 and H2, in the same way as is necessary for the tripartitioning diagrammed in [2a]). The shift of the 17-line repeaters from line-final in the first half to line-initial in the second half is one of the strongest cases for positing an initial-final interchange in line position as a central structural transformation in the architecture of this poem.

The final two repetitions I will treat together, as they form an A-B-B-A substructure in the last four lines of the poem. The interior repeater is *nós* 'us', which I have included in my discussion of repeating elements, even though it is not a lexical item, but rather a grammatical element. I make this analytical decision because of the way *nós* completes the pattern of repeaters in adjacent lines, which I have diagrammed in (6), and because of the saliency of the A-B-B-A ending of the poem, and also for some phonetic reasons, which I will turn to below. I emphasize, however, that this is a tentative conclusion. Possibly, more powerful symmetries can be shown to result from the exclusion of *nós*— I merely have found none thus far.

So we come, finally, to the repetition which closes the poem: *mito* 'myth'. This is, except for the two line-adjacent repeaters, *olhos* and *nós*, the only repetition in which there is neither a change of grammatical status nor of line position. In a structural sense, then, *mito* is unique, a fact which is congruent with the focal importance of the notion of myth in the interpretation of this poem.

For the poem concerns the relationship between boy and myth, between real and surreal, between Drummond's memory of his past—a part of his myth of himself—and the general myth of childhood, which all of us share, to a greater or lesser extent.

Let me summarize, in the diagram in (7), a skeletal version of (4) what I have said in the above discussion of the structure of this poem's repetitions.

The poem is halved by the placement of the two 17-line repeaters, each linking the second and fourth stanzas of its half, each changing in grammatical form, while remaining unchanged in line position. There are four repeating pairs in adjacent lines (these pairs are indicated by a prefixed '<'), two per half. The first half's pairs involve line-initial position; the second half's pairs are line-final. The first pair in each half involves a noun modifier and manifests a grammatical change, while the second pair in each half is nominal and does not change. The relationship of the two *types* of repetitions—and the 17-line re-

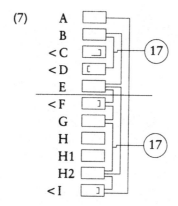

peaters on the one hand, and the line-adjacent pairs on the other—manifests the dance between beginning and end of line which characterizes this poem. Thus in the first half, while the 17-line repeaters on the root *caminh-* 'walk' are line-final, the two line-adjacent pairs involve the beginnings of lines. On the other hand, in the second half, the 17-line repeaters are line-initial, while the line-adjacent pairs are line-final.

Let us turn our attention now for a moment to the repetitions that involve a change in line position. As we proceed through the poem, the first members that we encounter of such pairs alternate with respect to where they occur in their lines, as shown in (8).

(8)   *menino*   occurs first line-finally
        cheir-   occurs first line-initially
        rod-   occurs first line-finally
        velho-   occurs first line-initially
        sopr-   occurs first line-finally

Note that all these alternations in line position begin in the first half—the last being one line before the mention of *o relógio inerte*. My guess is that there is a meaning to this distribution: that the dance of forms from one end to the other is an indexical sign of the passage of time. The lines of this poem are all of roughly the same length (they run from 5 to 8 syllables in spoken length), so moving back and forth in lines is a bit like moving in time. Is it too far-fetched to see the moves from one end of the line to the other as similar to the ticking of the pendulum of an abstract clock? And it is clear that the images in the first half of the poem, while they do contain some flashes of the surreal (especially in connection with the images surrounding *olhos* 'eyes'), are vastly different in flavor from those we find in the second half. When time stops, the present, active participles of E give way to the past, stative participles of F, and we enter the land of the surreal.

I will assume, then, that the two sectionings of the poem that I propose in (2) are to be held simultaneously in our consciousness. The residual clausal structure of the poem suggests, by the positioning of the poem's six copular verbs, a division into three 3-stanza sections, with a 3-line coda (cf. [2a]). The architecture of the eleven pairs of repeating words supports a division into two 5-stanza halves.

The question that immediately poses itself, however, is why? Why should this poem manifest a simultaneous 2- and 3-part structuring? Is there any other feature of the poem that can be tied into such a covalent sectioning? And why should the two sectionings be into 2 and 3 parts, rather into 2 and 5 parts, or 3 and 7, or any other conceivable pairing?

The tentative answer I wish to suggest is that the two most important words in the poem, *menino* [minínu] and *mito* [mítu], the only two lexical nouns in the last 3-line stanza, are so close in sound that Drummond has used their similarity to make what I can only call, for want of a better term, a deep pun. The 2-part sectioning corresponds to the two syllables of *mito*, the 3-part sectioning, to the three syllables of *menino*.

The painter Degas, bemoaning his lack of success as a poet to Mallarmé, said he was unable to understand his failure, since he had lots of ideas. Mallarmé's reply was: 'Ce n'est point avec des idées, mon cher Degas, que l'on fait des vers. C'est avec des mots.' ('It is not at all with ideas, my dear Degas, that one writes poems. It is with words.')[4]

What this means, among other things, is that the lexicon of each language makes certain poems possible that can 'work' only in that language, for only there are two concepts close enough in sound for a poet to use their verbal art to bring the words within hailing distance, let them dance together.[5] In this poem Drummond undertakes this task, to illuminate the concept of memory, of childhood, of our myths of ourselves, of the dream of reality, and the reality of dream.

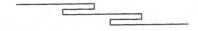

A great poem is like a hologram—it says its unsayabilities not once, or in one place, but throughout its structure, in many ways, on many levels, with many simultaneities.[6] We find the play of two and three in many places in this poem,

more than I will have space to trace in detail. I will begin with some of the most
salient manifestations.

The first stanza consists of three sentences, each two lines long. The number
of nouns per sentence does an alternating dance between two and three—in the
first sentence has 2, the second 3, the third 2 again. Each sentence contains a
noun phrase (NP) of the form shown in (9).

(9)   Article-Head Noun-Modifier-Prepositional Phrase (PP)

When we examine the sequence of the three head nouns, we find many ways
in which the message of alteration, a kind of interpenetration, is conveyed.

(10)	Definiteness	Number	Gender
o menino	+	singular	masculine
duas velas	–	plural	feminine
o rosto	+	singular	masculine

The nouns which head the PPs that follow the noun of (10), *memória* (fem),
fundo (masc.), and *estampa* (fem.) also alternate, but only in gender. Finally,
note how the central structural figure of the poem's repeated nouns—the dance
between ends of lines—is prefigured by the positioning of *talvéz*: early in line
A.1, final in line A.6. The two past participles of A, *suspenso* and *acesas*, make
the same transition from line-initial to line-final. Meanwhile, the three head
nouns of (10) move steadily from line-final position in line A.1, through line-
medial position in line A.3, to being one syllable from the beginning of line A.5.
One last comment on the first stanza: the other main structural and conceptual
figure of the poem—the A-B-A', the return changed, from the journey—is also
articulated by the three instantiations of the syntactic frame given in (9). Note
how the third sentence of A differs from the first not only in the positioning of
talvéz, but also with respect to the fact that while the first two postnominal
modifiers of the head nouns of (10) are past participles, the third modifier is
the poem's first adjective: *judaico* 'Jewish'. So the first stanza has a lot of work
to do: it exemplifies the interpenetration of two and three, it inaugurates the
dance of beginnings and endings of lines, and it simultaneously provides the
first instance of the A-B-A' figure of (5).

When we proceed to the second stanza, we know, from the discussion of (3)
above, that this stanza must have five lines, one less than the six lines of A, so
that the tripartitioning figure of (3a) can be served. How, then, will Drummond

keep the ball in the air of juggling threeness and twoness? The solution for this poem is to change from the three sentences of A to two sentences in B—the first, a sentence of two lines, the second, of three. And what of the number of nouns per sentence, which went from two to three and back to two, in three sentences of A? Well, we see that the first sentence of B has the expected number of nouns—three. But there is a difference—for the first time, we find an odd-numbered line, B.1, which has *two* nouns in it: *o cheiro do fogão* 'the smell of the stove'. To this point, the only two-noun line has been the even-numbered A.4. This is the first taste of another pervasive process we will find hologrammed throughout the course of this poem (and many others)—the decay of pattern.[7] The first pattern to decay in B is the one just mentioned—one noun per odd line. The next pattern to go is that of the triple alternation—in definiteness, number, and gender—of the head noun, which I called attention to in (10). The two head nouns of B, *o cheiro* (definite singular masculine) and *pés* (indefinite plural masculine), alternate in only the first two of these features. Thus the triple alternation becomes a double one.

However, the alternation in gender between the head nouns in odd lines has been replaced by a similar alternation in gender between the head nouns in adjacent lines: *cheiro* (masc.), *panela* (fem.), *pés* (masc.), *neve* (fem.), *sertão* (masc.), *imaginação* (fem.). Note that the last three of these six nouns are preceded by the same sequence of fused prepositions (*em* 'in') plus definite article (*a* [fem.], *o* [masc.]) which appears in the even lines of A. Thus what has happened in the transition from A to B is that the pairing of the syntactic figure given in (9) and the principle of alternation, which produces A-B-A (B-A...) structures, has begun to weaken. In A, the head noun in the odd lines was always of opposite gender from the noun that followed the preposition in the even line, and the gender alternation could be seen as working on three pairs of nouns *in tandem*. In B, on the other hand, while the structure of (9) is still in evidence in each of B's two sentences, the tandem structure has faded out. Thus a syntactic and conceptual structure has begun to decay.

When we consider the number of nouns per sentence, we see that the first sentence of B has three—the number we would expect, for the continuation of the 2-3-2 alternation of the sentences of A. But the second sentence of B has four nouns—and the 2-3-2-3 alternation in noun number in the first four sentences of the poem is never reestablished.

However, there is a larger pattern involving the dance of three and two, and it persists a bit further into the poem. This pattern is based upon the number of head nouns per stanza. The first stanza has three, as shown in (10); the second has two—*cheiro* and *pés*; the third has three again—*boneca* 'doll', *roda* 'wheel', and *trem* 'train'; and the fourth stanza again has two—*carta* 'letter', and *janela* 'window'. But this pattern, too, disappears—after the first four stanzas, I can detect no regularity in the distribution of the number of *head* nouns per stanza.

But let us examine one last numerical property of the distribution of nouns—the number of nouns per stanza. In A, there are seven, with a pattern emerging of one noun per line, except for one two-noun line, where the two nouns are in construction, the second subordinated to the first by the preposition *de* 'of' (contracted to *do* by a morphological rule: $de + o \rightarrow do$ 'of the'). The second stanza also has a total of seven nouns, and again, one line (B.1) manifests the constructional pattern N_1 *de* N_2. The third stanza has five unexceptionable nouns (*boneca, roda, jardim, trem,* and *ferro* [these last two again being linked by *de*]), one highly fishy noun, *brincada* (cf. the discussion above), and one stressed pronoun, *mim*—the first non-third-person nominal. I think we are justified in seeing a repetition of the number seven again here, so I will treat *mim* as a full NP, differently from the way I propose to treat the two occurrences of the unstressed first person singular clitic pronoun *me* in lines C.7 and C.8. These two lines thus constitute the first flaw in another strong pattern—every line of the poem contains (at least) one NP.

When we pass on to stanza D, we find another kind of perturbation in the basic pattern of seven NPs per stanza. There are indeed seven distinct nouns in D (*carta, letras, correio, selo, censura, janela,* and *olhos*) but there are eight NPs, because *olhos* occurs twice, as the head of two NPs in an appositional relationship with one another. So the seven per stanza pattern survives, but on tottery legs. Note, too, that the pattern of one N_1 *de* N_2 construction per stanza has also been weakened; there are no occurrences of *de* in D, and the closest approximation to a N_1 *de* N_2 construction is the conjoined NP in line D.4. Note also the further decay of the one NP per line pattern—in D, there are two more nounless lines—lines D.6 and D.9.

When we come to the two participial stanzas, which straddle the dividing lines of (2b), we arrive at the last places where it makes any sense to see a pattern of sevening for nouns. In E, there are in fact eight nouns, one per line, but seven *head* nouns, and one (*cadeira,* in E.2) subordinated to a preceding noun by the preposition *em* (fused with the article to produce *na*). In F, again there are seven head nouns (*cântico, vestido, doce, livro, banho, sonho,* and *viagem*), with ten other nouns subordinated to them in various ways. One point of similarity between the two groups of seven head nouns in E and F is that each stanza has six masculines, and one feminine (*barata* in E.5; *viagem* in F.11).

To conclude this section, let me summarize a bit. At the outset, I was concerned with demonstrating how Drummond helps fusion of the trisyllabic *menino* and the disyllable *mito* by constructing patterns that either are simultaneously three-ish and two-ish (cf. [2]), or alternate between three and two (as in the number of nouns per sentence, or the number of head nouns per stanza). In the course of discussing these latter patterns, it became necessary to document the general tendency of the poem to establish patterns and then to let them fade out.

I will conclude my discussion of the poem with a brief look at its sound structure. Unfortunately, it is such a long poem that I have only the rudiments of an understanding of the way this level of linguistic structure coheres with the syntactic, lexical, and semantic patterns I have discussed above.

I will start with the poem's meter. Of the poem's 86 lines, 60 are pronounced with six syllables, 18 with seven, 7 with five, and only one with eight. It would take too long to describe the various contraction rules which collapse adjacent vowels across word boundaries into single syllables, and for the level of detail with which I will be examining the poem's meter, this will not be necessary. But the interested reader will find the lone 8-syllable line in H.3, and the seven 5-syllable lines in lines A.6, C.5, D.1, D.9, G.4, I.1, and I.2. I note that the five among these seven that have final stress are all located in the first stanzas in the tripartitioning in (2)—in A, line A.6; in D, line D.9; in G, line G.4; and the first two lines of I. Thus this rare type of line supports the 3-part structure of (2a).

I have not yet found any rationale for the way the poem's 7-syllable lines are distributed, with the exception of the extremely regular pattern of alternating 6- and 7-syllable lines which begins in line H.1, and extends, with the exception of the lone 8-syllable line in H.3, uninterruptedly until line H.15, *a mina de mica*, a line highlighted by the repetition of the important syllable [mi] occurring under stress. I will return to the significance of [mi] presently. It is probably of significance that this line, which ends a sequence of extremely bizarre or surreal images, occurs immediately before the line *e esse caramujo*, 'and this snail', which contains the poem's only proximal demonstrative, possibly a signal of the poet's return to this world, the 'real' one. The conjunction *e* 'and' which begins this line is the first to occur between the lines of a two-line coordinate 'sentence' (I say 'sentence' here because for this poem, bare noun phrases correspond to sentences). The only other coordinating conjunction to occur between lines of a two-line sentence is located in the immediately following sentence, whose content seems to speak of the return from the land of dreams:[8] *A noite natural / e não encantada* 'The night [which is] natural and not enchanted'.

As an aside, I note that the function of the poem's twelve coordinating conjunctions seems to be to delineate the boundaries of the surreal (and also to articulate the halving structure of [2b]). Each half of the poem contains five line-initial conjunctions, and one line-medial one, in the first sentence of the fourth stanza of each half—in line D.4 and in the second line of H2. The conjunctions also manifest the phenomenon of structural decay—the first three introduce the fifth lines of the first three stanzas. This pattern is broken by the mediality of the next conjunction, in the *fourth* line of D, and by the fact that D is the first stanza to exhibit a doubled conjunction—the *e* of its final line. E returns to the pattern of one per stanza, again in the final line. F also has just one conjunction, not in the final line, to be sure, but before the head noun of the last main 'clause' of F—*viagem*. And then comes the most surreal third of the poem—stanzas G, H1, and H2. The first two of these lack coordinating conjunctions entirely, and the return of the line-initial occurrences of *e* before *esse* 'this' and *não encantada* 'not enchanted', followed, three lines later, by the poem's only *mas* 'but', seems to bespeak a return to normality, to the humdrum images of 'this' world.

I think, then, that the alternation of lines of seven syllables with lines of six (and, in the case of line H.3, of eight syllables) is a poetically significant use of syllable number, for it corresponds pretty closely with the peaking of the unreality of the imagistic content of the poem. Note also that precisely in this part of the poem there is the longest succession of two-line sentences—five in H1, and four in H2. The first eight of these all share the additional property of containing three nouns apiece, except that the fifth sentence of H1 has four nouns, and the first of H2 has two, possibly to highlight the important, but typographically unmarked, boundary between the two parts of H. I see this regularity of punctuation and noun population and the recurrence of the 6–7 syllable count alternation as counterpoints to the wildness of the journey through the land of imagination. It is as if this syntactic and metrical predictability were like a buffer against the onslaughts of the imagination—an anchor, a beacon, to guide the poet home.

However, aside from these first seven even-numbered lines of H1 and H2, I have been unable to discern any systematicity in the placing of 7-syllable (or 5- or 8-syllable, for that matter) lines within the overall fabric of the poem. But before leaving the topic of meter, I want to discuss briefly the basic metrical pattern of the predominant 6-syllable line.

To let the cat out of the bag quickly, the basic structure is that shown in (11).

$$(11) \quad wSw \quad wSw$$

There is a traditional, but rare, term for a 3-syllable foot whose middle syllable is prominent: amphibrach, 'two-armed'. Thus this poem is amphibrachic dimeter. Of the poem's 60 6-syllable lines, 26 are of the form shown in (11).

No other metrical structure has more than 26 occurrences, neither among the poem's 6-syllable lines, nor among the lines with more syllables.

But even in the lines of fewer or more syllables than six, there is a strong amphibrachic flavor present—in all, 85% of the poem's 86 lines end in the wSw sequence of an amphibrachic foot and 54% of the lines begin in an amphibrach. Moreover, it is often the case that the phonetic wSw sequence at the beginning or end of lines is supported by a syntactic boundary: 31 lines begin in an amphibrach followed by a syntactic break, and 27 lines end in an amphibrach that is preceded by one. Needless to say, the abstract pattern in (11) is a metrical analog of the fusion of two and three.

There is much more to be learned about Drummond's variations on the basic pattern shown in (11), but that will have to wait a fuller understanding on my part. And now, I wish to comment briefly on the segmental structure of this poem.

Here, too, I have taken only a few steps. This poem is a long and complex one, and its music seems to depend on principles which I have yet to grasp fully. I will start at the beginning, for it is at the beginning of the great poem that the ground rules for the music on which the whole poem will be built are laid down. It is a bit like the way classical musicians of India tune their sitar or sarod to the notes of the raga that they are about to play. The notes on which the raga is based are like the palette of colors with which the painter works—the great painter harmonizes her or his colors. Rembrandt's early self-portraits are painted in colors that are elastic, flexible, springy—like the young painter himself. And when his later years had weighed him down, the colors with which he painted himself rhymed in their somberness, their heaviness.

Thus said, what is the phonetic structure of the first stanza? Let us examine (12), where I show each syllable separately.

$$(12) \quad _1\varepsilon \text{ taw vé zu mi ní nu}$$
$$_2\text{sus pé su na me mɔ ryə}$$
$$_3\text{du əz vé lə za sé zəs}$$
$$_4\text{nu fú du du kwáh tu}$$
$$_5\text{yu hós tu žu dáy ku}$$
$$_6\text{nʌys tʌ́ pə, taw vés}$$

Possibly the first thing to catch my ear/eye here is the role of the [v]'s, probably because of the saliency of the repetition of the word *talvéz*, as the bearer of the first and last word stresses of this crucial opening stanza. There is already a play of sounds in this first repetition: in line A.1, the underlying /z/ which ends the word has been moved to the beginning of the next syllable, while in line A.6, it has remained in the final syllable, and been devoiced, by a regular phonetic process of Portuguese (and many other languages). Thus already in this first repetition, we are given the suggestion that among the parameters that will be relevant for the hearing of this poem's music are

(13) (a) voiced sound [z] ~ voiceless sound [s]
      (b) open syllable [ve] ~ closed syllable [ves]
           (or possibly better: syllable-initial [zu] ~ syllable-final [ves])
      (c) early in line ~ late in line

There is one more [v], in line A.3, opening the syllable [vɛ]. Thus each of the first three sentences manifests exactly one [v], a pattern which will persist three sentences more into the poem, in the words *vário*, *neve*, and *leve*. The sentences get longer, however, and the focality of the [v]'s is lost, in the general decay of pattern about which I have already spoken. But in A, the sequence [ve-vɛ-ves] already articulates the A-B-A' pattern which is so important for the interpretation of the poem on the level of image or semantics. And it adds one more alternation to the list in (13):

(14)   tense mid vowel [e] ~ lax mid vowel [ɛ]

If it is correct to identify the alternation in vowel height stated in (14) as one of the constitutive ground rules in holding the three sentences of A together vertically—that is, as participating in the one [v] per clause dance—then it is probably right to see this vowel alternation as also being at work in what we might refer to as the 'horizontal dimension' of the poem's construction—the sequence of segments within a line. This is rendered highly likely, it seems to me, because of the location of the two stressed vowels in line A.3 on the two vowels of (14)—on the syllables [vɛ] and [se]. And in line A.1, while we do not find these vowels under stress, we do find, as the first and third syllables, [ɛ] and [ve]. As I have argued above, this first syllable, being the verb *é* 'is', is highlighted structurally because of its salience in defining the tripartite sectioning of (2a). And in the second line of A, while we do not find the two mid vowels of (14), we find the nasalized mid vowel [ẽ], under stress, and a pretonic [e]. What this adds up to is a progression of these pairs of mid front vowels from the beginning toward the end of the first three lines of A, then two lines without any such vowels, with the final occurrence of [e] being the last syllable of line A.6. Thus these mid front vowels seem to be involved in articulating the initial-final dance which is so important to the structure of the poem's repeated lexical elements. The skeletal structure they figure in appears in (15).

(15) *Syllable*
   number: *1st*   *2nd*   *3rd*   *4th*   *5th*   *6th*   *7th*

	1st	2nd	3rd	4th	5th	6th	7th
1.	ɛ		é				
2.		ẽ			e		
3.			ɛ́			e	
4.							
5.							
6.					e		

I come now to a discussion of the poem's nasal consonants. In line A.1, we find the subsequence of the three syllables [mi ní nu], while in line A.2, we find the antisymmetric distribution (one [n], followed by two [m]'s), again on the three adjacent syllables: [na me mɔ]. These three syllables, however, have moved one syllable earlier in the line. Including also nasal vowels (in Portuguese, *m* and *n* always denote *nasalization* of the preceding vowel when postvocalic; they are pronounced as segmental nasals only when a vowel immediately follows them), the distribution of nasality in A is as shown in (16).

(16) *Syllable*
   number: *1st*   *2nd*   *3rd*   *4th*   *5th*   *6th*   *7th*

		1st	2nd	3rd	4th	5th	6th	7th
Line	→ 1.					mi	ní	nu
number	2.		pẽ		na	me	mɔ	
↓	3.							
	4.	nu	fũ					
	5.							
	6.	nʌys	tʌ̃					

As was the case with the distribution of mid front vowels, we see a kind of chiastic pattern, though not as clearly as in (15). Note also that the three occurrences of the preposition *em* 'in' articulate the A-B-A' pattern of (5): the first, *em + a*, is realized as [na]; the second, *em + o*, is realized as [nu]; while the third, *em + a* again, contracts with the following (deep) syllable [is], to produce [nʌys]—like and yet unlike the first [na].

I will digress for a moment to examine the words of the poem in which the sound [m] appears. They are listed in (17).

While I do not understand all of pies in which *m* has a finger, it is clear that it figures in words which are of great importance for the poem's meaning (*menino/mito, memória, imaginação, mim, me, isolamento*; (note that each of these contains an [m] followed by an [i] (or [y], in the case of *memória*), or preceded by an [i], *isolamento*, or both, *imaginação*) or structure (note that the

(17)

	First foot	Second foot	Stressed syllable	Unstressed syllable
A.		menino		mi
		memória	mɔ	me
B.		caminhando		mi
		imaginação		ma
C.		uma		mə
		mim	mĩ	
		me esmaga	ma	mis
		me recorda		mi
D.		caminhantes		mi
E.		dormindo	mĩ	
F.		missa	mi	
	mais			mays
	numa			mə
		mais		mays
G.		isolamento	mẽ	
		pasmo		mu
	mancha		mÃ	
		caramelos	mɛ	
H1.		música	mÃ	
		formigas	mi	
		mosquitos		mu
H2.	manchas	madeira	m	ma
	mina	mica	mi, mi	
		caramujo	mu	
	mas			mas
		mito	mi	
I.	menino			mi
		mito	mi	

two 17-line repeaters, *caminh-* and *mancha(s)* both contain [m], followed in each case by a palatal consonant, [ñ] and [š], in the onset of the next syllable). Remember also that the line *a mina de mica*, the first line to exhibit two stressed syllables beginning with [m], is also the last line of the 7-syllable~6-syllable alternating pattern that begins in H1. Thus this line marks an important structural boundary as well.

As I said at the beginning of the discussion of lexical repetitions, the longest span of a repetition is the move from *menino*, at the end of line A.1, to the *menino* at the beginning of line I.1. Thus [m] makes a long arc from second foot to first in this focal word, and we see in (17) that this transition is prefigured by the distribution of the poem's [m]'s: in the first half, there are no [m]'s in the first-foot syllables, while there are seven in the second half.

(17) also reveals the gradual emergence of the pivotal syllable [mi] under stress: [mi] occurs four times in unstressed syllables in the first half, but the closest we hear to this syllable under stress is the two [mī]'s of *mim* and *dormindo*. Significantly, the first line of the second half has the first stressed [mi]—in *missa* 'mass'. (Parenthetically, I feel that there is a flavor of Catholicism running through this stanza—the white dress, the prohibited book. But I have nothing to add to this observation at present. I feel this to be a loose end in my understanding of the poem.) Stressed [mí] reappears three times before *mito* in line H2.12, the last time *twice* in one line—*mina* and *mica*—with the second of these prefiguring *mito* in having the following syllable begin with a voiceless stop. And it is also obvious from inspection that while the [m]'s in the first half appear preponderantly before unstressed vowels, those in the second half not only occur more before stressed vowels, but are also more numerous than the [m]'s in the first half.

Summing up, then, if one follows the dance of the poem's [m]'s, it seems that they move from positions of lesser prominence to those of greater prominence, they figure centrally in the devices that section the poem into two halves, and their combinations with other segments and syllables are so arranged as to let the reader intuit the coming fusion of the poem's two central words *menino* and *mito*.

Another candidate for participation in a crossing pattern is the vowel [u], which appears twice in the last phrase of line A.1, and then twice in the initial word of line A.2, finally appearing just once in the initial syllable of line A.3. However, since this vowel occurs four times in each of the next two lines, in identical syllabic locations (syllables 1, 3, 4, 6—the four w's of the basic pattern [11]), I am not sure that I am correct in attributing to it a chiastic function. Note that it is just here—in line A.4—that the paired mid front vowels which have appeared in each of the first three lines stop, and while the first three lines have seven syllables apiece, lines A.4 and A.5 inaugurate the six-syllable amphibrachic pattern, both with a syntactic break between syllables three and four. So the appearance of the [u]'s in the four w-positions of these two lines may well be unconnected to the fronting 'motion' in which one observes the [u]'s participating in the first three lines of A. At present, I am too much a beginner in the understanding of the architecture of segment sequences in the lines of a stanza to be able to tell with any certainty. Accordingly, I will have to leave the matter open for the time being.

I will mention only one more candidate for a participant in the general pattern of phonetic crossing which I perceive to be of great importance in the ground rules of this poem. Consider the first two words of line A.1, and the first word of line A.2.

(18)   ɛ   taw   vez
        sus   pē   su

In the first line, we see an open first syllable, a half-closed second syllable (assuming that a post-vocalic glide makes the syllable a bit less open), and a third syllable which is, in underlying representation, closed by its final /z/ (phonetically, of course, this [z] will move to the onset of the next syllable, as shown in the first line of [12]). This sequence of syllable types—open, half open, closed—is precisely mirrored by the three first syllables of line A.2, except that the half-closedness of the syllable [pē] is not evident on the phonetic level, but only underlyingly, for there is strong synchronic motivation for assuming that the correct phonological representation for nasal vowels is a sequence of vowel and nasal consonant, as is the case in the orthography. The first and third vowels of the two sequences (18) are either close phonetically or identical, and their second syllables both start with voiceless stops. Finally, the major syntactic breaks of these two lines immediately follow the first three syllables. Thus the sequences in (18) also provide a case for the importance of chiasmus, on the phonological level.

Let us suppose for the moment that I am correct in my intuition that Drummond has chosen to use phonetic patterns that are chiastic to harmonize with the chiastic patterns I argued obtain in the structure of the poem's lexical repetitions. The question is: Why? What is the symbolic meaning of alternations that connect the beginning of one line with the end of another?

One answer suggests itself immediately—the irrelevance of temporal order, the transcendence of time. *O relógio inerte.*

If I am right in seeing this poem as being concerned with the blurring of boundaries—the boundaries of the 'real' boy in Drummond's past and the myth of that boy he carries within himself (or who carries Drummond within him?)—with the fusing of *menino* and *mito*, then it is only through a visit to a strange land, the land of paradox, of timelessness, of dream, that this fusion can be achieved. The poem is simultaneously tripartite and bipartite; it manifests many patterns that oscillate between twoness and threeness. Drummond's genius takes us from the A of our everyday humdrum life through the B of the surreal world of *imaginação*, where time is of no use to us, where our only lifeline to the person we thought we were before the journey is the regular beat of the meter—seven syllables, six syllables, seven, six—to return to A', to a world of temporality again. We come back dazed, to our present, but it is a richer present, because it is reflected. The myth in us is alive; we are alive in our myth. In the words of the Zen saying,

> Before I studied Zen, the tree was a tree, the lake was a lake, and the mountain was a mountain.
>
> After I had studied for some time, the tree was no longer a tree, the lake was no longer a lake, and the mountain no longer a mountain.
>
> I continued my study, and now the tree is again a tree, the lake again a lake, and the mountain again a mountain.

NOTES

[1] In this note, I wish to acknowledge that Rosalia Dutra was not only the one who introduced me to Drummond's poetry in general, but to this poem in particular. Throughout my work, her insights have been of fundamental importance in whatever I have learned about this poem. I would prefer to list her as a co-author, but I will defer to her preference that I not do so. So I will make do with these words of thanks for her holographic presence in the paper you have before you.

[2] This text is from Drummond (1964:181-82). I have changed the spelling, by removing certain diacritics over *e* and *o* (thus *selo* and *sobre* instead of *sêlo* and *sôbre*), in accordance with current spelling conventions. Otherwise, no change has been made.

[3] I have translated *menino* as 'boy', but it can equally well be used for 'child', especially when in the plural. I know of no way to resolve this ambiguity, nor do I think Drummond intends us to do so.

[4] This quote is taken from a masterful study of one of Yeats' poems (cf. Jakobson and Rudy [1980]).

[5] I argue in Ross (1981), that Frost does the same thing in his poem 'Out, Out—' where the noun *saw* is fused with the past tense of the verb *see*, in another deep 'pun'.

[6] This point has been apparent to everyone who has fallen under the spell of the structure of a poem, though I may have been the first to suggest the metaphor of the hologram to help with the visualization of the claim. Cf. Ross (1982).

⁷ This is the primary device I call attention to in the poem I study in Ross (1982).

⁸ In Ross (1981), I call attention to a similar linkage between coordinate structure and the predictability of everyday life.

REFERENCES

Drummond de Andrade, Carlos. 1964. Obra completa. Rio de Janeiro: Companhia Aguilar.

Jakobson, Roman, and Stephen Rudy. 1980. Yeats' 'Sorrow of Love' through the years. Poetics Today 2.1a, 97-125.

Lakoff, George, and Mark Johnson. 1980. Metaphors we live by. Chicago: University of Chicago Press.

Ross, Haj. 1981. Robert Frost's 'Out, Out—': A way in. In Wolfgang Klein and Willem J.M. Levelt (eds.), Crossing the boundaries in linguistics. pp. 265-82. Dordrecht: D. Reidel.

———. 1982. Poems as holograms, poetics as holograms. Poetics Journal 2, 3-11.

Snyder, Gary. 1980. The real work. New York: New Directions.

Index

abstract nouns, definite article with, 152

abstract pronoun, 89

amphibrachic dimeter, 185-86, 190

anaphoric items, 68, 77-78, 147, 150

antecedent, dislocated, 93

assertions, Brazilian Portuguese directives, 123-25

associative relations, 151-52

assumed familiarity, 144, 149-51

atonic vowels, 34, 39

authority, confronting, 123

auxiliary verbs, tense and, 73

Avoid Pronoun Principle, 70-71

Azores, ix

Bell Telephone Laboratories, 32

Berlitz, x

binding theory, 67-81

Brazilian Portuguese: coordinate structures and, 91-93; discourse-oriented, 96; empty subjects in, 87-100; inflection and, 98, 99; monophthongization and, 14-15; oxytones and, 23-36; politeness strategies and, 121-39; prepausal lengthening, 11-12; proparoxytones and, 23-36; relative clauses and, 93-94; stress and rhythm in, 3-29; subject pronominal and, 92-93; syllabicity shifts and, 15-19; transitional state, 98, 99; unstressed vowels, 31-41

Brazilian Portuguese directives, 121-39; avoidance of, 125-26, 128, 135; base form of, 126-29; force of, 122, 125, 126-28; learnability, 128-29; variation in form of, 123

Brazilian Portuguese stress, 3-29; alternating patterns, 25-26; degrees of, 10; diphthongization and, 9-10; instrumental evidence, 5-6; phonological evidence, 6-22; phonological processes, 9-22; primary, 24; secondary, 24; timing, 26-27

'A Cabra e Francisco' ('The Goat and Francisco') (Drummond de Andrade), 145, 154-59

Capeverdean diminutives, 53-63

Cape Verde Islands, ix

Carioca dialect, diphthongization and, 9-10

carnaval, 162

chiasmus, 191

child, directives to, 129-31, 136

children's speech, directives in, 128, 129

chromograph, 32

ABOUT THE EDITORS

DONALDO P. MACEDO is Director, Graduate Bilingual/ESL Program, at the University of Massachusetts, Boston. He earned his Ph.D. in Language Behavior at Boston University. A nationally recognized figure in linguistics, Macedo is the author (with Paulo Freire) of *Literacy: Reading the World and Reading the Word* (1987) and many other books and articles.

DALE A. KOIKE is Assistant Professor of Spanish and Portuguese at the University of Texas, Austin. She earned her Ph.D. from the University of New Mexico, and is the author of *Language and Social Relationships in Brazilian Portuguese: The Pragmatics of Politeness* (1992).

CPSIA information can be obtained at www.ICGtesting.com
Printed in the USA
BVOW06s2256191016

465513BV00004B/6/P